POSTFEMINISMS

Feminism, cultural theory and cultural forms

ANN BROOKS

R ROUTLEDGE

London and New York

First published 1997
by Routledge
11 New Fetter Lane, London EC4P 4EE

Simultaneously published in the USA and Canada
by Routledge
29 West 35th Street, New York, NY 10001

Reprinted 1998

© 1997 Ann Brooks

Typeset in Baskerville by Routledge
Printed and bound in Great Britain by Clays Ltd, St Ives plc

British Library Cataloguing in Publication Data
A catalogue record for this book is available from the British Library

Library of Congress Cataloging in Publication Data
A catalog record for this book is available from the Library of Congress

ISBN 0–415–11474–8 (hbk)
ISBN 0–415–11475–6 (pbk)

CONTENTS

ACKNOWLEDGEMENTS

I would like to acknowledge the support and enthusiasm of a number of people in this project. I would particularly like to thank Chris Rojek for his commitment to the initial project. At Routledge, Mari Shullaw's clarity of vision and careful judgement were invaluable to the success of the project. The enthusiasm of my postgraduate students to the course 'Postfeminism and Cultural Forms' at Massey University has been a constant source of encouragement. I would also like to thank Dr Lynne Star, Dr David Schlect, Dr Philip Barker and Professor Gregor McLennan for their encouragement and humour. I owe a debt to Stephanie Brennan for her incisive editorial skills and helpful and constructive criticism. A very special thanks to Heather Hodgetts, in the Department of Sociology at Massey University, for her patience, expert assistance and advice in all aspects of the production of this text. Wendy Lees at Routledge made the production process efficient and effortless.

INTRODUCTION

Postfeminism, as an expression of a stage in the constant evolutionary movement of feminism, has gained greater currency in recent years. Once seen, somewhat crudely, as 'anti-feminist', the term is now understood as a useful conceptual frame of reference encompassing the intersection of feminism with a number of other anti-foundationalist movements including postmodernism, post-structuralism and post-colonialism. Postfeminism represents, as Yeatman (1994: 49) claims, feminism's 'coming of age', its maturity into a confident body of theory and politics, representing pluralism and difference and reflecting on its position in relation to other philosophical and political movements similarly demanding change.

RELATIONSHIP BETWEEN POSTFEMINISM, POSTMODERNISM AND POST-COLONIALISM

The relationship between postfeminism, postmodernism and post-colonialism is an important one when understanding some of the central issues considered in the debates outlined in the following chapters. The concept of '*post*' common to all three discourses can be the subject of misconception in the popular interpretation of the terms. Postfeminism as in the case of post-colonialism and postmodernism is often used to signal a complete break in a previous range of usually 'oppressive' relations. 'Post' as used in these instances often implies that these relations have been overcome and replaced and in this context the emphasis is on a new range of temporal, political and cultural relations. This use of the concept of 'post' is highly problematic.

As it is understood in this book the concept of 'post' implies a process of ongoing transformation and change. As Spoonley (1995a: 49) comments, *post*-colonialism can be seen as marking 'a critical engagement with colonialism, not to claim that colonialism has been overturned'. In the same way, *post*feminism can be understood as critically engaging with patriarchy and *post*modernism as similarly engaged with the principles of modernism. It does not assume that either patriarchal or modernist discourses and frames of reference have been replaced or superseded. As Spoonley (1995a: 53) notes:

1

'The "post" of post-colonialism refers to a "continuous engagement with the effects of colonial occupation" '(Thomas, 1993: 8).

Postfeminism also occupies a similar 'critical' position in regard to earlier feminist frameworks at the same time as critically engaging with patriarchal and imperialist discourses. In doing so it challenges hegemonic assumptions held by second wave feminist epistemologies that patriarchal and imperialist oppression was a universally experienced oppression. As Gunew and Yeatman maintain, there is a need to

> organise around local allegiances in order to dismantle once again the universal models which however benign they may appear, work ultimately to confirm the old power structures, whether these be partriarchies or neo-imperialisms.
>
> (Gunew and Yeatman 1993: xiv)

Postfeminism, as with post-colonialism, 'represents one interesting possibility within the politics of difference that have emerged as an important site of political mobilisation...' (Spoonley 1995a: 64).

THE EMERGENCE OF POSTFEMINISM

The use of the concept of postfeminism is problematic for two reasons, which need to be clarified: first, the widespread 'popular' conception of postfeminism as a result of the appropriation of the term by the media; and second, the uneven development of postfeminism as a movement expressing change, and the resulting chronological and geographical distinctions that can be made. Alice (1995) claims that

> Postfeminism, (usually written as 'post-feminism') was coined in the period between the achievement of women's suffrage in the U.S. and the rise of 'second-wave' feminism during the 1960s. It denoted the successful outcome of struggles by women for the right to vote, hold public office and the choice to occupy many more personal spheres.
>
> (Alice 1995: 7)

There appears to be little in this definition of postfeminism to anticipate the way 'postfeminism' has become understood in the popular consciousness in the late 1980s and early 1990s where, as Alice contends, ' "postfeminism" has new currency, which is often hostile and directed towards feminists in particular' (*ibid.*).

One of the key proponents of this popular conception of 'postfeminism' is Susan Faludi, in her book *Backlash* (1992). Faludi draws on Brenda Polan writing in the *Guardian* to establish the credentials of her claim. Polan maintains that 'Post-feminism is the backlash. Any movement or philosophy which defines itself as post whatever came before is bound to be reactive. In most cases it is also reactionary' (Faludi 1992: 15).

Faludi claims that, whereas the media introduced 'the backlash to a national audience' in the 1980s through the use of terms such as 'the man shortage', 'the biological clock', 'the mommy track' and 'post-feminism' (*ibid.*: 101), in fact the press were expressing anti-feminist views much earlier. Faludi contends that:

> Post-feminist sentiments first surfaced, not in the 1980s media, but in the 1920s press. Under this barrage, membership of feminist organizations soon plummented, and the remaining women's group hastened to denounce the Equal Rights Amendment or simply converted themselves to social clubs. 'Ex-feminists' began issuing their confessions.
>
> (Faludi 1992: 70)

The agenda of the feminist movement was for Faludi clearly being set by the media and was designed to undermine feminist goals and achievements. She (1992: 14) claims that 'the media declared that feminism was the flavour of the seventies and that "post-feminism" was the new story – complete with a younger generation who supposedly reviled the women's movement'. The role of the media is clearly a powerful one in framing the generally negative and 'popular' understanding of 'postfeminism'. This view is shared by some feminists who elide the critically evaluative potential of postfeminism with the popular 'backlash model'. Book-marketing strategies, aimed to establish a generational antagonism to second wave feminism (see Faludi 1992), have reinforced the equation of postfeminism with 'the backlash' (see Walters 1995). As Alice claims:

> Perhaps the most persuasive message for *popular* postfeminism is that feminism has pushed women into wanting too much. Postfeminism is offered as an escape from the imposition of being 'superwoman' in order to fulfill a feminist image of success.
>
> (Alice 1995: 17, my italics)

The emphasis of much of the popular conception of postfeminism is focused on the attack on some of the most powerful cornerstones of the Women's Movement and second wave feminism more generally. More specifically it is about the issue of *equality*. This is apparent throughout much of Faludi's analysis:

> In the eighties, publications from the *New York Times* to *Vanity Fair* to *The Nation* have issued a steady stream of indictments against the Women's movement, with such headlines as 'WHEN FEMINISM FAILED' or 'THE AWFUL TRUTH ABOUT WOMEN'S LIB'. They hold the campaign for women's equality responsible for nearly every woe besetting women, from depression to meagre savings accounts, from teenage suicides to eating disorders to bad complexions... But what has made women unhappy in the last decade is not their 'equality' – which they don't yet have – but the rising pressure to halt, and even reverse, women's quest for equality.
>
> (cited in Alice 1995: 18)

The conceptual reference points of this popular postfeminism are clearly focused

3

on the issue of 'women's rights' and equal opportunities and thus on a white, Western, middle-class, mainly northern hemispherical, conception of feminism. This emphasis is not without value. Stacey (1990) has maintained, as Alice (1995: 22–23) notes, that such a 'framing' of postfeminism 'is useful to signify how feminism becomes rewritten, depoliticised and incorporated into media accounts of contemporary culture and that postfeminism is not necessarily antifeminist'.

Popular 'post-feminism's' conceptual repertoire provides a useful point of distinction from the way postfeminism is framed within the feminist academic community, particularly those drawing on postmodernism, poststructuralism and post-colonialism to inform their understanding of feminism in the 1990s.

Postfeminism as understood from this perspective is about the conceptual shift within feminism from debates around equality to a focus on debates around difference. It is fundamentally about, not a depoliticisation of feminism, but a political shift in feminism's conceptual and theoretical agenda. Postfeminism is about a critical engagement with earlier feminist political and theoretical concepts and strategies as a result of its engagement with other social movements for change. Postfeminism expresses the intersection of feminism with postmodernism, poststructuralism and post-colonialism, and as such represents a dynamic movement capable of challenging modernist, partriarchal and imperialist frameworks. In the process postfeminism facilitates a broad-based, pluralistic conception of the application of feminism, and addresses the demands of marginalised, diasporic and colonised cultures for a non-hegemonic feminism capable of giving voice to local, indigenous and post-colonial feminisms.

Postfeminism, as it is discussed in the chapters of this book, is about the challenges posed to what has been identified as 'hegemonic' feminism (Sandoval 1991) with its roots clearly located in the Anglo-American influences so powerful in the conceptualisation of second wave feminism. It has become, as Alice (1995: 11, n. 6) notes, 'the dominant and colonising voice of feminist theory through publishing and academic influences'.

As will be shown in the unfolding of the debates around postfeminism, the 'mapping' of the major moments within postfeminism is both complex and multifaceted, with significant chronological and geographical distinctions. Many of the writers, theoreticians and practitioners discussed in the chapters of *Postfeminisms* are writing at the point of intersection of a number of theoretical, conceptual and disciplinary influences (Gayatri Chakravorty Spivak; Trinh T. Minh-ha; Meaghan Morris; Chandra Talpade Mohanty; Sneja Gunew). Others are writing out of an experience of the unacceptable face of 'hegemonic' feminism in different cultural and geographical contexts (bell hooks; Roberta Sykes; Caroline Ramazanoglu; Chela Sandoval). Many more have drawn on a range of debates in the area of cultural theory to frame their more critical feminisms (Teresa de Lauretis; Judith Butler; Rosi Braidotti; Linda Nicholson; Nancy Fraser; Michèle Barrett; Sophie Watson; Ien Ang; Anna Yeatman; Annemarie Jagose).

4

What all postfeminist writers, theoreticians and practitioners have in common is an understanding of feminist theory which as de Lauretis (1988: 130) claims 'became possible as such ... in a post-colonial mode', that is by a commitment to 'feminist theory which can be distinguished by *process* rather than simply its origins or manifestos' (Alice 1995: 11). De Lauretis reflects the changing emphasis within feminism which she claims has moved feminist theory into a position which she sees as 'resisting closure of definition' (*ibid.*). It is this shift in direction and emphasis within feminism, with the emergence of postfeminism, which frames the debates outlined in this book.

The ten years between 1980 and 1990 proved to be much more than a decade in terms of the historical development of feminism as a body of theoretical and critical practice. The gulf between second wave feminism[1] and what is described here as postfeminism became more clearly defined and focused around the issues of feminist theory and theorising.

Postfeminism has been seen by some theorists to be the culmination of a number of debates and fiercely fought arguments from both within and outside feminism. As Michèle Barrett (1992) argues in her important text with Anne Phillips, *Destabilizing Theory: Contemporary Feminist Debates,*

> To say this is not to pose a clear distinction between the collapse 'from the inside' of the 1970s feminist consensus and theoretical developments 'outside' feminism for the interaction and dialogue have been more profound than that would suggest ... [I]t is to point to important parallel lines as well as links between feminist and non feminist strands of contemporary social, political and cultural theory.
>
> (Barrett and Phillips 1992: 5)

The collapse of consensus from within feminism formed around issues of theorising. Concepts such as 'oppression', 'patriarchy', 'sexuality, identity and difference' as used by white middle-class feminists were increasingly challenged. These issues were thrown into relief and highlighted by feminism's intersection with cultural theory, specifically with postmodernist and poststructuralist dimensions of cultural theory. As Barrett argues,

> the key thinkers of 'post-structuralism' – Derrida, Foucault and Lacan have in combination as well as individually mounted a devastating critique of the main assumptions on which much social and feminist theory was previously based and it has proved to be a critique from which neither has emerged unscathed.
>
> (Barrett 1992: 201)

Postfeminisms: Feminism, Cultural Theory and Cultural Forms seeks to situate and investigate the relationship between second wave feminism and postfeminism. In the process it will become evident that a clear gap is emerging between the two. Feminism's intersection with poststructuralism and postmodernism had led to a shift of emphasis, both theoretically and conceptually, within feminist theory. Sylvia Walby maintains that

> Postmodernist arguments for the fragmentation of concepts used in 'modernist' social theory have produced a tendency to shift the central theoretical concept away from structure to 'discourse'. This is represented in the increasing significance of Foucault rather than Marx in social theorizing. The consequences of this are to conceptualize power as highly dispersed rather than concentrated in identifiable places or groups.
>
> (Walby 1992: 48)

Walby's position represents a view within feminism which is reluctant to see a shift away from structural analysis and metatheorising typical of the 'earlier feminist waves'. Other feminist theorists such as Barrett (1990, 1992) recognise that the relationship between feminism, poststructuralism and postmodernism has been both dynamic and productive for feminism and social theory more generally. She maintains that

> Feminist theory has been able to take up a number of issues outside the classically 'materialist' perspective...Poststructuralist theories notably Derridian deconstructive readings, Lacanian psychoanalysis and Foucault's emphasis on the material body and the discourses of power have proved very important in this. Feminists have appropriated these theories rather than others for good reasons: these theories address the issue of sexuality, subjectivity and textuality that feminists have put at the top of the agenda. In considering the debates that now ramify around feminism and poststructuralism it is clear that the classic materialist presuppositions are increasingly harder to apply usefully.
>
> (Barrett 1992: 215)

To what extent feminism's intersection with postmodernism and poststructuralism has produced a definable postfeminism will be considered below. McLennan (1994: 113) argues that the need for feminism to become postmodern, as is proposed in the work of Linda Nicholson (1992) and Fraser and Nicholson (1990), implies there is a conceptual equivalence in postmodern feminism and postfeminism. McLennan makes the point that it is difficult to see how postmodern feminism can be labelled feminist in any meaningful sense. As he maintains, 'if gender is only one strand amongst many, and within the matrix of the uniform features of gender identity are definitely subsidiary to other differences, then that stance is, as the authors imply *post*feminist' (*ibid.*).

Postfeminisms: Feminism, Cultural Theory and Cultural Forms sets out to achieve a number of objectives. First, it seeks to contextualise the debates which are currently redefining feminism in the context of the historical and critical development of feminism as a body of theoretical and political practice. It sets out to establish the basis of the distinction between second wave feminism and postfeminism around issues of feminist theory and theorising. 'Postfeminism', as it is used here, refers to the current state of feminist thinking – the culmination of a number of debates within and outside feminism. Specifically it refers to feminism's intersection with elements of cultural theory, particularly post-modernism, poststructuralism and psychoanalytic theory, as well as with the theoretical and political debates around post-colonialism.

The second objective is to investigate the nature and form of postfeminism and postfeminist debates. This is contextualised within an analytic framework which considers debates surrounding feminism's 'turn to culture' (Barrett 1990) and whether the culmination of such debates has produced a 'paradigm shift' (Barrett 1992) within feminist theorising.

The third objective builds on and takes forward many of the issues raised above. It considers postfeminism's intersection with a number of 'cultural waves', including postmodernism, poststructuralism, psychoanalytic theory, discourse theory and semiotics, contextualised around specific cultural and media forms and substantive fields. These debates are investigated within the areas of cultural politics, popular culture, representations and cultural space.

The book is divided into three parts. Part I, *Challenging and fragmenting the consensus of the 'second wave'*, investigates the apparent consensus which characterised second wave feminism. This consensus was focused around a number of areas: the need to establish theories of social causation; the question of the establishment of a feminist epistemology; the relationship between theory and practice; and the relationship between experience, subjectivity and theory. As Barrett and Phillips (1992: 2) note, 'behind all the sharp disagreements over what was primary or secondary, feminists united in the importance they attached to establishing the fundamentals of social causation'. Despite the identification of a number of causes, feminists united around the need to establish theories of social causation and to specify 'sites of oppression' for 'women' as an oppressed group. However concepts such as 'sites of oppression' as well as 'women' and 'patriarchy' remained unchallenged in terms of their validity and general application within feminist theorising. As Barrett and Phillips note:

> 1970s feminism assumed one could specify a cause of women's oppression. Feminists differed substantially as to what this cause might be – male control of women's fertility, a patriarchal system of inheritance, capitalism's need for a docile labour force – but did not really question the notion of cause itself. Nor was there any difficulty with the idea of oppression which seemed to have self evident application. Important too was the assumption shared by most feminists that the cause being sought lay at the level of social structure.
>
> (1992: 2)

Part I considers the issue of theorising within second wave feminism, in particular the issue of theorising concepts such as 'oppression', 'patriarchy' and 'women', and the intersection of feminism with class, race and ethnicity as reflected in a number of feminist perspectives. It also considers some of the challenges raised within feminism itself to this consensus and looks at the fragmentation of this consensus. The debates are framed within feminism's location within the modernism–postmodernism, modernity–postmodernity dichotomy.

Chapter 1 considers how the consensus of second wave feminism was increasingly challenged from both within and outside feminism. As indicated, a clear distinction between pressures from 'inside' and 'outside' feminism cannot be made because of the overlap in areas of critique in conceptual and theoretical terms. The breakdown in consensus came from three directions:

- From within feminism itself – the political impact of women of colour's critique of the racist and ethnocentric assumptions of a largely white, middle-class feminism.
- The issue of sexual difference was highlighted as an area that had not been sufficiently articulated within feminist theories of the first and second wave, and the work of the French feminist deconstructivists was an aspect of a growing interest in the area of psychoanalytic theory around issues of sexual difference and identity.
- The intersection of feminism with postmodernism, poststructuralism and post-colonialism.

Part II, *Feminism's 'turn to culture' – a paradigm shift in feminist theorising?*, explores the challenges to feminism as a result of its intersection with cultural theory.

The phrase 'feminism's turn to culture' was used by Michèle Barrett (1990) in an article of that name. In a later work, Barrett outlines what she means:

> In the past ten years we have seen an extensive 'turn to culture' in feminism... Within this general shift we can see a marked interest in analysing processes of symbolisation and representation – the field of 'culture' and attempts to develop a better understanding of subjectivity, the psyche and the self.
>
> (Barrett 1992: 204)

Feminism's intersection with different dimensions of cultural theory, including postmodernism, poststructualism and psychoanalytic theory, has led some theorists to pose the question of whether there has been a 'paradigm shift' within feminism.

Barrett (1992: 206) argues that 'many feminists might regard the shift from "equality" to "difference" models of feminism which has characterised the past decade of Western feminism, as a shift of that order'. This section of the text will consider to what extent such a shift has taken place and whether we should talk about 'postfeminism' or a 'postmodern feminism'. The intersection of feminism with issues emerging from debates in the area of post-colonialism has further shaped the political focus of these debates.

Part II considers 'feminism's turn to culture' (Barrett 1990) in two ways: in terms of the increasingly vigorous debate around the significance, nature and validity of a feminist epistemology in the face of an increasingly 'fragmenting feminism'; and in terms of feminism's intersection with postmodernism, poststructuralism, discourse theory and psychoanalytic theory as ultimately leading to the emergence of postfeminism, as an example of what Barrett (1992) calls a 'paradigm shift' in feminist theorising. As she argues,

> contemporary Western feminism, confident for several years about its 'sex/gender distinctions', analysis of 'patriarchy' or postulation of the 'male gaze' has found all these various categories radically undermined by the new 'deconstructive' emphasis on fluidity and contingency.
>
> (Barrett 1992: 202)

Chapter 2 considers the challenges facing the feminist epistemological project in the light of critiques emerging from within feminism, alongside a parallel range of critiques from the area of cultural theory.

Chapters 3, 4 and 5 further develop these debates, and consider a number of issues surrounding the emergence of postfeminist debates. They include:

- the intersection of feminism, postmodernism and post-colonialism
- feminist theory and poststructuralism
- postfeminism, discourse, power and resistance
- psychoanalytic theory, subjectivity and identity.

Part III, *Postfeminism and cultural forms*, investigates these debates in a number of areas, including cultural politics, popular culture, and representational and cultural space. This third section considers postfeminism's intersection with a number of 'cultural waves' contextualised or focused around specific cultural and media forms and substantive fields. These include: cultural difference and cultural politics, popular culture, media and film theory (including semiology, 'pleasures' and spectatorship), and pornography and cultural space.

Chapter 6 considers issues emerging from debates in the area of cultural 'politics of difference' and the cultural politics of the academy. This chapter highlights the impact of feminism's intersection with modernist and postmodernist discourses, and considers the implications for the articulation of postfeminist discourses within the academy. The chapter looks at issues surrounding dominant male figures in the emergence of postmodernism in the academy and the concept of 'cultural space', or the issue of 'the place' from which women may 'speak' or represent themselves. The work of a number of feminist/postfeminist theorists and writers, and the positioning of Women's Studies as a forum for feminist intellectual debate, are used to highlight and articulate the potential for postfeminist discourses within the academy. Chapter 7 considers the intersection of postfeminism and popular culture, and considers popular culture's potential as a 'site of contestation and struggle' for issues of representation and identity. Feminism in its intersection with dimensions of cultural theory has re-evaluated popular cultural forms, including music, dance, style and film from a postfeminist position. This chapter focuses on the redefinition of popular cultural forms as 'sites of struggle' for postfeminist theorists and writers.

Feminist theorists and practitioners have long been involved in media and film theory. Current postfeminist interventions into filmic and media discourses can be seen as an outgrowth and development from feminism's involvement in this direction. Chapter 8 considers feminism's traditional involvement in both film production and scholarship. It further considers postfeminism's critique of these traditional feminist models, particularly those drawn from psychoanalytic theory. This chapter examines postfeminism's intersection with models emerging from post-colonialist and anti-racist debates, and considers their significance for the establishment of 'multiple voices' in feminist film and media theory.

The final chapter draws together many of the issues developed in earlier chapters, particularly those surrounding popular cultural forms, representations, cultural space and identity. In this context popular cultural forms can be seen as 'sites of resistance' for a number of groups who wish to 'open up' the possibility for the creation of new sites of meaning and new identities. This point is particularly significant in relation to issues around sexuality, subjectivity and identity which have been highlighted by postfeminist debates. In Chapter 9 the issues of pornography and cultural space are contextualised within the broader debates surrounding representations, sexuality and identity.

Postfeminisms: Feminism, Cultural Theory and Cultural Forms examines a range of theoretical debates which describe the current state of feminist theorising, conceptualised within this text as postfeminism. The text examines postfeminist writers, theorists and practitioners in the area of cultural theory and cultural forms. Postfeminist theorists and practitioners do not set out simply to demystify the whole concept of the representation of women in different cultural forms. They seek to 'rupture the coherence of address' to 'dislocate meaning' to destabilise theory and 'to open up a space of contradiction in which to demonstrate the non coincidence of woman and women' (de Lauretis 1984: 7). Postfeminist theorists of cultural forms identify 'sites of oppression', but they also actively articulate 'sites of resistance' within both cultural theory and cultural forms.

Part I

CHALLENGING AND FRAGMENTING THE CONSENSUS OF THE 'SECOND WAVE'

1

CONSENSUS AND CONFLICT IN SECOND WAVE FEMINISM

Issues of diversity and 'difference' in feminist theorising

INTRODUCTION

This first chapter investigates feminism's location at the intersection of modernity and postmodernity, and examines some of the debates which have been leading feminism towards a possible paradigm shift. As it confronts critiques from within and outside its own discourses, contemporary feminism is reassessing its epistemological foundations within modernism. This chapter considers some of these critiques and assesses the implications for feminist theoretical and political debates in the 1990s.

FEMINISM, MODERNITY AND POSTMODERNITY

Feminism has always engaged with the 'master' discourses with which it has found itself allied, whether they are the discourses of modernity or postmodernity. It cannot be denied that the theoretical frameworks and principles of operation which have characterised feminism have been the result of feminism's intersection with these discourses, either the 'metanarratives' of modernity, e.g. Marxism, or the postmodernist and poststructuralist discourses of postmodernity.

The relationship between feminism and modernity is not a straightforward one. Marshall (1994: 148) notes the relationship of women to modernity and to social theory as a modern project is one riven with contradictions and ambiguities. She claims that feminism 'constitutes both a critique of *and* a defence of modernity, so has a great stake in the modernity–postmodernity debates which are at heart about the possibility of a "subject" for social theory'. The failure of theories of modernity for feminism has been their inability to come to grips with 'difference' adequately. Thus, on the one hand, as an emancipatory politics and a body of critical and political theory, feminism continues to use 'egalitarian rhetoric as the basis of most of its political demands'. In this sense, as Marshall contends, 'feminism is wedded to the modern by virtue of its rootedness in the space opened up by rights discourse'. However, she notes that, at the same time, its commitment to 'difference' and diversity and its sceptical stance towards reason call forth the postmodern.

Moira Gatens (1986) highlights the significance of feminism's deconstructive relationship to modernist theory, in this case philosophy:

> By *self-consciously* demonstrating that any philosophical paradigm is *not* neutral these feminists make themselves, both as philosophers and women, visible. By making themselves visible, they in turn throw into question the legitimacy of claims and assumptions in philosophy that have been taken as axiomatic. Insofar as the approach questions the very foundation and status of philosophy it also reveals the investments and concerns of philosophy. It does this by demonstrating not only *what is* excluded from a particular philosophy but also *why* it is crucial for the very existence of that philosophy, to exclude it.
>
> (Gatens 1986: 25)

Gatens' comments identify two dimensions to feminism's critique of modernism: first, feminism's approach to theoretical deconstruction, as Yeatman (1994: 17) claims, 'evinces unwillingness to evacuate the ground of knowledge production, to leave a particular discipline to its phallocentric leadership'; second, it anticipates feminism's critique of modernism's metanarratives. Central among such metanarratives has been Marxism and the 'production-paradigm'. Feminist philosophical critique as outlined by Benhabib and Cornell offers a direct challenge to the production paradigm. They raise the question of whether

> the concept of production, which is based on the model of an active subject transforming, making and shaping an object given to it, can adequately comprehend traditional female activities, such as childrearing and caregiving, which are so thoroughly intersubjective.
>
> (1987: 2)

The challenge to metanarrative as an explanatory framework came from within and outside feminism, perhaps the most serious critique being that of the theorisation of the 'subject'. Marshall (1994: 96), drawing on the work of MacDonald (1991), contends that it is in their questioning of the 'subject' that Marxists, feminists and poststructuralists have found some intellectual affinity. Marshall notes that 'there is increasing doubt cast on the premise of orthodox Marxist theory that an individual's identity, consciousness and in essence social being, are derived from one's position in the social division of labour' (*ibid.*).

Feminism's critique of modernist metanarratives has been thrown into relief by feminism's engagement with postmodernism. Fraser and Nicholson's (1990) work in this area has been seminal.[1] They argue that feminist theorists must abandon their own versions of the modernist metanarratives which have inspired the great general theories of modernity.[2] Yeatman (1990b: 290) contends that if 'postmodernism empowers, as in a sense it is empowered by, feminism and feminist-inspired democratic visions, feminist theorists will have to give up their own "trained" subscription to modernist perspectives which sustain monovocal, monological constructions of authority'.

Fraser and Nicholson (1990: 31) cite the work of Nancy Chodorow (1979) as one of a number of feminist social theorists who 'has constructed a quasi-metanarrative around a putatively cross-cultural, female-associated activity'. In addition, Yeatman notes that they identify a number of second wave feminists whose work has followed a similar pattern. She identifies Ann Ferguson and Nancy Folbre, Nancy Hartsock and Catherine MacKinnon (among others), who 'have built similar theories around notions of sex-affective production, reproduction, and sexuality respectively' (Yeatman 1990b: 291). The difficulty with these theories is their biological essentialism, their lack of a cross-cultural component, and their tendency towards social constructionism. She argues that 'a genealogical' construction of the 'categories of sexuality, reproduction and mothering would avoid the universalistic assumptions inherent in these models'.

The response of feminist theorists to postmodernism and poststructuralism has not been characterised by consensus. Sylvia Walby (1990, 1992) has been in the forefront of critics of feminism's theoretical incursions into postmodernism. She contends that 'postmodernists are correct to point out that many of the existing grand theories of patriarchy have problems in dealing with historical and cultural variation. But their solution of denying causality itself is necessarily defeatist...' (Walby 1992: 36). While Walby herself rejects a return to modernist metanarratives, with their 'totalizing' frameworks, she contends that 'postmodern critics go too far in asserting the necessary impossibility and unproductive nature of investigating gender inequality'. She argues that the problem with a traditional Marxist framework is that it attempts to incorporate all forms of social inequality into that of class, utilising 'a simple base-superstructure model of causal relations'. Walby's solution is to be found in theorising more than one causal base. She contends that the 'ability to theorize different forms of patriarchy is absolutely necessary to avoid the problem of simple reductionism and essentialism'. However, Yeatman (1990b: 291) points out that it is important to emphasise that, if postmodernism means abandoning universalistic, general theories and instead exploring the multivocal worlds of different societies and cultures, 'this is *not* the same thing as abandoning the political-ethical project of working out the conditions for a universal pragmatics of individualized agency'.

It is the issue of agency and of subjectivity more generally, which lies at the heart of feminism's ambiguous 'positioning' between modernity and post-modernity. As Marshall (1994: 148) notes, 'feminist analysis must recognise and build upon the insight that it can fully embrace neither an unreconstructed modernism's subject nor postmodernism's rejection of the subject, by virtue of the fact that women as subjects have never been accorded the coherence, autonomy, rationality or agency of the subject which undergirds an unreconstructed modernism, and which postmodernism has deconstructed out of existence.'

The fragile consensus of second wave feminism was increasingly challenged from both within and outside feminism. One of the key texts that brings together these two sets of pressures is Michèle Barrett and Anne Phillips' book *Destabilizing Theory* (1992).[3] Barrett and Phillips outline three reasons why feminism has gone through a period of radical self-criticism: the political impact of women of colour within feminism; the issue of sexual difference, highlighted as an area that had not been sufficiently articulated within feminist theories of the second wave and more generally the whole area of subjectivity, diversity and difference within feminist theorising; and the impact of poststructuralism and postmodernism on feminism. The shift of emphasis from 'equality' to 'difference' emerging from within feminism's own ranks as a result of critiques from women of colour, Third World feminists and lesbian feminists has been described by Barrett (1992) as 'paradigm shift' of the same order as that of feminism's intersection with poststructuralism and postmodernism.

THE POLITICAL IMPACT OF WOMEN OF COLOUR WITHIN FEMINISM

Postmodernism and poststructuralism, with their emphasis on 'deconstruction' and difference, reinforced critiques that had already been directed at the 'essentialism', ethnocentrism and 'ahistoricism' of branches of feminist theory. The problematic nature of terms such as 'patriarchy', 'women' and 'oppression' was for those 'at the margins' of feminism further highlighted in the debates within the feminist movement instituted initially by women of colour. Carby (1982) and hooks (1984) comment on the universalisation of terms by an essentially white, middle-class, heterosexual, feminist movement as if they referred to the experiences of all women. As hooks (1984: 4) argues, 'Race and class identity create differences in quality of life, social status and lifestyle that take precedence over the common experience women share – differences which are rarely transcended.'

The universal application of 'black' as a concept was shown to lack any cultural and historical specificity in the way it had come to be used. In Britain the use of 'black' had a political dimension and was used in a 'generic' sense to apply to groups who shared an experience of colonialism and racism. Its application in terms of both race and ethnicity was imprecise and was applied to 'Afro-Caribbean' and 'Asian', ignoring national, regional, cultural, ethnic and linguistic particularities. In the United States, 'black' was again used in a generic sense, but usually applied to Afro-American and Afro-Caribbean groups who had a shared experience of slavery. In Australia, 'black' was frequently applied to Aborigines as an indigenous group (see Pettman 1988).

Writers such as Carby (1982), hooks (1984), Sykes (1984) and Ramazanoghu (1986) have raised different issues around the limitations of second wave feminism for women of colour. All acknowledge that second wave feminism has neglected the 'lived experience' of racism. This neglect renders second wave feminism's theoretical framework and categories inappropriate and its practices problematic. Many of the critiques have coalesced around the theorising and application of the concept of 'patriarchy'.

Just as critiques of second wave feminism by women of colour have pointed to limitations in the application of the concept 'black' as not recognising cultural and historical specificity, so women of colour maintain that 'patriarchy' is equally ethnocentric in its application. As Carby (1982: 217) states, 'black men have not held the same patriarchal position of power that white males have established'. At a more general level of critique, Michèle Barrett (1988) argues that the term 'patriarchy' has lost all analytic or explanatory power, and is now used synonymously with 'male dominance'. Both Carby and Barrett, while approaching the issue from different positions, agree that a more contextualised, culturally specific concept of patriarchy must be developed in order to more accurately reflect a range of experiences of oppression. Ramazanoglu (1986) claims that, while an understanding of ethnocentrism is important in feminist theory, this alone does not lead to an understanding of black women's experience of oppression, further that the failure of feminist theory arises not only from its ethnocentrism but also its failure to address the issue of racism.

Roberta Sykes, in speaking for/of Aboriginal women, raises the same issues for indigenous women. As Sykes claims:

> White women merely have less power and control than white men. I do not doubt that white women experience this state acutely but in comparison to both black women and black men white women are extremely powerful and have control over many resources.
>
> (1984: 63)

The intersections of race, ethnicity and class within second wave feminism, and the implications for feminist theory and practice, have been shown to be problematic. Second wave feminist theory failed to address the fact that there are different 'sites of oppression' and potentially different 'sites of struggle'. It is at this level of analysis that, Walby (1990: 16) maintains, 'postmodern critics have made some valuable points about the potential dangers in theorizing gender inequality at too abstract and general level'. She notes that sites of oppression for women of colour may be different from those of white women, and this may change the basis of gender inequality. Elsewhere Walby claims that

> some black feminists such as hooks, have argued that since the family is a site of resistance and solidarity against racism for women of colour, it does not hold the central place in accounting for women's subordination that it does for white women.
>
> (1992: 34)

It is not only 'a question of recognizing ethnic inequality, and the different sites of oppression for women of different ethnicities, but the particular ways in which ethnic and gender relations have interacted historically change the forms of ethnic and gender relations' (*ibid.*). However, Walby raises doubts about postmodernist critiques of feminist theory, and maintains that there is sufficient evidence of commonly shared oppressions among women to identify 'patriarchy' as a significant source of oppression in advanced Western capitalist society. However it is clear that 'patriarchy' is experienced in different ways by different women and results in different 'sites of oppression' and 'sites of resistance'.

The critique raised by women of colour to feminist theory and practice has been one of a number of critiques the history of feminist theory has undergone. De Lauretis (1993: 86) charts some of the periods of conflict within feminism, and notes that in the 1970s the debate in the US was characterised by a debate between academic feminism versus activism defined as an opposition between theory and practice, which led to a polarisation of positions either *for* theory or *against* theory. De Lauretis identifies a further fragmentation within feminism with the subsequent internal division of the movement over the issue of separatism or 'mainstreaming', which 'recast the practice/theory opposition in terms of lesbian vs heterosexual identification and of women's studies vs feminist cultural theory...' (*ibid.*).

The issues of pornography and representation were the focus of conflict within feminist debates in the mid-1980s. De Lauretis (1993: 87) contends that 'the so-called feminist sex wars...have pitched 'pro-sex' feminists versus the anti-pornography movement in a conflict over representation that recast the sex/gender distinction into the form of a paradoxical opposition'. As she notes, on the one hand sex and gender are collapsed together and become both analytically and politically indistinguishable as can be seen in the work of Catherine MacKinnon and Nancy Hartsock. On the other hand sex and gender 'are severed from each other' and are recombined in a series of 'boundary' crossings such as 'transsexualism, transvestism, bi-sexualism, drag and impersonation (Butler), cyborgs (Haraway) etc' (*ibid.*). Central to all these areas are issues of identity, subjectivity and difference within feminist theoretical debates.

ISSUES OF SUBJECTIVITY, DIVERSITY AND DIFFERENCE WITHIN FEMINISM

The issues of subjectivity and identity within feminist theorising are closely related to issues of epistemology within feminist theoretical analysis and the relationship between feminist knowledge and women's experience. Feminist debates in the 1990s are more reflective of the ongoing debates around feminist epistemology and theory both from within and outside feminism (see Chapter 2). Sandra Harding's 'Reinventing Ourselves as Others: More New Agents of History and Knowledge' (1993) is a case in point, reflecting on her earlier work

(1986) on the relationship between experience and knowledge, her latest writing 'examines the kinds of subjects or agents of history and knowledge and the kinds of projects that are generated by the "logic" of standpoint theory' (Harding 1993: 142). She characterises these as 'reinventing ourselves as "other"'. Harding argues that some feminist epistemological positions have claimed that only women and women's experiences can generate feminist knowledge. Her work is clearly informed by the feminist debates of the 1980s and goes much further than previously in making problematic the concepts of 'experience' and 'oppression'.

Harding (1993: 148) amplifies this position in arguing that it is maintained that only those who are African-American, or lesbian, or working-class, or Third World, can originate anti-racist or anti-homophobic or anti-bourgeois or anti-imperialist insights. She asks whether it is true that only the oppressed can generate knowledge, and proceeds to question whether an understanding of oppression can only come out of an experience of oppression. As she maintains, the perspectives of those outside 'of the fiercely fought struggles to claim legitimacy' can often appear illegitimate or even 'monstrous', and gives examples of 'male feminists; whites against racism, colonialism and imperialism; heterosexuals against heterosexism; economically over-advantaged people against class exploitation' (Harding 1993: 144). Her point is that there is a real danger in equating of certain types of 'experience' with 'the truth' and with valid knowledge, and that it is important to understand the concept of 'contradictory identities' and 'contradictory social locations' for feminist theorising.

Harding has redefined aspects of feminist standpoint epistemology (see Chapter 2) to incorporate more fully the concept of contradictory identity and contradictory social locations within feminist methodological analysis. She notes that

> The kind of contradictory identity and social location that is a consequence of following standpoint logic in fact has already appeared in a number of analyses, with the assistance of analyses that began in lesbian lives (and were almost always first generated by lesbians), lesbians and heterosexuals have learned to 'read against the grain' their otherwise spontaneously heterosexist experience.

(Harding 1993: 156)

In discussing the contradictory nature of experience, Harding maintains that it is not 'experience' itself, but thinking from a contradictory position, that produces feminist knowledge. As such, feminist knowledge is not something that need only be generated by women, or oppressed women: it can also be generated by men and other groups:

> the point is to develop strategies that encourage men as well as women, whites as well as people of colour, straights as well as gays and lesbians, the

19

economically over-advantaged as well as the working class and the poor to become active agents of historical understanding.

(Harding 1993: 158)

Harding's interpretation of the contradictory and contested nature of feminist epistemological and methodological debate in the 1990s might be surprising to some feminist theorists, but Harding is not alone in being influenced by such debates. Marshall (1994: 104) contends that feminist theories of the subject have flourished in 'exposing the androcentric bias of grand theories of "unencumbered selves" ', but have 'floundered in implicitly or explicitly replicating gender polarity…or the binary opposition of male and female, rooted in bodily existence'. As Alcoff (1988) maintains, in feminist theories of the subject it has become an opposition between 'essentialism' and 'nominalism'.

FEMINIST THEORIES OF SUBJECTIVITY: ESSENTIALISM VERSUS NOMINALISM

Despite its familiar caricature, feminist essentialism is not a unitary system of thought. Marshall (1994: 104) maintains that three types of essentialist thinking can be identified, 'each resting on different sorts of argument about how biological difference is transformed into subjective difference – biological essentialism,[4] philosophical essentialism and historical reification.' Biological essentialism is usually associated with the work of Shulamith Firestone, Mary Daly and Adrienne Rich. Philosophical essentialism is represented by the work of Simone de Beauvoir. Both groups of writers are identified as making influential contributions to theories of gender-differentiated subjectivity in which women's sense of self is seen to be located in the particularity of the female body. The historical reification of women's experience and the corresponding reification of 'gender identity' is most clearly stated in socialist feminist theory.[5] Marshall (1994: 107) maintains that 'the historical reification and conflation of public/private, production/reproduction, male/female, also characterises the bulk of Marxist feminist theory which focused on the gendered division of labour in capitalism as rooted in the exigencies of biological reproduction.'

FEMINISM, POSTSTRUCTURALISM AND SUBJECTIVITY

Feminist epistemological and methodological debates of the 1980s and 1990s have been both informed and transformed by feminism's interrogation of postmodernism and poststructuralism. Chris Weedon's *Feminist Practice and Poststructuralist Theory* (1987) sets out the relationship between feminism, poststructuralism and subjectivity, and comments that feminism and poststructuralism are both centrally concerned with the issue of subjectivity. Weedon argues that poststructuralism, like feminism, has been keen to 'deconstruct' the concept of the 'subject' within the liberal humanist tradition in order to

20

understand, theorise and make problematic the nature of meaning produced within this tradition. Feminism's intersection with postmodernism (and in particular poststructuralism) has provided feminism with a range of critical frameworks, including 'discourse', 'deconstruction' and 'difference', which have been used to challenge and refine traditional assumptions of identity and subjectivity.

Weedon claims (1987) that the poststructuralist concept of discourse is centrally important for feminism. She maintains that discourse refers to ways of constituting meaning which are specific to particular groups, cultures and historic periods. It is drawn from the work of Michel Foucault (see Chapter 3) who used it to highlight the multifaceted nature of power. In developing a feminist poststructuralist perspective, Weedon contends that feminism must investigate the discursive 'sites' of male power as they are articulated and legitimised in institutional structures of power and forms of knowledge.

Feminists are aware of the significance of the concept of 'discourse'. In discussing the impact of Foucault's concept of discourse for the development of a feminist historiography, Gail Reekie (1994: 1) comments: 'More than any other writer associated with poststructuralism, Michel Foucault has provided feminist historians with a legible set of guide maps for this always hazardous journey out of structuralist and modernist thinking.' She goes on to note that for many academic women 'trained in social history and women's history, the shift from experientially grounded accounts of historical reality to discourse theory has produced something like a crisis of faith in our home discipline' (*ibid.*). Within Foucauldian analysis discourses are multiple, and suggest competing, potentially contradictory ways of giving meaning to the world. They offer 'subject positions' for individuals to take up. Discourses vary in terms of the power they offer individuals, and also vary in their authority.

In contrast to the liberal humanist assumptions of the unified, rational self, poststructuralism – and more specifically feminist poststructuralism – proposes a subject which is fragmentary and contradictory. Feminist poststructuralists reject the concept of an essential, unified female nature, and feminist poststructuralism offers, according to Weedon (1987: 125), 'a contextualisation of experience and an analysis of its constitution and ideological power'. As Weedon suggests, the advantage of this strategy lies in the fact that an awareness of the contradictory nature of subjectivity highlights the possibility of choice in different situations and between different discourses.

FEMINIST POSTSTRUCTURALISM OR POSTFEMINISM?

Poststructuralist theories thus reject the concept of the humanist subject, and feminist poststructuralism poses a radical challenge to essentialism. The 'subject' is no longer a fixed entity, a manifestation of 'essence' but 'a "subject-in process" never unitary, never complete' (Marshall 1994: 108). This anti-essentialist position culminates, as Fraser (1992: 66) contends, in a postfeminist stance where a conception of a collective feminist identity may be perceived as totalitarian and dangerous.

Michel Foucault's deconstructive approach to the 'subject' has been influential for many feminists and feminist poststructuralists. Foucault's 'subject' is decentred and dispersed and Foucault insists that we reject 'totalizing' discourses and the model of the rational humanist subject. Judith Butler (1990a: 136) draws on Foucault's 'genealogical' method to deconstruct the 'subject' of feminism. She contests the 'reification' of gender implicit in the binary conception of masculine/feminine subjectivity and rejects any notion of feminine identity. Thus, for Butler, gender is *performative*, it is an effect of performance and is constituted in performance, so, as Butler notes, 'it has no ontological status apart from the various acts which constitute its reality' (see Chapter 9). As Marshall indicates, Butler's 'feminist strategy, is to disrupt the performance, to "trouble" the congealed categories of gender through parody'. She notes that 'Butler's work is important in its insistence that there is no "essence" reflected by gender – it only takes on a guise of naturalness through repeated and discursively constructed performances' (1994: 110).

For feminist poststructuralists such as Chris Weedon (1987), neither the attempt to redefine the truth of women's nature within the terms of existing social relations – as in liberal feminism's attempt to establish equality with men – nor the radical-feminist emphasis on fixed difference expressed as separatism, is politically adequate.

Feminist poststructuralism is thus a significant advance over second wave feminism because it addresses historical and cultural specificity in the experiences of women. Weedon outlines the position as follows:

> For a theoretical perspective to be politically useful to feminism, it should be able to recognize the importance of the *subjective* in constituting the meaning of women's lived reality. It should not deny subjective experience, since the ways in which people make sense of their lives is a necessary starting point for understanding how power relations structure society. Theory must be able to address women's experience by showing where it comes from and how it relates to material social practices and the power relations which structure them...In this process subjectivity becomes available, offering the individual both a perspective and a choice, and opening up the possibility of political change.
>
> (Weedon 1987: 8–9)

Poststructuralist accounts have addressed some of the criticisms raised by women of colour to feminist essentialism. bell hooks (1990: 29) suggests 'critiques of essentialism which challenge notions of universality and static over-determined identity within mass culture and mass consciousness can open new possibilities for the construction of self and the assertion of agency'.

However, while feminist poststructuralist 'alliances' have opened up a range of possibilities, there are problems with poststructuralism's conceptualisation of the subject. As de Lauretis contends in her analysis of Linda Alcoff's (1988) contribution to the debate,

> if the poststructuralist critique of the unified, authentic subject of humanism is more than compatible with the feminist project 'to deconstruct and de-essentialize' woman [Alcoff], its absolute rejection of gender and its negation of biological determinism in favour of a cultural-discursive determinism results, as concerns women, in a form of nominalism.
>
> (de Lauretis 1993: 83)

She goes on to note that, if the concept of woman is a fiction, then the very concept of women's oppression is obsolete and feminism's *raison d'être* disappears.

There are other criticisms that can be made of poststructuralism's position on the subject. Poststructuralist critiques of the feminist subject are often predicated on a model of 'feminist essentialism's' failure to take into account differences such as those of sexual orientation, class and race. However, there is rarely any discussion of the materiality of these differences, Modleski (1991: 18) notes, 'once they have served their theoretical purpose of dissuading feminists from claiming commonalties across class and racial lines'.

This raises an additional important issue around the crucial role that marginalised groups have played in critiquing the whole area of identity and subjectivity, and highlights the difficulty of establishing the relationship between experience, social power and resistance. De Lauretis (1993: 81) claims 'that the notion of experience in relation both to social–material practices and to the formation and processes of subjectivity is a feminist concept not a poststructuralist one'. Waugh (1989) draws attention to the fact that many of the critiques of identity and subjectivity emerged from within subjugated groups both inside and outside feminism. As Waugh suggests,

> for those marginalized by the dominant culture, a sense of identity as constructed through impersonal and social relations of power (rather than a sense of identity as the reflection of an inner 'essence') has been a major aspect of their self-concept long before poststructuralists and postmodernists began to assemble their cultural manifestos.
>
> (Waugh 1989: 3)

Poststructuralist critiques have been valuable in problematising the notion of the 'subject' as constructed through language, and in providing a vocabulary for feminists struggling with the limitations of earlier approaches. However, as Marshall (1994: 111) notes, 'the refusal of a "subject" for feminist theory leads to serious problems with the status of poststructuralist feminism as a political project'. Marshall goes on to note that, not only does it have difficulty 'in accounting for its own emergence as a non repressive discourse, but its inherent relativism poses clear difficulties for the inherently normative character of feminism'.

Barrett (1988) defines the essentialism versus nominalism debate in terms of a 'continuum', with neither extreme being particularly satisfactory. Alcoff (1988: 421) maintains that the way out of the contradictions for feminism lies in 'a theory of the subject that avoids both essentialism and nominalism'. Alcoff recommends the development of the notion of 'woman as positionality'. By this Alcoff (1988: 431) suggests that we need 'to construe a gendered subjectivity in relation to concrete habits, practices and discourses while at the same time recognizing the fluidity of these'. She identifies de Lauretis (1986) and Riley (1983) as exemplars of this approach and argues that the notion of positionality is useful in drawing together both subjectivity and structure. Alcoff (1988: 434) suggests that from this perspective gender identity is not only relational to a given set of external conditions, but that 'the position women find themselves in can be actively utilized ... as a place from where a meaning is constructed, rather than simply the place from where a meaning can be discovered (the meaning of femaleness)'.

Marshall (1994) contends that conceiving of identities as interpreted allows us to negotiate the path between essentialism and nominalism and between agency and determination. She argues there is an inherent tension between the term 'woman' as a theoretical construct which implies gender as universally constitutive of the subject, and the realities of really existing 'women' who may or may not share a unified 'gender identity'. Thus the concept of 'gendered identities' is useful in implying a recognition of plurality and difference which does not abandon the notion of gender as playing a part in constituting the subject. As Marshall (1994: 12) notes, it is 'precisely the conflict and tension between the centred and decentred conceptions of the subject in feminist theory that contains the potential for theorizing resistive agency, on the part of both collective and individual subjects'.

FEMINISM AND THE 'POLITICS OF DIFFERENCE'

The issues of subjectivity and experience within feminist theory have been deconstructed by poststructuralism and postmodernism. Feminist poststructuralism challenges feminism's tendency to view both subjectivity and women's experience as 'unitary', monovocal, and characterised by a unified discourse. Poststructuralism, specifically feminist poststructuralism, establishes 'experience' as contradictory and identity as plural. Yeatman notes that, even where 'feminist theorizing remains tied into the distinctly essentialist presuppositions of liberal, radical and socialist feminism, this theorizing cannot continue, innocent of postmodern feminist theorizing and its embrace of the politics of difference' (1994: 13). Yeatman goes on to note that, 'to the extent that postmodernism appears to be the discursive terrain on which the politics of difference is currently being played out, feminism and postmodernism can be understood, as in a relationship of reciprocal interpellation' (*ibid.*).

The intersection of feminism with poststructuralism and postmodernism has, in the multiplication of the grounds of difference, permitted difference as such to emerge. As Yeatman notes, 'it is not swallowed up in the monological politics of inversion which a binary political contest requires' (1994: 15). Difference poses a new set of requirements for feminism and, as Yeatman goes on to argue, contemporary feminism 'as it is refracted through a politics of difference may be seen as responding to this challenge' (*ibid.*). As has been apparent from the preceding arguments, and as Yeatman contends, 'the emergence of the category of difference has permitted feminist theory to investigate the materiality of the discursively interpellated female subject, and thereby to open the significance of difference in embodiment for the politics of difference' (*ibid.*).

CONCLUSION

Contemporary feminist theory is the product of epistemological upheavals which have characterised its own as well as other disciplinary areas, such as the social sciences and the humanities. Felski (1989: 35) raises the question: 'How, then, is feminism to legitimate and sustain its own critique of patriarchy, once it recognizes the existence of a more general legitimization crisis which questions the grounding and authority of all forms of knowledge?' Contemporary feminist theory in its intersection with postmodernism and poststructuralism is having to reassess its previously held epistemological assumptions. It is in the process of having to come to terms with its affinity with postmodernism, and it is therefore confronted with issues of how to situate its own value commitments in relation to the pluralistic and relativistic implications of postmodernism and poststructuralism. As Yeatman (1990b: 284) contends, 'feminism lies on the cusp of a paradigm revolution and the features of the alternative emergent paradigm are not yet clear'.

Part II

FEMINISM'S 'TURN TO CULTURE' – A PARADIGM SHIFT IN FEMINIST THEORISING?

2

CHALLENGING THE BASIS OF THE FEMINIST EPISTEMOLOGICAL PROJECT

INTRODUCTION

Feminism has been centrally concerned with the question of epistemology since its inception. Feminist writers/scholars have sought to challenge the basis and characteristics of epistemologies which posit a conception of 'truth', which is essentially 'reality' interpreted from a male perspective. In the necessarily intense and vigorous debate which has resulted – on the significance, nature and validity of a feminist epistemology – feminism has challenged the concept of a traditional 'Enlightenment', rationalist epistemology whose characteristics including rationality, objectivity, reason and language are seen by some branches of feminism as essentially masculinist. This chapter examines the current state of feminist epistemological debates and feminist theorising.

FRAMING THE DEBATES AROUND A FEMINIST EPISTEMOLOGY

The emancipatory goals and epistemological assumptions of second wave feminism based on the interrelationship between knowledge and liberation can be clearly traced to the liberal humanism of enlightened modernity. McNeil (1993: 149) maintains that

> The women who gave birth to second wave feminism can be thought of as daughters of the Enlightenment in that they seemed to have inherited some Enlightenment assumptions. In its early heady days of the late 1960s and 1970s they created a movement which held out the promise of increased and better knowledge of gender relationships and through this knowledge, women's liberation. Knowledge and liberation were regarded as incremental and inter-related goals: as women gained more knowledge of their position in the world, it was presumed that their power to transform it would increase accordingly.
>
> (McNeil 1993: 149)

The key strategies employed by second wave feminists were designed to expose

29

the nature of 'patriarchy' and 'oppression' and to establish 'women only spaces', new patterns of relationships between women through the practice of consciousness-raising. McNeil (1993: 150) indicates that some feminists, notably Catherine MacKinnon (1982) (among others), saw this process as the 'linchpin of feminism and the foundation of a distinctive feminist epistemology'.

In the 1980s and 1990s the debates surrounding the issue and form of feminist epistemology have taken a number of different directions. The view of the essential female experience has been criticised from within feminism by 'women of colour', lesbian feminists and Third World women. Other branches of feminism have explored more fully feminism's intersection with psychoanalytic theory and cultural theory, particularly poststructuralism and postmodernism, and have questioned the very existence and relevance of a feminist epistemology. Halberg (1992) investigates the nature and feasibility of the feminist epistemo-logical project; and in doing so, she raises obstacles of a theoretical and practical kind facing feminism in its epistemological quest. Halberg maintains that there are three inherent tensions in the feminist project which cannot be resolved at the theoretical level. These are the issues of objectivism versus relativism, that of women's and men's thinking, and of 'difference' in feminist thinking. Halberg recognises that there are also problems at another (practical) level, in terms of the applicability of the concept of 'experience' within the feminist project. While Halberg notes that the most obvious concept to draw on is 'the common experience of women', in practical terms the concept is too vague and differentiated to accommodate the theoretical demands required of it.

Writers like Walby (1990), while sympathetic with the notion of 'experience' as the basis for an alternative epistemology, are critical of the lack of a thoroughgoing analysis of the social and political contextualisation of experience, and argue for the need to combine elements of discourse analysis within a model of social and political change. Feminist debates in the 1980s and 1990s have highlighted the social constructedness and social locatedness of experience (Harding 1993).

The debate within some branches of feminism has developed around what are seen to be the competing concepts of 'reason' versus 'experience' as significant variables in the emergence of a feminist epistemology. Grant (1987) maintains that some feminists reject 'reason' as a basis on which to construct a feminist epistemology, on the grounds that it is 'male'. This view of 'male reason' is highly problematic. Halberg (1992) argues that much of the feminist critique of 'malestream' science presupposes that modern epistemology is a product of a 'male way of knowing', which results from a specific male way of thinking. Halberg contends that the feminist view of knowledge and reason as 'male' emerges from the feminist view that the fundamental dichotomy of Enlight-enment thought is rooted in the mind/body, male/female dichotomy. Halberg asserts that feminism

> tends to see every idea (in, for example, philosophy or meta-theory) about
> everything as male biased, as if the hegemony of dominant conceptions

were complete. Patriarchy appears free of conflicts and contradictions, totally dominated by a unified masculinity.

(1992: 374)

She argues that there are 'incompatible tendencies in feminist epistemologies' (Halberg 1992: 373) and, as a result, she cannot see any feasible way of grounding feminist epistemology. Halberg, while identifying the tensions involved in feminist epistemological debates, does not engage with the debates in any meaningful sense. Nor does she consider the implications of the increasing feminist 'pluralism' of the 1980s and 1990s. Halberg's model of feminism, at least at her level of engagement, is a 'univocalist' model.

Further, for feminists the question of philosophy as outlined by Halberg has always been subordinate to social criticism. Consequently, feminists have begun by developing critical social and political perspectives and from there have drawn conclusions about the status of philosophy. The work of Linda Nicholson (1990, 1992), among others, is representative of feminism's more plural, self-reflective stance in epistemological terms. Nicholson (1990) argues that feminists have understood and exposed the political power of the academy and of knowledge claims. They have, in this context, challenged the supposed neutrality and objectivity of the academy. In so doing, feminists have recognised that universal knowledge claims by the academy only really serve the interests of, and have value for, men of a particular culture, class and race. Nicholson further notes that the philosophical underpinnings of these views reflect an historically specific set of masculinist values. Thus, most feminists, in approaching the establishment of a feminist epistemology, have been motivated by the demands of a political practice not by an overriding concern with the status of philosophy. As Nicholson (1990: 26) argues, 'Women whose theorising was to serve the struggle against sexism were not about to abandon powerful political tools as a result of intra-mural debates in professional philosophy.'

Feminist responses, while varied in their approach, have sought to 'develop new paradigms of social criticism which do not rely on traditional philosophical underpinnings' (Fraser and Nicholson 1990: 26). The crucial issue for feminism, in its consideration of epistemological debates, is whether, in addition to criticising 'male ways of knowing', feminism requires the articulation of a single alternative way of knowing.

Some second wave feminists were led, on the basis of political imperatives, to establish their own 'metatheories'. These metatheoretical models formed very large social theories, encompassing theories of history, society, culture or psychology, which had a universalistic, cross-cultural application. As Nicholson argues, 'Such theories share some of the essentialist and ahistorical features of meta-narratives. They are insufficiently attentive to historical and cultural diversity' (Fraser and Nicholson 1990: 27). The criticisms levelled at such feminist metatheories are based on the fact that theorising at this level presupposes some commonly held but unwarranted and essentialist assumptions

31

about human nature and the conditions for social life. Critiques levelled at such metatheories have emerged from feminism's own discourses, and from feminism's intersection with elements of cultural theory, particularly postmodernism and poststructuralism.

CHALLENGING CONVENTIONAL EPISTEMOLOGIES

Feminists have sought to challenge conventional epistemologies by developing alternative paradigms. Within the social sciences, Walby (1990: 16) argues that feminist challenges to mainstream social science have invoked a variety of approaches to knowledge. She maintains that some branches of feminism have argued that orthodox accounts are empirically incorrect on their own terms, while others have claimed that the very way that men have constructed what counts as authoritative knowledge is itself patriarchally constructed.

Sandra Harding's (1986) analysis of feminist theories of scientific knowledge identifies two models. She labels the first model 'a feminist empiricist model', which employs a traditional empiricist method to feminist concerns. Walby (1990), in discussing the feminist empiricist model, maintains that feminists operating within this position adopt a 'methods'-led approach, arguing for a return to an empirically grounded scientific approach to knowledge. Feminist empiricists see what they insist is a 'false scientificity', of the traditional 'scientific' approach to knowledge, as essentially framed by 'patriarchally' biased knowledge.

Walby (1990: 17) claims that 'feminist standpoint epistemology', offers a more far-reaching critique and argues that 'the way that men have typically constructed what counts as authoritative knowledge is itself patriarchal. This second school . . . argues that the only basis of unbiased knowledge of the world is women's own direct experience'. Feminist standpoint epistemologists assert that we need a new feminist methodology which is closer to women's own experience. As Halberg (1992) maintains, feminist standpoint epistemology is the feminist version of 'objectivism'. It is founded on the claim that women have 'a cognitively privileged position' in society so that their knowledge is superior to men's knowledge and that this 'privileged' position is taken to be rooted in women's experiences. Harding (1990: 96–97) maintains that 'In claiming that inquiry from the standpoint of women (or the feminist standpoint) can overcome the partiality and distortion of the dominant androcentric/bourgeois/western sciences, it directly undermines the point of viewlessness of objectivism while refusing the relativism of interpretationism'.

There are different branches of feminist thinking within this broad epistemological model, including radical feminists, cultural feminists and French feminist deconstructivists. Radical feminists claim that true knowledge is intuitive and female, and that 'reason' or rationality is simply an ideological weapon that men use against women. Cultural feminists have taken the argument further in juxtaposing the masculine and culture, to feminine and nature. Grant (1987), in summarising the key elements in this position, states that within this position 'male logic' is seen as one aspect of a broad-based, masculinist hegemony. A group of theorists and writers who can be loosely identified as French feminist deconstructivists, while not representing either position directly, attack traditional theorising as patriarchal and locate language as the site of political struggle within the context of a psychoanalytic theory of meaning. They include Julia Kristeva, Luce Irigaray and Hélène Cixous and take as their starting point Jacques Lacan's psychoanalytic theory of language and subjectivity.

Moira Gatens (1994) warns against the dangers of the position taken by Irigaray and others. For these theorists, the very activity of theorising or constructing conceptual categories is an intrinsically male endeavour. Gatens argues that such writers effectively exclude women from the domain of intellectual discourse. The point made by Gatens is that feminists who attack all 'grand categories' fail to diagnose tensions or contradictions in the texts produced by male philosophers.

The conclusions of these different branches of feminist theory are: that the basis of 'masculinist theory' is partial, incomplete and assumes a knowledge base which is neutral; that direct experience is a necessary precondition for knowledge, and what counts as knowledge must be grounded in women's experience; that women's experience is systematically different from men's experience; and that knowledge and theory are incorrect or biased to the extent that they exclude women's experience.

The crucial issue for feminist standpoint epistemology in assessing its plausibility is the extent to which it is tenable to use women's experience as the basis for a theory of knowledge. Halberg (1992) notes that recent critiques of feminist epistemology have recognised and admitted that women's experiences are not unitary, and that epistemologically different groups of women – for example black women, working-class women, Third World women and so forth – all have different and 'group-specific' knowledge, which requires that we postulate different groups of interests.

In a recent further development of the 'feminist standpoint' position, Harding (1993) elaborates on the relationship between feminist knowledge, experience and oppression. Harding's (1993) work goes further than previously in making problematic the concept of 'experience' and 'oppression', and her work is clearly informed by the feminist debates of the late 1980s. She argues that some feminist epistemological positions have claimed that only women and women's experiences can generate feminist knowledge.

Harding (1993: 155) maintains that having women's experiences, and being a woman, is clearly not sufficient to generate feminist knowledge; all women have women's experiences but only at historical moments do any of us ever produce feminist knowledge. She states that it is thinking from a contradictory position that generates feminist knowledge. The key problem with Harding's somewhat redefined 'standpoint' position is that, while it attempts to address the criticisms of the 'essentialist' character of women's experience, and in addition offers a more refined view of the relationship between feminist knowledge and experience, it does not explain how feminist knowledge is to be 'grounded' epistemologically.

So what are the implications for a feminist epistemology based on a feminist standpoint position? Grant (1987) rejects essentialism and experience as a basis for feminist epistemology on the grounds that it is too difficult to operationalise the idea of women's experience. Halberg (1992) agrees, in maintaining that there is no feasible way of grounding a feminist epistemology within the boundaries of a 'feminist standpoint'. Halberg argues that feminist standpoint epistemology, through its privileging of 'multiple experiences', leads to a highly relativist view of knowledge. From this perspective, the existence of various, sometimes contradictory, women's standpoints means that there is no possible way of deciding between them.

The logic of 'feminist standpoint epistemology', as Harding (1991) argues, was to interrogate the 'male' subject of knowledge and to replace it with a different knowing subject. However, as has been indicated, feminist standpoint epistemology is characterised by inconsistencies which make the possibility of 'grounding' a feminist epistemology logically impossible. In addition, Halberg notes that the concept of 'experience' is a very vague term and the context of experience is never coherent or identical for all women. Halberg concludes in saying that, even if all women shared 'determining experiences', this would not necessarily give rise to the same kind of knowledge.

EPISTEMOLOGY, FEMINISM AND CULTURAL THEORY

The 1980s and 1990s saw the debate around the establishment of a feminist epistemology come under a number of pressures from within and outside feminism. The 'totalising' tendencies of earlier feminist theorising was challenged from within feminism by marginalised, colonised and indigenous women, who objected to feminist theories which failed to address their problems. Alongside the critiques emerging from within feminism emerged a parallel range of critiques from the area of cultural theory challenging the basis of a feminist epistemology. As Halberg (1992: 373) argues, 'the contours of feminist epistemologies had hardly acquired a distinct identity when they were challenged by postmodernist/anti-foundationalist thinking'. As Halberg goes on to assert, postmodernism is particularly challenging for feminist thinking because it questions the very idea of a foundation for knowledge. Halberg maintains that what follows from these objections is the idea that the concept of 'truth' is always plural and situated, and that the very basis of epistemology has to be questioned. Both postmodernism and poststructuralism have assisted feminism's attempts to take this debate forward through the concepts of 'deconstruction' and 'difference'.

For poststructuralist philosophers like Derrida and Foucault, knowledge is produced discursively. Nash (1994: 66) claims that 'Within such systems reason and experience are themselves no more than discursive constructions legitimating certain statements and denying others authority.' She notes how Derrida's critique of 'the metaphysics of presence' has problematised the conception of experience as simple and 'transparent':

> What this means is that experiences can never be isolated from the context in which they reveal themselves and every experience involves undecidability... Derrida's work shows, how no two categories or cognitions are identical because of the way identities depend minutely on the contexts in which they appear.
>
> (Nash 1994: 66, 67)

This has important implications for feminists focusing on the construction of gender identity. Judith Butler (1990a) emphasises how gender identities are contested and subverted through repetition in very different contexts from those in which they have hitherto been used and considered appropriate. As Butler notes, there may be opportunities, and occasions for subversion, in everyday social practices.

Nash (1994: 67) points out that Foucault's work similarly abandons the aim of achieving transparent truth, though for somewhat different reasons. One of the most important aspects of his work for feminists is that which has been concerned with the way the modern body and subjectivity have been constructed. Nash comments that 'Although, notoriously, Foucault has very little to say about the construction of the gendered body and gendered subjectivity' (*ibid.*), his approach has been developed by a number of feminists working in the area (Diamond and Quinby 1988; Bartky 1990; Bordo 1990).

More generally, the importance given to detail and context in the theory and method of deconstruction (see Nash 1994: 67) is valuable for feminism at a time when 'feminism's distrust of monocausal theories of women's oppression' is centrally positioned for feminist theoretical debates. As Nash (1994: 68) notes, 'the central categories of grand theories are both too abstract and also too fixed in their theoretical framework to allow the specific positions of women to be considered'. In addition, a 'second important feature of deconstruction for feminism is the way it emphasises how the modern ideal of knowledge has always been closely connected with the desire for control' (*ibid.*). Foucault's influence in this respect has been particularly important. His work emphasises the way power and knowledge are inextricably linked in modern societies. Foucault shows how 'the extension of truth is always an extension of power', and he alerts us 'to recognize the inherent danger of the assumption that knowledge is simply a disinterested reflection of reality and that the use of reason will lead to progress (Foucault 1980)' (*ibid.*). Nash goes on to point out that 'the Foucauldian emphasis on the interdependence of knowledge and power alerts us to the possibility that our formulations of women's position may contribute to the techniques of normalisation he describes in his work (see Butler 1990a: 3–6)'. Feminism's contribution to the normalisation of gender relations is clearly 'a problem for feminist standpoint epistemology which privileges women's special access to knowledge' (Nash 1994: 68). In this respect, such a position seems to contribute to 'the regulation and reification of gender identities, a regulation and reification that feminism set out to disrupt' (Nash 1994: 69).

A final element emerging from debates around deconstruction is, as Nash notes, 'the critique of knowledge as a reflection of the world in the reason and experience of the knowing subject'. From this perspective, 'knowledge is not elaborated by a knowing subject as modern philosophy would have it; rather knowledge positions subjects within certain discourses by enabling certain possibilities and excluding or repressing others' (ibid.). This fits well with the conclusions emerging from feminist epistemological critiques of knowledge produced during the last decade.

Feminist theorists who accept much of the postmodernist and poststructuralist critique of Western rationalism are critical of earlier feminist ventures. As McLennan (1995a: 16) notes, 'Thus, to some people, earlier monistic expressions of feminism have resulted in a restricted frame of reference which looks increasingly outdated.' As he goes on to note, 'Feminist theory has become "a prisoner of gender" in that sense [Flax 1990b: 52] and the "essentialist" identification of women's oppression as a uniform condition now looks precisely what is problematic' (ibid.).

POSTMODERNISM, FEMINISM AND AGENCY

The clearest statement of feminism's postmodernist character comes from Jane Flax (1990b), who argues (that feminist theory is typical of postmodern philosophy and, as such, reveals many of its characteristics. Flax maintains that feminist theory has contributed to the debates and growing uncertainty within Western intellectual circles about 'the appropriate grounding', and methods for explaining and interpreting human experience. She (1990b: 41) argues that 'Contemporary feminists join other postmodern philosophers in raising important metatheoretical questions about the possible nature and status of theorising itself.'

However, it is clear that, as Halberg (1992), Walby (1990) and others maintain, postmodernism challenges the primacy of epistemological discourses and thus undermines the 'feminist epistemological project'. In addition, there is concern among some feminists that the intersection of feminism and postmodernism might result in feminism becoming incorporated into post-modernism, and losing its distinctive character as a body of critical theory and practice. Others reject feminist postmodernism's challenge to feminist theory, on the grounds that, as Walby (1990) argues, most feminist postmodernists attack the very basis of consensus in feminist theorising: that is, the emphasis on the commonalities shared by women. Walby further notes that some postmodern theorists (e.g. Baudrillard) may be considered anti-feminist in their thinking.

In addition to the problematic relationship between feminism and postmodernism already outlined, the inescapable fact remains that the primary motivation of postmodernism is philosophical, while the primary motivation of feminism is political. Nicholson's (1990) position on the intersection of postmodernism and feminism is sometimes ambiguous, but she characterises the theories well. Fraser and Nicholson (1990: 19–20) argue that 'Postmodernists offer sophisticated and persuasive criticisms of foundationalism and essentialism but their conceptions of social criticism tend to be anaemic. Feminists offer robust conceptions of social criticism but they tend at times to lapse into foundationalism and essentialism.'

This surely must be seen as the essential impasse for the development of a postmodern feminism. As Fraser and Nicholson (1990) maintain, within postmodern theoretical thinking primacy is given to theoretical issues determined by the contemporary status of philosophy rather than by social criticism and political practice and engagement. Hekman (1990), like Nicholson (1990), argues for the importance of the intersection of feminism and postmodernism and wants to preserve the feminist concern about power, but at the same time Hekman (1990: 156) maintains that feminists cannot simply turn to postmodernism and take away from it what they want. McLennan, drawing on Hekman, maintains that 'The mission of feminism within the postmodern is thus to *politicise* it conceding that postmodernism can in turn assist feminism in the process of de-essentializing itself' (McLennan 1994: 108).

McLennan (1994) contends that the ambiguity and confusion manifested in the work of many of the feminists seeking a 'partnership' (Nicholson and Hekman), as opposed to a 'marriage' (Flax), between feminism and postmodernism is highlighted in the later work of Nicholson, who (1992) argues that feminists can produce a better and politically stronger theory by abiding by their postmodern inclinations. At the same time, she suggests 'that the new postmodernist directions for research ... "must not violate recognised political mandates of feminist research" ' (Nicholson 1992: 98). However, as McLennan (1994: 116) argues, it is clear that 'postmodernism does violate' those political mandates by 'pluralizing the number of such mandates', and by failing to identify political priorities.

Feminists have approached the issue of theorising with a view to avoiding essentialism and reductionism in ways other than establishing either a marriage or a 'partnership' with postmodernism. Sylvia Walby (1990, 1992) has been one of the most consistent opponents of feminism's 'paradigmatic shift' (Barrett 1990, 1992). She argues:

[In] the face of the complexity of the social world the postmodernist response is to deny the possibility of causality and macro-social concepts ... [R]ather than abandoning the modernist project of explaining the world, we should be developing the concepts and theories to explain gender, ethnicity and class. Not only is the concept of 'women' essential to grasp the gendered nature of the social world but so is that of 'patriarchy' in order that we do not lose sight of the power relations involved.

(Walby 1992: 48)

Walby (1992) does not deny that postmodernism has been valuable in terms of its interrogation of feminist theory, and in its critique of feminism's lack of historical and cultural specificity in the use of terms such as 'patriarchy'. She recognises the validity of postmodernism's claim that much of the metatheorising around 'patriarchy' has been problematic in terms of dealing with historical and cultural variation. However, as she notes, the solution of postmodernists is to deny causality, which she sees as 'defeatist'. Walby advocates a form of 'pluralism' based on a theorisation of different 'patriarchal bases' or 'sites' to overcome the critique of essentialism and reductionism.

One of Walby's main criticisms of both postmodernism and poststructuralism concerns their failure to consider power at a level of structural analysis. However, she does recognise the usefulness of the concept of discourse within poststructuralist theory and the centrality of the concept of power in Foucault's analysis of discourse within poststructuralism. As Weedon (1987: 13) notes in her analysis of the Foucauldian concept of discourse and power, 'if Foucault's theory of discourse and power can produce in feminist hands an analysis of patriarchal power relations which enables the development of active strategies for change, then it is of little importance whether his own historical analyses fall short of this'.

The intersection of feminism with poststructuralism can be seen to provide feminism with a useful analytical and critical device in the establishment of the relationship between experience and knowledge. In its critique of the 'rational autonomous self' of mainstream liberal social theory, poststructuralism has challenged many of the assumptions on which second wave feminism was based. As Weedon (1987: 33) maintains, 'In making our subjectivity the product of the society and culture within which we live, feminist poststructuralism insists that forms of subjectivity are produced historically and change with shifts in the wide range of discursive fields which constitute them.' Barrett (1992) argues that feminism's 'turn to culture' (1990) has created a more critical and reflexive feminism. She notes that second wave feminism was characterised by a consensus and confidence around issues of 'patriarchy', distinctions along sex/gender lines, as well as issues of 'subject' positioning and sexuality. Barrett goes on to indicate that these categories and ways of thinking within feminism have been challenged by the emphasis on 'deconstruction' and 'difference' – characterising debates in the field of cultural theory.

Poststructuralism offers feminism the means of moving beyond the analysis of power within social structures, to an analysis of power within a range of discursive fields. In this context, Barrett (1992) argues that the Foucauldian concept of discourse, within poststructuralist analysis, facilitates an analysis of the 'epistemological power' of different discourses. That is, she is arguing that the analysis of discourse 'opens up' an understanding of the nature and location of power within different discursive regimes. Feminism's intersection with the Foucauldian concept of 'power-knowledge' locates the analysis of power at a number of different levels (see Chapter 3).

DISCOURSE, DIFFERENCE AND THE IMPLICATIONS FOR FEMINIST EPISTEMOLOGY

Feminist poststructuralism, in focusing on the issue of power in subject positions and discourses, addresses the critiques that have been made of different branches of feminist theory, for their uncritical application of terms such as patriarchy and for their essentialist views of concepts such as 'women' and 'oppression'. Poststructuralism can also, through its analysis of discourse and power, locate feminist questions and issues, discursively and institutionally.

Many feminists have looked to the work of Michel Foucault, particularly his analysis of power, as a resource. Rosemary Pringle and Sophie Watson (1992) examine the relationship of power and the state, using a Foucauldian model of power. They argue that power should not be analysed in terms of a metatheoretical model of power either in sociopolitical or economic terms. Power, as drawn from a Foucauldian analytic frame of reference, facilitates an analysis of power in terms of local and institutional context and establishes the possibility of 'resistance' and contestation. McLennan notes that

> a feminism suitably influenced by the work of Michel Foucault would see power as a micro-level phenomenon and a socially pervasive one, its multiple forms and effects saturating not only official political institutions, but being 'immanent in all social relations' [Pringle and Watson 1992: 65].
>
> (McLennan 1995a: 18)

However, one of the questions facing Foucauldian feminism as raised by McLennan (1995a) is whether this approach involves a 'theory' of power at all. McLennan argues,

> ... the most that emerges is a pan-societal vision of micro-conflict, ... It is just this analytical 'pointillism' that has led more structurally inclined feminists to warn that 'fragmentation has gone too far', and that overly postmodernist feminism leads in effect 'towards mere empiricism' [Walby 1992: 31].
>
> (McLennan 1995a: 19)

Barrett and Phillips (1992), while acknowledging the significance of feminism's 'turn to culture', and while recognising the importance of concepts such as 'discourse' and 'difference' and 'deconstruction' for feminist theorising, have some reservations about feminism's intersection with cultural theory. Anne Phillips (1992) maintains that, in the context of a rethinking of contemporary political theory, feminist theory cannot afford to situate itself, in any total sense, for 'difference' and against 'universality', for in doing so feminism's epistemological challenge to the 'power-knowledge' base of the academy is undermined.

FEMINISM, FOUCAULT AND THE POLITICS OF THE ACADEMY

Feminism's intersection with Foucauldian analysis and concepts has changed the content and focus of the 'power-knowledge' debate within feminism. Understanding patriarchy – 'the knowledge project' – within feminism has become both more complex and diversified. In addition, the nature and application of feminism can be seen to mean different things to those inside and outside the academy. On one level, empirical work around gender inequality and gender relations has continued. However, more theoretical research drawing on poststructuralism in particular now has a prominent profile within feminist debate. Foucault has been a major, though by no means the only, influence in this increasingly theoretical focus within the feminist 'power-knowledge' project.

Feminism's investigations of the categories 'woman' and 'gender', as well as 'patriarchy' and 'oppression', are, as McNeil (1993: 158) notes, 'recent exemplary feminist forays involving the interrogation of feminism's own discourses inspired by poststructuralism in general and often Foucault in particular'. As Judith Butler (1990a: 5) maintains, these investigations constitute 'a feminist genealogy of the category woman'. One of the reasons why feminism has started to investigate or deconstruct its own categories is the relative failure of 'the equality trajectory of feminism' (McNeil 1993) to realise its goals. There are still strong gender divisions within established professions and within the academy, with men continuing to occupy powerful decision-making positions. In addition, previously established categories have been shown to be inadequate in reflecting inequalities, as the opening up of global research has exposed inequalities amongst women, particularly differences of class, race, sexual orientation and physical ability.

Feminist knowledge has not only become more diverse but has also shifted in emphasis. McNeil (1993: 159) notes that 'the extended channelling of the feminist emancipatory drive for knowledge into diverse forms of therapy (including psychoanalysis) and into an intensified feminist theory (drawing most notably on poststructuralism and psychoanalysis) has transformed feminism'. While the increasing specialisation and diversification within feminism might have been expected, what was perhaps surprising was the shift away from empirical investigations around gender relations and patriarchy, to a more purist theoretical domain uncluttered by the exigencies of empirical research.

Feminist theoretical analysis, particularly within the academy, has become more specialised. This is partly the result of feminist academics gaining entry into the academy and establishing feminist discourses within traditional academic domains, e.g. feminist literary criticism, feminist philosophy, feminist history, etc.

While it is important that feminist discourses should proliferate within the academy, writers such as Toril Moi (1989b), Tania Modleski (1991) and Kate Campbell (1992) have all warned that there is a tendency for feminist intellectuals to become ever more distanced from the mass of women whom feminism set out to liberate. Further, there is an increasing tendency towards the creation of 'a body of feminist knowledge which circulates more or less within the academy' (McNeil 1993: 162). Both Cornell West (1992) and Nancy Hartsock (1990) have shown that the intellectual becomes distanced from political movements in Foucault's version of critical intellectual work. Hartsock has argued more generally that Foucault speaks from a position of power. 'As a white male member of the intellectual elite he is, to use Hartsock's borrowing from Albert Memmi (1967), "the colonizer who refuses and thus exists in a painful ambiguity... the colonizer who refuses to become a part of his group" [Hartsock 1990: 164]' (McNeil 1993: 161). There is a need for a fuller, more rigorous analysis of the 'professionalisation' of feminism and of the nature of feminist intellectual labour.

A number of feminists writing in the 1990s have expressed concern about the direction of feminism. McNeil (1993) maintains that feminist theoretical knowledge has become somewhat detached from the goal of the women's movement as a liberatory political movement. Tania Modleski (1991) attacks feminist 'theoretical discourse' particularly as it is linked to poststructuralism. She maintains that feminism has turned in on itself, particularly in its critique of the categories of 'woman' and 'gender'. As McNeil maintains, although Modleski's book is not posed in this way, it can be read as a protest against the breaking down of the 'power-knowledge' project which once preoccupied feminism. As McNeil (1993: 115) notes, the question which reappears continually in Modleski's book is, 'What is the relationship between the elaborate development of knowledge associated with feminist theory and women's power in the world?'. Kate Campbell has shown how feminist theory has helped some women realise power in the academy but often not directly challenging the patriarchal power of the academy. She writes of the academy 'harbouring feminism: building it up and replenishing it in some ways, yes; but at the same time given to running it dry, keeping it within walls seeing to its overall containment' (1992: 2).

Ramazanoglu (1993) warns of the dangers of 'the politics of relativism' if feminism follows a Foucauldian or poststructuralist model too closely. She maintains that, 'Just as feminism is becoming a significant intellectual force in the production of knowledge it is in danger of being thwarted by an elitist but academically respectable relativism and pluralism which ignores gender, disempowers women and diminishes difference' (Ramazanoglu 1993: 8). She goes on to argue that feminism is in danger of being shifted from an 'emancipatory global movement' to a philosophical specialism which she maintains legitimates a political pluralism leading to fragmentation. She sends out this warning:

Feminists need to take seriously the political uses Foucault's thought can be put to, and the possible uses of his work in supporting male dominance by ignoring 'gender' in social relations and appearing to rise above the political implications of social divisions between women'.

(Ramazanoglu 1993: 8)

FEMINISM, 'PLURALISM' AND THE POLITICS OF RELATIVISM

At an epistemological level, there is a need for a radical and critical feminist epistemology to challenge the male monopoly of knowledge and exclusion of women from both the production of knowledge and positions of power. However, feminism's intersection with poststructuralism and postmodernism has led some feminist theorists to voice concern about the direction of feminist theory. Patricia Waugh (1992) explores the relationship between feminism and postmodernism. She argues that feminism clearly emerged from Enlightenment modernity, with its conceptions of justice and subjectivity as being 'universal' categories. However, Waugh maintains that feminist discourses, in articulating issues of sexual difference, weakened the extremes of universalism in modernist thought. She argues that, in this sense of articulating 'difference', feminism can be seen as postmodern. Waugh notes that feminism does recognise a contradiction in its attempt to establish an epistemological base, in that women look for equality and recognition based on cultural and ideological formations which feminism seeks to challenge.

Feminism, like postmodernism, argues Waugh, has provided its own critique of essentialist and foundationalist assumptions. However, as a political practice, feminism cannot completely turn its back on 'enlightened modernity', she says: to be effective as an emancipatory movement it must have a belief in an effective 'human agency', in the importance of historical continuity and historical progress. She argues that feminism has been engaged in a struggle to reconcile context-specific difference or situatedness with universal political aims, and she makes the important point that 'totalities', such as the concept of political unity, need not mean uniformity. Waugh argues that the postmodern espousal of decentring as liberatory says little about women as beings in the world who may continue to find themselves displaced even within a critique of epistemology which has supposedly deconstructed the centre and done away with the margins.

Seyla Benhabib (1994) offers a critical overview of the alleged convergence between feminism and postmodernism. She argues that many feminists have accepted three main theses associated with postmodernism. One is the concept of the 'death of man', or the end of humanism, which means the dissolution of philosophies that begin with 'the subject', subjectivity, or human consciousness. A second theme identified by Benhabib is 'the death of history', which refers to the disappearance of 'grand narratives'. The third element is the 'death of metaphysics', which means the end of the attempt 'to discover absolute truth, or the "essences of things"' (Benhabib 1994: 230). While Benhabib recognises the importance of these issues within feminist theorising, she expresses a concern that, if they are engaged with too uncritically, they threaten not only to eliminate feminist theory as a distinct enterprise, but to dissolve its emancipatory goals in the process. Benhabib maintains that in their 'weak' versions these theories are useful, but in their 'strong' versions they are counterproductive for feminist theory, politics and practice. Benhabib maintains that a 'weak' version of the 'death of man' thesis 'situates' the subject in context, and is valuable in stressing variability and diversity. The more radical version, however, reduces 'the subject' to an endless state of flux. This latter position is both unhelpful and damaging to feminism: as Benhabib maintains, it provides no means of understanding how women could become more autonomous and change the circumstances of their lives. Similarly, Benhabib points out that much the same position exists for 'the death of history'. While it is important to recognise that there are no absolutes in historical change, if all forms of theorising about patterns of change are rejected, then there is no way of promoting successful emancipatory struggles.

Benhabib maintains that, while postmodernism can illuminate certain problems for feminism, any attempt to link feminism with a 'strong' postmodernism would lead to incoherence and would make effective theorising impossible. Benhabib argues that a 'strong' postmodernism leads feminism into a position where it is reticent to formulate a feminist ethic or concept of autonomy because of a fear of lapsing into essentialism. She argues that this has produced in feminism 'a retreat from utopia'. She maintains that 'Postmodernism can teach us the theoretical and political traps of why utopias and foundational thinking can go wrong, but it should not lead to a retreat from utopia altogether. For we, as women, have much to lose by giving up the utopian hope in the wholly other' (Benhabib 1994: 230).

Barrett (1991) has maintained that postmodernism's tendency to deconstruct and fragment some of the central concepts used in 'modernist' social theory has shifted the focus of theoretical debate from structural analysis to an analysis of 'discourse'. The implications are to produce a highly dispersed and fragmented analysis of power, which fails to locate the source of power in any specific location or social group. The implications for feminist theory and epistemology are, as a result, highly problematic because of a denial of causality within the plurality of sources of power articulated through this model.

Barrett argues that the significance of poststructuralism, in particular for feminist thinking, has made 'classic materialist' models of social power seem less politically useful for feminist analysis. She recognises that poststructuralism challenges traditional notions of causality, but maintains that Foucault's concept of discourse is valuable in this respect because it facilitates an analysis of the nature of epistemological power of discursive regimes. Barrett (1992: 204) points out that the new critical feminism that has emerged has moved away from the more 'determinist' models of 'social structure (framed as capitalist, patriarchy or gender-segmented labour market) and focuses on culture, sexuality and political agency'.

Barrett maintains that evidence of a 'paradigm shift' within feminism can be seen to have taken place already. She claims that the debate within feminism around 'equality/difference' which has characterised the past decade of Western feminism can be seen as a paradigmatic shift of that order. However, Barrett argues that feminism is too indebted to 'modernist' values to be able to totally reject the context in which it was formed. She maintains that a total postmodern abandonment of binary structures would be rejected by many feminists. She argues that we can speak of 'a gendering of modernity' (Barrett 1992) as a new critical enterprise, and maintains that it is becoming increasingly possible to identify debates on the implications for feminism in the various critiques of modernism and modernity.

Barrett's generally positive view of feminism's intersection with poststructuralism does contain reservations. She argues that debates around ideology and subjectivity have shown that we need a better conception of agency and identity than has become available in either anti-humanist poststructuralist thought or its humanist/modernist predecessors. Barrett and Phillips (1992) recognise there is now a concern that the process of self-criticism operating within feminism might lead to a move away from the goal of production of accurate and systematic knowledge, and that feminism may lose sight of the hierarchies of 'white male privilege'. They make the point that more recent theory does not equal better theory. However, they argue that it should not be assumed that nothing new can ever be added to the debate. As Barrett and Phillips (1992: 7) maintain, 'To claim transcendence is to ignore our own position in history; to reduce debates to their essential context is to deny the power of context and discourse.'

The question facing feminist theorists is how far feminism should go in engaging with contemporary theoretical debate around postmodernism and poststructuralism. As Barrett (1992: 215) notes, 'in legitimate critique of some of the earlier assumptions we may stray too far from feminism's original project'. Barrett (1992: 6) cites Bordo's (1990) comments in this regard: 'Susan Bordo . . . has argued that too relentless a focus on historical heterogeneity . . . can obscure the transhistorical patterns of white male privilege that have informed the creation of the Western intellectual tradition.' Bordo recognises the new scepticism about the use of 'globalising' categories within feminist theory. She recognises, and considers, feminism's appropriation of 'deconstruction' and the call from within feminism for new 'narrative' approaches aimed at the adequate representation of 'difference'. She maintains that the influence of poststructuralism has shifted the central concerns of feminism from a specific practical 'political' emphasis to questions of adequate theory. Bordo (1990: 152) argues that, as a result, feminism has been diverted from an analysis of 'professional and institutional mechanisms through which the politics of exclusion operate more powerfully in intellectual communities', and she goes on to say that, at the same time, feminism deprives itself of analytical tools for critiquing those communities.

However, Bordo claims (in a note) that her main criticism is directed at the programmatic adoption or appropriation of poststructuralism. She maintains much poststructuralist thought – particularly as manifested in the work of Foucault – is useful in terms of offering interpretive tools and analytical devices rather than theoretical frameworks for analysis.

Bordo argues that, while in theory all 'totalising' narratives may be equal, in the context of Western history and actual relations of power characteristic of history, there are significant differences between the 'meta-narratives' of gender theory, and those in the white male intellectual tradition. The latter, argues Bordo, being located at the centre of three axes of privilege – race, class and gender – had more to lose in giving recognition to 'difference'. Feminist theory, as Bordo points out, is not located at the centre of cultural power. She maintains that feminism, being an 'outsider discourse' and a movement born out of the experience of marginality, has been far more attuned to issues of exclusion and invisibility. She warns against the dangers of the paralysis that could accompany the self-doubt and criticism that feminism is experiencing, and maintains that a decade ago feminist academics were preoccupied with the concept of 'otherness'. However, she argues that feminist academics have been 'accepted' within a masculine patriarchal academy, and concludes that 'our language, intellectual history and social forms are "gendered"; there is no escape from this fact and from its consequences on our lives' (1990: 152). She maintains that academic institutions have only just begun to absorb the messages of 'modernist' social criticism, to allow them to escape any further challenge to their epistemological and power bases.

The process of self-reflection, which has characterised feminist thinking in the 1980s and 1990s, has accompanied changes in both the nature, and form, of patriarchy in a range of cultural, social, political, economic and institutional sites. One of the results has been a breakdown in the consensus of second wave feminism and a movement towards a 'feminist pluralism'. As Ramazanoglu notes,

> since academic social theorists are increasingly under some pressure to acknowledge feminist social theory, those unsympathetic to feminist politics are offered a level of engagement between feminism, poststructuralism and postmodernism which is intellectually challenging but extremely abstracted and also insensitive to the political point of feminism.
>
> (Ramazanoglu 1993: 8)

CONCLUSION

What conclusions can be drawn with regard to any fundamental shift in orientation for feminism? McLennan (1994: 118) argues that 'feminism cannot completely give up on a critical rationalist conception of *ideology*'. As he continues, '[Postmodernism,] immensely valuable as it has been as a kind of conceptual *agent provocateur*, . . . will, I think, be superseded by a more rounded and positive theoretical orientation' (McLennan 1994: 120). Both postmodernism and poststructuralism can be seen as valuable theoretical interventions in a feminism which, while superficially characterised by coherence, was internally riven by divisions based on race, ethnicity, class and sexuality. However, it is argued by some branches of feminism that there needs to be an articulation of feminist epistemologies for feminism to pose a significant challenge to the academy. As Elizabeth Grosz contends:

> The choice . . . is not between maintaining a politically pure theoretical position (and leaving the murkier questions of political involvement unmasked); or espousing a politically tenuous one which may be more pragmatically effective in securing social change. The alternatives faced by feminist theorists are all in some sense 'impure' and 'implicated' in patriarchy. There can be no feminist position that is not in some way or other involved in patriarchal power relations; it is hard to see how this is either possible or desirable, for a freedom from patriarchal 'contamination' entails feminism's incommensurability with patriarchy, and thus the inability to criticise it.
>
> (Grosz 1990b: 342)

She notes that feminism's engagement with patriarchy not only provides the conditions under which feminism can become familiar with what it criticises, but it also provides the means by which patriarchal dominance can be challenged. Thus, from the perspective of second wave feminism, postmodernism and poststructuralism's effective denial of the status of all epistemologies renders feminism politically and epistemologically powerless, and must ultimately lead to feminism's rejection of a 'long term relationship'.

3

FOUCAULT AND POSTFEMINISM
Discourse, power and resistance

INTRODUCTION

Poststructuralism, along with postmodernism and psychoanalytic theory, has been among the most important theoretical developments of the twentieth century. Poststructuralist theorists such as Derrida and Foucault have challenged traditional epistemological assumptions about knowledge and truth, in terms of how knowledge can be apprehended and whose knowledge is valorised. The origins of poststructuralism can be traced to a number of theoretical strands as noted by Weedon (1987: 13), including 'the structural linguistics of Ferdinand de Saussure and Emile Benveniste, Marxism, particularly Louis Althusser's theory of ideology and the psychoanalytic theories of Sigmund Freud and Jacques Lacan'. Weedon comments that they also

> include Jacques Derrida's theory of '*différance*' with its critique of the metaphysics of presence, in which the speaking subject's intention guarantees meaning, and language is a tool for expressing something beyond it, deconstruction based on Derrida's theory and Michel Foucault's theory of discourse and power.
>
> (Weedon 1987: 13)

Thus the term 'poststructuralism' is plural and incorporates a range of theoretical positions.

As has been indicated, Weedon (1987) develops a version of poststructuralism which she calls 'feminist poststructuralism'. She recognises that there are different forms of poststructuralism and that not all forms are productive for feminism, but she contends that its different forms share certain fundamental assumptions about language, meaning and subjectivity. Weedon maintains that the least 'a feminist poststructuralism can do is explain the assumptions underlying the questions asked and answered by other forms of feminist theory, making their political assumptions explicit' (1987: 20). She contends that poststructuralism can identify the type of discourse from which particular feminist questions emerge and can locate them socially and institutionally. For a theory to be useful it needs to be able to address questions of how social power is exercised and how social relations structured around gender, class and race might be transformed. She recognises that this requires an historical perspective, which she notes is absent in many theories of poststructuralism but is central to the work of Michel Foucault.

Foucault's analysis of power, as outlined by Weedon, presents historical explanations of the development of power as repression and looks to the specific forms taken. As Weedon explains, Foucault understands hegemonic control by the State to extend to a range of interests and investments in different forms of power. Foucault understands the operation of power through institutional arrangements e.g. education, work, the law. Weedon outlines how the operation of social control through these agencies disciplines the body, mind and emotions, constituting hierarchial forms of power such as gender, ethnicity and class. The practices learned in institutional contexts constitute 'subjective identity'.

The implications for 'structural' models of power are clear in Foucault's analysis. As Weedon (1987: 124) argues, in considering 'patriarchy', explanations which attempt to account for it only 'in terms of privileged forms of power such as the capitalist mode of production, the nuclear family or male violence against women, offer necessarily, partial politically limited analyses'. She goes on to consider the implications for a feminist poststructuralist perspective, and maintains that through an analysis of the nature of power and subjective identity created through different discourses, feminism can establish an alternative knowledge base. As Weedon maintains,

> the knowledge produced for women through the process of subjugation to such discourses can be the basis for the articulation of alternative meanings which do not marginalise and subordinate women, and which in the process transform the hegemonic structures of masculinity.
>
> (Weedon 1987: 127)

This chapter explores the relationship between feminist theory and the Foucauldian concepts of discourse and power. It has been argued that discourse, as used in Foucault's work, provides for an analysis of power at a more differentiated level and facilitates an analysis of the nature of epistemological power of discursive regimes. The use of the concept of discourse will be considered for feminist theory and politics, and for a broader-based conception of power and oppression as analysed within feminist poststructuralism.

FOUCAULT, POWER AND DISCOURSE

The first part of the chapter investigates the significance of Foucault's concepts of power and discourse for feminist theory. In order to understand the impact of the Foucauldian model for feminist theory and politics it is important to contextualise Foucault's work within the broader debate within social theory around the epistemological and methodological implications of poststructuralism in general. The relevance of Foucault for feminist theory will be considered in terms of both the contradictions within Foucauldian analysis itself and between feminist theory and Foucault's model of power and discourse. Some of the problems emerging for feminism in adopting a Foucauldian model of power and discourse will be assessed, as well as the intersection of feminism and poststructuralism more generally for issues such as 'patriarchy', 'oppression' and resistance.

CONTEXTUALISING FOUCAULT: POWER, TRUTH AND DISCOURSE

Michèle Barrett, in her text *The Politics of Truth: From Marx to Foucault* (1991), contextualises Foucault's concept of 'discourse' as the focus of an alternative theoretical model to that of ideology. She defines Foucault as an exemplar of the poststructuralist critique of the theory of ideology, and frames the Foucauldian model within the broader shift from ideology to 'discourse' in social theory. Foucault, Barrett argues, rejects the concept of ideology because it has implications for concepts of absolute truth, because it rests on a humanist model of the individual subject, and because it is enmeshed in the Marxist base and superstructure model.

Barrett makes a distinction between 'discourse' as it relates to textuality (Barthes, Derrida), and Foucault's theory of discourse which describes discourse as central in the nexus of relations of power and which is the focus of concern at this point. As Barrett (1991: 126) points out, 'in direct contrast to the concerns associated with "textuality", Foucault's use of the concept of discourse and of what we would call discursivity in general is very much related to context'. The key element to grasp about Foucault's use of the concept of discourse is that it enables us to understand how what is said has its own social and historical context and is a product of specific conditions of existence. His concept of discourse is explained in his major methodological work *The Archaeology of Knowledge* (1972).

Barrett shows how Foucault's concept of discourse is embedded in a theoretical system which has developed a range of categories involving an explicit rejection of classical Marxist categories. Peter Dews (1984) reinforces Barrett's view that Foucault's concept of power was developed in part as a polemic against Marxist structuralism. Dews (1984: 73) maintains that Foucault's thought represents a highly individual historical vision and is 'specifically concerned with forms of knowledge and modes of social organisation characteristic of capitalist modernity'. Dews argues that Foucault's *The Birth of the Clinic* (1973a) can be seen as an oblique polemic against the Marxist view.

Barrett indicates that her analysis of Foucault's concept of discourse is framed in the context of categories, including: the issue of determinism; issues concerned with epistemology and the question of knowledge, truth and power; and issues concerned with the definition of the subject and agency. Barrett, having outlined these three issue areas, focuses first on the problem of

49

determination and the issue of discourse and the non-discursive in Foucault. She maintains that in *The Order of Things* (1973b) Foucault distinguishes between dependencies which are: intra-discursive, i.e. between the objects, operations and concepts within one discursive formation; inter-discursive, i.e. between different discursive formations; and extra-discursive, i.e. between discursive and non-discursive formations. She points out that the way Foucault thought of the relations between the discursive and non-discursive was profoundly different from the conventions of Marxism.

As Foucault (1991: 60) himself argues, his approach to the analysis of discourse is 'To investigate not the laws of construction of discourse as is done by those who use structural methods, but its conditions of existence'. He goes on to say that discourse is related 'not to a thought, mind or subject which engendered it, but to the practical field in which it is deployed' (Foucault 1991: 161). Foucault refers to this as a 'discursive field', which consists of a whole group of regulated practices, so for Foucault 'discourse' is a set of 'practices' rather than structures. Barrett outlines Foucault's analysis of discourse in *The Archaeology of Knowledge* as the production of 'things' by 'words': i.e. as Barrett (1991: 30) indicates, 'discourses are composed of signs, but they do more than designate things, for they are "practices that systematically form the objects of which they speak" '. She maintains that, in a reversal of the classical materialist hierarchy, Foucault says that the rules of discursive practice 'define not the dumb existence of a reality, nor the canonical use of a vocabulary, but the ordering of objects' (Foucault 1972: 49).

Barrett highlights some of the significant issues that Foucault's concept of discourse raises. First, his questioning of the hierarchy of determinism found in Marxism. As Barrett indicates, Foucault saw determination as polymorphous rather than unilinear and he wanted to claim 'the determinative powers of discourse in constituting practices that are ultimately responsible for – as Said put it – "how people thought, lived and spoke" ' (Barrett 1991: 131). Second, Barrett notes that Foucault opposed the conception of social structure although he developed an equally general concept: that of power.

Barrett indicates that Foucault's concept of discourse was closely connected with his concept of truth, knowledge and power. Foucault's concept of power as outlined by Barrett does not locate it in agencies – e.g. State, economic forces, or individuals – but sees it in terms of 'micro' operations of power. Barrett (1991: 135) points out that Foucault's concept of power was 'developed as a critique of Marxism's theory of power as an instrument of class dominance'. Foucault saw power as something that is exercised rather than possessed, i.e. power is not attached to agents and interests but is incorporated in numerous practices. As Barrett (1991: 136) notes, 'the object of analysis changes in Foucault, from power as an absolute, to power in terms of power relations'.

Foucault's disagreements with Marxism were profound. He rejected the realist epistemology on which the ideology/science distinction had been founded: he also rejected the notion of the subject which Marxism assumed (both individual agent and class subject). Barrett (1991: 138) argues that 'one would say that Foucault is working outside the Marxist problematic of determinism, rather than seeking to retrieve a polymorphous model of causality within it'. As Barrett (1991: 139) notes, the materialist premises of Marxism are inadequate as a basis for thinking about political, cultural and social life in late twentieth-century society 'whose determinations are so different from those of mid-nineteenth century manufacturing capitalism'.

Barrett draws on Barry Smart's 'The Politics of Truth and the Problem of Hegemony' (1986) to extrapolate the relationship between power, ideology and Foucault. As Smart maintains,

> Foucault by virtue of critical distance from the limitations of the Marxist problematic has been able to transform the terms of the debate from a preoccupation with the ambiguous concept of 'ideology' and its effects, to a consideration of the relations of 'truth' and power which are constitutive of hegemony.
>
> (Smart 1986: 160)

In discussing Foucault on hegemony, Smart suggests that Foucault's project was to show 'the complex multiple processes from which the strategic constitution of forms of hegemony may emerge' (1986: 160).

Nancy Fraser (1989) draws comparisons between Foucault's concept of genealogy and the concept of ideology. Genealogy and the genealogical method was Foucault's method of studying history through the analysis of discourse. McNeil (1993) argues that the genealogical method was designed to explore not who had power, but rather the patterns of the exercise of power through the interplay of discourses. Cain (1993) shows how, through his genealogical method, Foucault arrived at the position that it was the exercise of power that created knowledge. The genealogical method enables Foucault to chart the discontinuities of history and the play of power relations in the production of knowledges. Fraser claims that Foucault, in opposing genealogy to ideology, maintains that

> genealogy does not concern itself with evaluating the contents of science or systems of knowledge or for that matter with systems of beliefs . . . Rather it is concerned with the processes, procedures and apparatuses whereby truth, knowledge, belief are produced, within what Foucault calls 'the politics of the discursive regime'.
>
> (1989: 19)

Fraser proceeds to develop systematically the links between discourse, power/ knowledge, truth and ideology in Foucault's work. She argues that the functioning of 'discursive regimes' in Foucault's model involves forms of social constraint which can take different forms, such that the constraints themselves and their application will vary depending on the regime. Such forms of heterogeneous constraint, or in Foucault's terms 'power', circulates in and through the production of discourses in societies. Thus, as Fraser (1989: 20) maintains, 'what Foucault is interested in when he claims to be studying the genealogy of power/knowledge regimes [is]...networks of social practices involving the mutual interrelationship of constraint and discourse'.

On the question of ideology, while the terms of the debate may have shifted from the concept of ideology (or the 'economics of untruth' as Foucault describes it) to the 'politics of truth' in his own work, this is problematic. As Fraser (1989) notes, Foucault's approach to the study of power/knowledge regimes sidesteps or ignores the categories truth/falsity or truth/ideology. Fraser argues that Foucault does not address the question of whether the knowledge emanating from the discursive regimes he studies is true, adequate or distorted. Rather than assessing the legitimacy of epistemic content, Foucault describes the procedures, practices, apparatuses and institutions of knowledge production.

Barrett (1991) outlines Foucault's position on the 'subject', arguing that Foucault maintained that 'the subject should be thought of as constituted rather than a given and his interest in the practices constituting that subject (discursive, social, etc.) was much broader than that of many other modern theorists' (Barrett 1991: 146). She focuses on the reasons why Foucault has been so significant for feminism and puts forward two reasons: Foucault's displacement of social class from the theorisation of subjectivity; and 'Foucault's implacable critique of the "sovereign" subject of humanist discourse' (Barrett 1991: 147). Biddy Martin locates Foucault's critique of humanism in the context of feminist theory, and argues that

> feminist analysis demonstrates ever more convincingly that women's silence and exclusion from struggles over representation have been the condition of possibility for humanist thought: the position of women has indeed been that of an internal exclusion within Western culture, a particularly well-suited point from which to expose the workings of power in the will to truth and identity.
>
> (Martin 1988: 13)

In the *The Archaeology of Knowledge*, Foucault wrote:

> discourse is not the majestically unfolding manifestation of a thinking, knowing, speaking subject but, on the contrary, a totality in which the dispersion of the subject and his discontinuity with himself may be determined...[I]t is neither by recourse to a transcendental subject nor by recourse to a psychological subjectivity that the regulation of its enunciations should be defined.
>
> (Foucault 1972: 55)

Barrett (1991) points out that Foucault's rejection of the myth of the transcendental subject, his anti-humanism and his analysis of individualisation in modern society is quite different from Derridean and Lacanian poststructuralism. She argues (1991: 150) that 'the breadth of the Foucauldian perspective means that Foucault's insights can be set to work across a whole spectrum of work in historical, textual, sociological and critical debates'.

It is the issue of agency, Barrett says, that causes most scepticism about the relevance of Foucault's concept of power, among both feminists and social theorists generally. Anthony Giddens (1987) outlines the contradictions apparent in Foucault's work around the question of agency. He argues (1987: 98) that Foucault's history is a history with no active subject. It is a history with the agency removed; the individuals who appear in Foucault's analyses seem impotent to determine their own destinies. Moreover, as Giddens comments, that reflective appropriation of history, basic to history in modern culture, does not appear at the level of the agents themselves.

THE SIGNIFICANCE OF FOUCAULT FOR FEMINIST THEORY: CONTRADICTIONS AND COMPROMISE

On one level Foucault appears to hold much significance for feminism. As Ramazanoglu (1993) notes, he has enabled feminists to look in new ways at the control of women. At another level, Foucault can be said to challenge or even undermine feminism, in that, as Ramazanoglu states, he questions many of feminism's conclusions about the nature of social life and in the process deconstructs both feminism's emphasis on collective action as part of the transformative process and the nature of gendered power itself.

Foucault's work was not directly supportive of feminism, nor did he offer a direct challenge to feminism. In fact, Foucault personally seemed sympathetic to women's desire to change power relations. His work does have particular implications for feminist thought and feminist politics: Foucault challenges traditional feminist conceptions about the nature of knowledge and power and, in particular, challenges feminists' understanding about the nature of men's power over women. Foucault challenges a range of concepts, including reality and truth, cause and effect, freedom and the nature of human agency, which, as Ramazanoglu notes, are intrinsic to the Western liberal humanistic tradition and which many feminists have uncritically adopted. Foucault challenges and subverts these concepts of truth.

The obvious tensions between Foucault and feminism highlight fundamental problems in explaining the nature of power relations which both feminism and social theory have failed to solve. These contradictions and problems should not be linked necessarily to any specific weakness in feminism, but, as indicated above, rather to feminism's pragmatic approach to some of the most profound problems confronting social theory. Caroline Ramazanoglu, writing in *Feminism and the Contradictions of Oppression* (1989), argues that the contradictions and inconsistencies of feminist thought are indicative of the fact that feminism is deeply contradictory because women's lives are contradictory.

Thus, in addressing the significance of Foucault for feminism and feminist theory, it is, as Grimshaw notes,

> not so much a question of whether Foucault can be useful to feminism (or vice versa) or whether some 'synthesis' of the two can be found. It is rather a question of what affinities there are between some of the questions that feminist theory has addressed and those that Foucault addresses and what sort of dialectic can be created between these.
>
> (Grimshaw 1993: 52)

There are a number of issues resulting from Foucault's work which are significant for feminist theory, practices and politics. Feminism's interrogation of theory, especially since the 1970s, has already begun to question 'the implicit or sometimes explicit misogyny of theories, disciplines and intellectual frameworks' (Grosz 1990a: 91). As Grosz notes, Foucault finds problematic any aspirations to truth as an objective, verifiable and eternal value, and his adoption of theory as a strategy both confirmed and enhanced feminists' doubts about the 'epistemological politics invested in truth' (*ibid.*). The implications for 'resisting' feminist discourses have been profound. Foucault's critique of the concept of truth, and his suggestion of theory as a strategy or tool, has contributed to the development of alternative feminist discourses. French feminist deconstructivists (Hélène Cixous, Luce Irigaray and Julia Kristeva) have developed a body of writing which does not claim a truth status but positions women's writing between theory and fiction. In addition, some feminist challenges to phallocentrism do not aim to replace patriarchal discourses with feminist truths, but 'to reveal the investments patriarchal knowledges have in both representing and excluding women' (*ibid.*). As Grosz goes on to note, a range of feminist voices do not claim a universal objective value, but reflect particular views written from specific perspectives.

A second major area of interest for feminists in relation to Foucault's work is the structure/agency debate. Fraser (1989) argues that, like Foucault and Habermas, she has wanted to avoid what she describes as 'functionalist models that purport to show how "systems reproduce themselves" '. The limitations of these models based on structural analysis is that they screen out ' "dysfunctional": actions that resist, contest and disrupt social practices' (1989: 9). In addition, argues Fraser, they tend to neglect the actions of social agents and more generally social processes and the ways in which even 'the most routinised practice of social agents involves the making and unmasking of social reality'. However, while Fraser accepts the poststructuralist critique of 'totality' when applied to what she describes as 'ahistorical philosophical metanarratives', she is less convinced of this critique when applied to empirical theories about historically specific social formations, which, she maintains, can be 'both epistemically possible and politically useful'.

Foucault's approach to understanding power can offer feminists new and productive insights into relations of dominance and subordination both within masculinist discourses and within feminism itself. As Ramazanoglu (1993: 2) notes, while feminists have been developing theories of the social construction of gender, sexuality and the body, Foucault has opened up a parallel but rather different theory of social construction through new ways of deconstructing history and of analysing power relations. Fraser is positive about Foucault's approach to understanding the operation of power, which she describes as 'productive' rather than prohibitive. In addition, she argues, Foucault's account of power demonstrates that modern power is 'capillary' in that it operates at the lowest extremities of society in everyday social practices. Further, Fraser (1989: 18) notes that 'Foucault's genealogy of modern power establishes that power touches people's lives more fundamentally through their social practices than through their beliefs.' In addition, Foucault's emphasis is on the practices of the operation of power and, as Fraser points out, this facilitates an understanding of power which is both broad and 'anchored in the multiplicity of what he calls "micro practices", the social practices that constitute everyday life in modern societies' (*ibid.*).

Foucault's understanding of the nature and operation of power has a number of implications for feminism. Foucault's notion of knowledges and truths as the bearers of power has raised a number of issues around feminist politics and practices, and has challenged key assumptions about the nature and causes of women's subordination on which various versions of feminism are based. Ramazanoglu (1993) argues that the implications of Foucault's analysis suggests that feminist political practices are based on a misunderstanding of the power relations that feminism aims to transform. As Grimshaw (1993) notes, Foucault's work is useful in pointing out that theories of emancipation such as feminism, tend to be blind to their own dominating tendencies, and feminism itself is not innocent of power.

Jana Sawicki (1991) argues that a Foucauldian approach can offer a useful alternative to feminist analyses which adopt over-monolithic notions of male power and male control of women. Sawicki argues that feminism's recognition of its own potentially dominating and oppressive tendencies is crucial for feminism for a number of reasons. Women are themselves implicated in many forms of domination and oppression along class, occupational and ethnic lines. In addition, feminist thinking and practice has not been innocent of divisive, exclusionary and oppressive tendencies resulting in the marginalisation of groups of women. Grosz (1990a) notes that feminist practices are neither more nor less neutral and value-free than any other, and feminist research is as implicated in power relations as any other.

Foucault's pluralistic and localised conception of power, reflected in his account of marginal political struggles and subjugated discourses, facilitates an understanding of 'resistance' in terms of challenging patriarchal discourses at a 'micro' level. Grosz maintains:

> while Foucault's marginalised, localised struggles rule out the concept of 'The Revolution' smashing patriarchy in one fell swoop, he makes clear that a revolution of sorts is already under way. Patriarchal relations can be

transformed, not through reformism but in strategically located strikes at power's most vulnerable places.

(Grosz 1990a: 92)

It is clear that Foucault is significant for feminism. Ramazanoglu (1993) notes that feminism cannot afford to ignore Foucault, because the problems he addresses and the criticisms he makes of existing theories and their political consequences identify problems in and for feminism. However, she also notes that feminist knowledge poses a challenge to the validity of Foucault's work. As Ramazanoglu contends, there has been growing interest in Foucault's work among academic feminists who have been both enthusiastic and critically evaluative of his work. Some examples are Barrett and Phillips (1992), Bartky (1990), Braidotti (1991), Butler (1990a), Diamond and Quinby (1988), Fraser (1989), Hekman (1990), Nicholson (1990) and Sawicki (1991).

One of the ways feminism has challenged Foucauldian analysis revolves around 'the question of truth'. As Ramazanoglu points out, while Foucault might criticise feminism for the limitations and rigidities of its conception of the truth of patriarchy, feminists could equally criticise Foucault because he did not recognise that his supposedly neutral analysis of the discourses of truth, power and sexuality comes from a male perspective. As Ramazanoglu (1993: 45) maintains, it is not simply a question of confronting Foucault's 'masculinist analysis' with one which is woman-centred. The difficulty is the interaction between Foucault's understanding of the nature and operation of power, and feminism's reliance on women's experiences as a grounding for its explanations.

While feminism cannot afford to ignore Foucault, feminists need to be aware of the dangers of too close an engagement with Foucault. Feminists who wish to draw on Foucault must realise that his position shifted in some respects between his major works and again in many later interviews and discussions with him. Further, if feminists are looking for consistency, as Ramazanoglu (1993: 8) notes, 'feminists are at risk of being lured into some version of political pluralism in which feminist politics are undermined by political relativism'. Feminists therefore need to be wary of Foucault and to take seriously the political uses Foucault's thought can be put to and the possible uses of his work in supporting male dominance by ignoring gender in social relations.

POWER AND DISCOURSE IN FOUCAULT

Foucault sees all of his work contributing to outlining the intricate and highly variable forms of power in discursive and non-discursive practices. McNeil (1993) notes that at the centre of all Foucault's enquiries is his concern with the power–knowledge relationship. This can be seen to begin within his early methodological texts, notably *The Archaeology of Knowledge* (1972), and carries through to his specific historical studies (case studies on madness, criminality and sexuality). However, there is a tension in Foucault's work, as Ramazanoglu

(1993: 17) notes, between his later emphasis on the fractured and unstable nature of power which is both productive and accessible, and his earlier emphasis on a more stable and concentrated conception of power.

Peter Dews (1984) maintains that Foucault introduces and begins to elaborate his theory of power in his text *Discipline and Punish* (1977), establishing a theoretical distance from his more narrowly focused methodological concerns of the late 1960s. During the 1970s, he says, Foucault begins to develop a view of power which clearly indicates disillusionment with structuralism. His inclination is to play down the repressive and negative aspects of power and to present the operation of power as primarily positive and productive. This shift of emphasis in Foucault's work creates tensions between a feminist and a Foucauldian concept of power. As Ramazanoglu (1993) notes, Foucault's early work is concerned with domination and physical power, but he moved increasingly to a position which denied that power was repressive or resulted from a single source of domination or oppression. While feminists identify male power as repressive, Foucault moved towards a position which defined all power as productive.

In fact, Foucault does not present a 'theory' of power, but develops a series of methods for examining the operation of power. He describes his work as an 'analytics of power', a series of methods which make no claim to lasting or eternal truth. However, as Grosz (1990a: 87) indicates, although Foucault does not consider power either as a uniform or homogeneous thing, it is possible to extract a number of 'methodological theses' from his work to assist an examination of power relations. Grosz notes that, for Foucault, power is not possessed, given or seized, rather it is exercised and exists only in actions: 'It is . . . a moveable substratum upon which the economy, mode of production, modes of governing and decision-making, forms of knowledge, etc., are conditioned' (*ibid.*). As a result of this position, Foucault refuses to equate power with social structures such as patriarchy. His deconstruction of theories of power such as patriarchy or capitalism led him to emphasise the unstable ways in which power is constantly created. As Ramazanoglu (1993: 5) indicates, 'He conceptualised people's experiences of domination and subordination as "effects" of power, rather than as proceeding from a specific source of power.'

For Foucault, negotiations or struggles within society are not essentially about the possession of power, but rather the contested terms of the deployment of power. Thus Foucault implicitly contests a notion of men's possession of power over women. As Ransom (1993: 129) indicates, this theory of power underpins Foucault's pluralism; power is understood as plural, not operating on 'a single trajectory' or with reference to specific questions. Foucault understands power as 'capillary, spreading through discourses, bodies and relationships in the metaphor of a network' (*ibid.*).

Foucault did acknowledge men's exercise of power over women but denied that men hold power. Ramazanoglu and Holland (1993) argue that there has been insufficient analysis of the middle ground of power relations, i.e. between the micro-politics of everyday life and the consolidation of deeply entrenched male privilege throughout social life. Foucault (1988: 103) himself states that the way in which power operates and is exercised was little understood. He suggests focusing on specific techniques of power to show how those in power arrive at particular decisions.

Fraser (1989: 22) argues that Foucault's empirical studies of modern societies focus on the nature of modern forms of power. She states that, for Foucault, modern power is unlike earlier power in that it is local, continuous, productive, capillary and exhaustive. Foucault maintains that the nature of modern power/ knowledge developed gradually in local piecemeal fashion largely in what he called 'disciplinary institutions' beginning in the late eighteenth century. Fraser (1989: 24) argues that in describing power as 'capillary' Foucault meant that power did not emanate from a single source 'but circulates throughout the entire social body down to even the tiniest and apparently most trivial extremities'. Fraser contends that this emphasis on the 'capillary' character of modern power denies a crude ideological critique of power and emphasises the 'politics of everyday life'.

Foucault does not deny feminist concepts of women as an oppressed group, nor Marxism's concept of the oppression of the working class. As Grosz (1990a) indicates, he 'demassifies' and localises the categories 'woman' and the working class so that these categories are no longer universal categories. Ramazanoglu (1993) argues that Foucault's deconstruction of power releases feminism from rigid conceptions of universal patriarchy, racism or heterosexism. However, she goes on to note that, by seeing power as everywhere and at some level accessible to everyone, it could result in a lack of acknowledgement of women's systematic subordination to other women, as well as systematic domination by men. Ramazanoglu makes the important point that using Foucault

> means acknowledging the multiplicity of difference and claiming the end of 'woman' as a universal category. But it can also lead to a tendency to revert to speaking in abstracted terms of deconstructed 'women' because of the absence of . . . class, racism or gender as categories of power relations in his thought.
>
> (Ramazanoglu 1993: 10)

POWER, FEMINISM AND FOUCAULT

There are a number of tensions in feminism's engagement with the Foucauldian conceptualisation of the operation of power. Because power in Foucault can be conceptualised as ever-changing, generating points of intensity, it can also be seen as generating points of resistance. While many forms of feminism are committed to an organisation of the mass of women, united by a common oppression and a common struggle against patriarchy, Foucault would argue that even if such mass movements were possible, they may not be the most effective forms for change. As Grosz (1990a) argues, smaller groups of well-positioned militants may well be more successful in effecting change than large-scale organisations. Foucault does recognise the necessity for links between local and global forms of power. As he maintains, 'the local and the global mutually condition each other...No local form of power can sustain itself for any length of time without the broader context of global overarching alignments' (Foucault 1980: 94).

Soper's 'Productive Contradictions' (1993) maintains that the paradoxes in Foucault's account of power-knowledge are responsible for some specific tensions between feminism and Foucault. Soper argues that Foucault says relatively little about the sources of power and does not offer an account of women's oppression or women's resistance to oppression. However, as she notes, he does encourage feminism to think more deeply and more self-critically about both oppression and liberation. Grimshaw (1993) maintains that since Foucault sees power as everywhere, it is difficult for him to distinguish between different forms of power and this makes it problematic to develop an adequate theory of women's resistance to power. Fraser also notes that Foucault does not interrogate power regimes from the standpoint of their legitimacy or illegitimacy. However, she argues that Foucault's conceptualisation of power has brought to light some neglected features of the operation of power in modern life. Further, Fraser (1989: 28) argues that Foucault's account of modern power 'constitutes good grounds for rejecting some fairly widespread strategic and normative political orientations and for adopting instead the standpoint of a "politics of everyday life" '.

Ultimately the tensions between feminism and Foucault can be traced to conceptual ambiguities in Foucault's notion of power. Fraser maintains that Foucault calls too many different sorts of things 'power'. While she agrees that there can be no social practices without power, this does not imply that all forms of power are normatively equivalent, nor that all social practices are equivalent. Fraser (1989) argues that it is essential to Foucault's own project that he is able to distinguish between sets of practices and forms of constraint. However, she maintains that this requires greater normative resources than Foucault possesses, and ultimately the crucial defect in Foucault's conception of power is the absence of a clear, normative framework.

DISCOURSE AND THE EXTRA-DISCURSIVE

The tensions raised by feminism's engagement with Foucault emanate in part from what are seen as ambiguities or inconsistencies in his analysis of discourse. Soper (1993) explores the relationship between discourse and oppression. Soper maintains that if Foucault is saying that oppression is constituted in discourses and therefore cannot exist prior to (or outside) discourses, then Foucault's accounts of discourse become arbitrary in their distancing from material circumstances. The nature of Foucault's understanding of both discourse and the relationship between discourse, the 'pre-discursive' and the 'extra-discursive' is explored below.

Foucault argues, throughout his work, that discourse is not merely a concept, but that discourses have an objective reality and so, for Foucault, they have a quality of 'exteriority' (Foucault 1991: 60). In the article 'Politics and the Study of Discourse', Foucault outlines the patterning of 'discursive regimes' and 'relations' in society as follows:

> ...(a) intra-discursive dependencies (between the objects, operations and concepts of a single formation); (b) inter-discursive dependencies (between different discursive formations, such as the correlations which I studied in *The Order of Things* between natural history, economics, grammar and the theory of representation); (c) extra-discursive dependencies between discursive transformations and transformations outside of discourse (e.g. between medical discourse and a whole play of economic, political and social change).
>
> (Foucault 1991: 58)

The difficulty with this definition of discourse and 'discursive regimes' is how exactly to describe the relationship between discourse and the human subject. It is a problem which Foucault consistently refuses to address in his work. He describes discourse as 'a space of differentiated subject positions and subject functions' (*ibid.*) and, as a result, Foucault claims, it is identifiable without reference to subjective experience or intentionality. As Hartsock (1990: 167) argues, 'this has the effect of "generating a language" where things move, rather than people'.

Perhaps the most thoroughgoing and engaging critique of the relationship between discourse and the 'extra-discursive' (or what, if anything, exists outside 'discursive regimes') is located in Maureen Cain's article 'Foucault, Feminism and Feeling: What Foucault Can and Cannot Contribute to Feminist Epistemology' (1993). Cain explores Foucault's work by considering whether it is possible for relationships to exist which are not wholly within discourses. She comes to the important conclusion that it is no longer possible to leave discourse analysis out of feminist research, nor can feminists leave relationships out of discourse analysis. She sees Foucault as proposing a radical methodology which allows discursive powers and processes to be made available as never before.

Cain (1993) sets out to establish where Foucault stood on the question of the 'ontological primacy of discourse', that is, on the question of whether or not only those relationships exist which are somehow or other known in discourse. She argues that the relationship between discourse and the 'extra-discursive' is an uneasy and changing relationship. Cain describes the 'extra-discursive' as a ~~tion~~ of social reality or existence which cannot be grasped in the analysis ~~ourse~~; it is literally what exists outside discourse.

~~ult's~~ major methodological work, and the one in which he addresses the ~~ip~~ between discourse and the extra-discursive, is *The Archaeology of* ~~972~~). Foucault is primarily concerned with the internal relations of ~~at~~ is, he wants, as Cain (1993: 76) argues, to explore the internal relationships between the 'elements', such as subjects, objects, relationships, etc., which make any specific discourse what it is. As Cain maintains,

> Foucault's aim is to make these relations more visible through the process of deconstruction. Thus, from this perspective a discourse must be understood in terms of the operation of its elements, that is, in terms of the rules governing the relations between its constituent elements.
>
> (Cain 1993: 76)

Cain argues that, given this position, a discourse cannot be explained in terms of anything except its own internal relationships:

> it is easy to see how this can be interpreted as proposing a radical autonomy for discourse...His alternative method of 'mapping' as displayed in 'The Archaeology' leaves his work open to the interpretation that discourses are not only self-generating but also generative of all relationships of which they speak.
>
> (Cain 1993: 77–78)

Cain goes on to locate 'discourse' within what she sees as Foucault's broader purpose. She prefers to interpret Foucault as proposing a 'radical methodology'; one which enables discursive processes and powers to be made more apparent.

In *The Archaeology of Knowledge* (1972), Foucault distinguishes between discursive relations and primary and secondary relations as outlined in the following passage:

> 'primary' relations..., independently of all discourse or all objects of discourse, may be described between institutions, techniques, social forms, etc. After all, we know very well that relations existed between the bourgeois family and the functioning of judicial authorities and categories in the nineteenth century. They cannot always be superimposed upon the relations that go to form objects: the relations of dependence that may be assigned to this primary level are not necessarily expressed in the formation of relations that makes discursive objects possible. But we must also distinguish the secondary relations that are formulated in discourse itself: what, for example, the psychiatrists of the nineteenth century could say about the relations between the family and criminality does not reproduce, as we know, the interplay of real dependencies; but neither does it reproduce the interplay of relations that make possible and sustain the objects of psychiatric discourse. Thus a space unfolds articulated with possible discourses: a system of *real* or *primary relations*, a system of *reflexive* or *secondary relations*, and a system of relations that might properly be called *discursive*. The problem is to reveal the specificity of these discursive relations, and their interplay with the other two kinds.
>
> (Foucault 1972: 46)

From this passage it can be seen that Foucault does not understand primary relations as necessarily expressed in discursive relations at all, and it is clear, in recognising an organising role for discourse, that he does not imply that other relations do not exist. Foucault (1972: 46) in fact argues that his enterprise, or the problem he faces, is to specify the nature of these discursive relations and the interaction between the two. As Cain elegantly notes, the autonomy or uncaused character of discursive relations does not mean that their articulations with primary and secondary relations cannot be charted. However, this is a largely uncharted area for Foucault and, as Cain (1993) elaborates, these points of intersection or articulation between the discursive and the extra-discursive can be seen as sites of resistance, power, struggle and political action. It is here that feminists can become pro-active in taking the Foucauldian debate forward and exploring and charting the 'moments of articulation' (Cain 1993: 79) and nature of resistance. However, in discussing the nature of resisting discourses, or as Foucault called them 'reverse discourses', Soper (1993: 34) warns that it is important not to be seduced by the dialectic of 'reverse discourses' into forgetting that the implications for groups experiencing oppression cannot be determined through an analysis of competing discourses.

The significance of the Foucauldian analysis of the relationship between discourse and the extra-discursive for feminists is an interesting one as outlined by Cain (1993). She argues that the nature of discursive relations, as described in Foucault, does not preclude the possibility of relationships of which 'no discourse speaks'. Cain is here concerned with the 'repressed knowledges', i.e. the voices of those silenced by, or excluded from, dominant discourses. Cain's analysis of the nature of the discursive and the extra-discursive raises a number of opportunities, spaces or 'sites of resistance' for feminists in the area of theory, methodology and epistemology.

FOUCAULT, POWER AND SUBJECTIVITY: AGENCY AND RESISTANCE

Foucault's primary concern in a great deal of his work has not been power as such, but the development of an analytical approach to the subject. In 'The Subject and Power' (1982), he begins by stating that the goal of his work has not been to analyse 'the phenomena of power, but rather to create a history of the different modes by which, in our culture, human beings are made subjects' (Foucault 1982: 208). A key feature of the Foucauldian analysis of power is that a challenge to power does not come from the outside but from calling into question 'the mechanisms of the constitution of subjectivity' (Foucault 1982: 216–217).

Foucault proposed that 'subjects' are created in and through discourses and discursive practices. Hekman (1990: 68) argues that he developed what has been characterised as 'the most sustained critique of the notion of the subject'. The 'subject' that Foucault was intent on deconstructing was the subject or 'self' of the Enlightenment. Grimshaw (1993) comments on Foucault's opposition to the

Enlightenment conception of 'man' as an autonomous self-determining human subject and explains his conception of the 'self' as an historical product created by discourses. Foucault, in 'Truth and Power' (1980), clearly situates the subject within a discursive framework:

> I don't believe the problem can be solved by historicising the subject as posited by the phenomenologists, fabricating a subject that evolves through the course of history. One has to dispense with the constituent subject, to get rid of the subject itself, that's to say to arrive at an analysis which can account for the constitution of the subject within a historical framework. And this is what I would call genealogy, that is, a form of history which can account for the constitution of knowledges, discourses, domains of objects, etc., without having to make reference to a subject which is either transcendental in relation to the field of events or runs in its empty sameness throughout the course of history.
>
> (Foucault 1980: 117)

Feminists, argues Grimshaw, can find his approach useful in analysing the extent to which women are constructed as subjects in discourses and so in power relationships. She notes that, while some feminists have found Foucault's deconstruction of subjectivity useful, others have suggested that there are dangers and gaps in Foucault's analysis of power and subjectivity.

The concept of power in Foucault as both productive and pluralistic can be seen as supportive of different forms of power, while at the same time as producing sites of resistance, struggle and change. The concept of 'resistance' is, as Ramazanoglu (1993) notes, part of Foucault's definition of power since he defines all power as producing resistance. Resistance to power, argues Ramazanoglu, can take the form of new discourses producing 'new truths'. Ramazanoglu goes on to note that these may be 'counter discourses' which oppose dominant truths or 'reverse discourses'. Both have considerable significance in their application for different aspects or dimensions of feminism. Counter discourses can be identified in feminist epistemologies and practices which challenge dominant patriarchal discourses in terms of knowledge, practices and procedures. Challenges to dominant patriarchal discourses of sexuality as heterosexist and phallocentric come from lesbian feminists, and Foucault himself recognised homosexuality as a 'reverse discourse'.

Some feminists, however, have challenged the relationship between power and resistance in Foucault. Grimshaw (1993: 54) asks whether Foucault can adequately theorise resistance, for if the subject is constituted within discourse and by relations of power, then what opportunity can there be for resistance? As she notes, if the norms of femininity are simply imposed, where does the opportunity for resistance come from? Foucault, aware of these criticisms, attempted to deal with the questions in his later work, maintaining that power and resistance go together and that there is never power without resistance.

This solution has not satisfied many feminists, who argue that Foucault 'dissolves the agency of the human subject and replaces it with a passive conception' (Ransom 1993: 134). Feminists adopting this view see Foucault's work as problematic in identifying the production of subject positions within discourses and, as a result, in being unable to account for human experience and consciousness as actively involved in changing the nature of discursive regimes. Other feminists, more sympathetic to elements of Foucault's work (Weedon 1987; Fraser 1989; Hekman 1990), have challenged this critique. Weedon maintains that, while the subject is constituted by discourse, she still exists 'as a thinking, feeling and social subject and agent capable of resistance and innovations produced out of the clash between contradictory subject positions and practices' (1987: 125). From Weedon's standpoint, Foucault does not undermine women's potential for resistance and agency but sees, as Ransom (1993: 134) comments, 'subjectivity as contested within discourse'.

Hekman (1990: 73) maintains that 'the constituted subject is a subject that resists' in Foucault's work, and that those who argue that Foucault's concept of subjectivity disempowers women can themselves be seen to be operating within a humanistic framework of subjectivity. As Hekman goes on to note, Foucault is not attacking nor attempting to undermine the agency of the subject, but challenging the liberal essentialist conception of the subject which lies at the centre of humanist thought. Hekman (1990: 72) argues that Foucault's view of the discursive location of subject positions and subject functions 'serves as an important corrective to the tendency among some feminists to define the essentially female'. Thus, the constitution of subjectivity within social and historical discourses does not limit women's agency. As Ransom (1993: 135) notes, it is precisely our 'embeddedness in discursive practice' that empowers political action.

SUBJECTIVITY, 'REASON' AND NEUTRALITY

Feminists have found Foucault's critique of liberal humanism not only crucial in terms of recognising the flawed conception of the human subject which characterised Enlightenment thought, but also in his overturning of the objectivity of such thought. Feminist pluralists challenge the claims to universality, value neutrality, impartiality and objectivity of knowledge characteristic of liberal humanism, which they argue results in particular versions of reality being privileged over others and 'in the denial of particular realms of experience crucial to the process of making sense of the world' (Ransom 1993: 137).

The crucial issue is to what extent Foucault's model of subjectivity and discourse establishes an interaction between experience and material reality. As Ransom (1993: 138) notes, the relationship between feminism and Foucauldian analysis depends on whether 'the relationship between reality and experience can be understood through an analysis of discourse which does not address political agency based on experience'. Bordo (1990) maintains that the neutralisation of power within discourse, or the pluralisation of the bases of power, effectively undermines the recognition of a shared relationship to oppression. In this position the significance of gender itself is undermined. Ransom notes that, when Foucault describes discourse as 'neutral', it does not mean that he is ignoring the fact that the location of subject positions is not a function of dominant positions and dominant groups. However, she argues, feminism needs a more complete sense of how power penetrates subjectivity. She notes that feminists have been concerned not merely to reject the basis of epistemologies and a reality which has claimed reason, truth and objectivity, but to understand and articulate challenges to the basis of their plausibility.

SUBJECTIVITY, SUBJUGATED KNOWLEDGE AND FOUCAULT

Foucault understands subjugated knowledges as holding the potential for resistance. Ransom (1993) argues that this point is crucial in understanding the relationship between feminism and Foucault. She maintains that it is this shared conception of oppression held by a subjugated group that creates friction in the relationship between Foucault and feminism. Ramazanoglu (1993) notes that, in moving beyond the liberal humanist assumptions of the Enlightenment, Foucault had no need to think in terms of the agency of the human subject, and consequently the nature of a shared conception of oppression remains unaddressed in his analysis of subjectivity and power. Foucault did not understand power as repressive, rather as productive, and people are both constituted as subjects in discourses and discursive practices but also act in the process of establishing themselves as particular kinds of subjects. It is clear there are ambiguities in the Foucauldian model of power and discourse, plus contradictions for the relationship between feminism and Foucault around the nature of subjectivity, power and discourse. However, the fact remains, as Soper (1993: 35) notes, that Foucault has raised issues around both the nature and operation of discourses of resistance which are significant for any emancipatory politics.

FOUCAULT AND FEMINISM – SOME PROBLEMS FOR FEMINIST POLITICS

What could be more seductive for feminists than a discourse which, like that of Michel Foucault in *La Volonté de Savoir* (*The History of Sexuality*), focuses on the complex interaction of power and sexuality?...Alluring as they may seem, however, the apparent parallels between Foucault's work and feminism ought not to deceive us. Feminists ought to resist his seductive ploys since, as I shall argue in this essay, the price for giving in to his powerful discourse is nothing less than the depoliticisation of feminism. If we capitulate to Foucault's analysis, we will find ourselves caught up in a sado-masochistic spiral of power and resistance which, circling endlessly in heterogeneous movement, creates a space in which it will be quite impossible to argue that women under patriarchy constitute an oppressed group, let alone develop a theory of their liberation.

(Moi 1985b: 95)

Toril Moi's damning indictment of the impact of Foucault's work on feminism, while certainly highlighting some of the pitfalls of Foucauldian analysis, tends to ignore the fact that both feminism and Foucault are characterised by contradictions and problems. The following summary considers some of those problems as well as considering some of the advantages of feminism's engagement with Foucault.

Nancy Fraser (1989) argues that Foucault's work has made it possible to understand the nature and operation of power and political problems in new ways. However, she goes on to note that Foucault's work is beset by difficulties and raises a number of philosophical questions which, she argues, it is not equipped to answer. Fraser contends that Foucault's analysis of power lacks a normative framework, resulting in a model of power where all forms of power are seen as normatively equivalent. However, Sawicki (1991) argues that those critics who have viewed Foucault's work as lacking any normative framework have seen it wrongly and he wanted to defamiliarise and challenge dominant discourses and discursive practices. As Sawicki notes in interpreting Foucault,

> Freedom lies in our capacity to discover the historical links between certain modes of self-understanding and modes of domination, and to resist the ways in which we have already been classified and identified by dominant discourses. This means discovering new ways of understanding ourselves and one another, refusing to accept the dominant culture's characterisations of our practices and desires, and redefining them from within resistant cultures.
>
> (Sawicki 1991: 44)

Sawicki's analysis of Foucault highlights the fact that feminism and feminist practices have not been 'innocent' or free of power relationships.

Feminist theories that maintain a metanarrative of male power, argues Ramazanoglu (1993: 9), fail to address the issue of women who are marginal or framed as 'other' in mainstream feminist discourse. Such a position ignores women who themselves hold power over other women based on class, racism, sexual orientation or domestic service. Ransom develops this point more fully in establishing feminism's theorising of difference as the central difficulty in feminist debate today. She notes that there is a problem of developing a theory within feminism which can translate and articulate both differences and commonalities in the experiences of women (1993: 125). As she comments, this has been a major area of difficulty in providing coherence within feminism.

The failure of a feminist politics based on essentialism was its advocacy of a feminist politics based on sameness and an inherent disregard for difference. Ransom argues that the possible range of differences between women are infinite, and forms of differentiation which are analytically distinct from the categories of gender, race and class 'stake their claim to the coherence of political agency' (1993: 125). The problem with theorising difference is that it is difficult to conceptualise in a coherent way, as commonalities and differences intersect along lines of gender, class, ethnicity, sexuality, etc. Foucauldian analysis has, for many feminist pluralists, provided a framework for identifying and articulating difference and commonality. Feminism thus becomes translated into 'feminisms' or 'postfeminism' and becomes, as Ransom (1993: 127) points out, one set of subversive discursive strategies amongst others, which Foucault (1980: 81) identifies as 'the insurrection of subjugated knowledges'. As Hartsock (1990) notes, these provide, according to Foucault, the only form of potentially radical knowledge or political action in the contemporary world.

The question is whether Foucault's discursive analysis assists feminism's need for a theory to accommodate plurality and difference. Foucault's analysis of power and discourse has already been considered. Through his analysis of the exercise and operation of power, he attempts to show that the exercise of power cannot be reduced to a single causal factor. As Ransom (1993: 128) comments, Foucault aims to subvert the basis of humanistic thought and to provide 'a pluralistic methodology' which can accommodate this process.

However, as Ramazanoglu (1993) notes, the conceptual deconstruction of difference is too easily removed from practical politics rooted in the nature of women's differences and in women's common interests. She contends that the political problem with this approach

> is that it does not 'discover' the hidden and institutionalised power relations which differentiate the lives of black lesbian women in Britain from those of white heterosexual women or the lives of middle class housewives with ethnic roots in the Indian sub-continent from those of say service workers from the African diaspora, or the lives of such service workers from 'black British' professionals. Without some systematic understanding of such inter-relationships we cannot grasp the complexity, the contradictions and the unpredictability of the interplay of social differences.
>
> (Ramazanoglu 1993: 9)

Thus, if analysis is abstracted from a feminist grounding in women's different experiences, as Ramazanoglu has noted, we are left with the problem of an undifferentiated sense of 'women'. It is this relationship between the significance of women's experience and the theorising of the discursive nature of subjectivity which is problematic for feminism's relationship with Foucault. Ransom (1993: 138) argues that Foucault tries to 'resolve the tension between the social embeddedness of the subject who experiences oppression and the generation of knowledge by the historical theorist by positing a distance between the theorist and the object of study'. However, the tension between difference and commonality between women and within feminism cannot fully be resolved by the adoption of a Foucauldian method. Ransom argues that Foucauldian analysis does not offer feminism an adequate theory which addresses the ways in which women differ.

Contradictions within feminism will inevitably persist, because women's experiences and the way in which women understand and articulate diversity is contradictory. At the same time, as Ramazanoglu (1993) notes, there are common threads in women's experiences of gender relations and in the persistence of dominant male discourses exercising power over women, which are not adequately explained by Foucault's analysis. Women's experience of male power reinforces feminism's critique of Foucault and, as Ramazanoglu (1993: 22) indicates, leads feminists to suggest two aspects of power which appear to conflict with Foucault's model of power. First, women's experiences suggest that men do hold power and that their power constitutes a form of domination. Second, the nature of the domination cannot be understood simply as a product of discourse because, as Ramazanoglu indicates, it must be understood as 'extra-discursive', that is, as relating to realities outside those of discourse. Thus, for Ramazanoglu, from a Foucauldian perspective a feminist politics defined in terms of oppression and emancipation has no direct relevance. She claims that for Foucault it does make sense to establish new discourses and identify new forms of power and new forms of the self as mechanisms for transforming political relations.

CONCLUSION

Foucault's vast range of work provides a powerful resource for feminists, particularly feminists who are interested in a feminist pluralism based around a more reflexive feminist epistemology and practice. While Foucault's work can be seen to resonate with feminism's search for a greater degree of pluralism in its articulation of difference and in its search for new discourses and discursive practices, there are limitations to feminism's engagement with Foucault. Foucault's pluralistic model of power and difference does not in itself offer a theoretical framework which can adequately distinguish between the kinds of differences that cut across women's lives. In order to reflect fully the diversity of women's lives and experiences, it is important to retain the capacity to identify the structural contradictions 'in difference'. The nature of such contradictions cannot be accounted for in discursive analysis alone. As Ransom (1993: 144) notes, both in terms of what women share and the cultural and structural factors which divide women, feminism requires the development of a methodology that acknowledges the presence of the speaker in what is spoken.

4

PSYCHOANALYTIC THEORY, SEMIOLOGY AND POSTFEMINISM

INTRODUCTION

This chapter investigates the intersection of psychoanalytic theory and semiology with feminist theory and considers the implications for postfeminist debates. There are two spheres where these debates have made an impact. The first is the impact of psychoanalytic theory and semiology within the French intellectual tradition, particularly as a result of feminism's engagement with the work of Jacques Derrida and Jacques Lacan. Debates in the area of feminism, sexuality and textuality have been explored and 'dramatised' in the work of the French feminist deconstructivists – Luce Irigaray, Julia Kristeva and Hélène Cixous – in their dialogue with the work of Derrida and Lacan. The second major area of impact is in the area of film and media theory, in particular the intersection of debates in the area of psychoanalytic theory and semiology with feminist theoretical debates as applied to these areas. The work of E. Ann Kaplan and Teresa de Lauretis has made powerful contributions to this area and will be explored in this chapter.

THE FRENCH INTELLECTUAL TRADITION AND FRENCH FEMINIST DECONSTRUCTIVISTS

Feminism, sexuality and textuality: Derrida, *'différance'* and deconstruction

Feminist theory in the 1970s was strongly influenced by psychoanalytic models of sexuality and subjectivity, which were in turn influenced by Freud's work and by the French psychoanalytic theorist Jacques Lacan. As Weedon notes,

> many feminists have attempted to make psychoanalytic theory the key to understanding the acquisition of gendered subjectivity, either by accepting the terms of Freudian discourse, or by advocating psychoanalytic theory as a way of understanding the structures of femininity and masculinity under

69

patriarchy, together with the social and cultural forms to which these structures give rise.

(Weedon 1987: 43)

Psychoanalysis investigates the complex ways in which psychosexuality is bound up with unconscious processes. Freudian psychoanalysis can be divided into two related areas, the first a theory of the genesis and development of male and female sexuality and the second area an analysis of the operation of the unconscious. Rowley and Grosz (1990: 177) note that

> [Freud] never claimed expertise about the sexual life of women which he referred to as a 'dark continent' for psychology. He wrote only three major essays about women – all near the end of his life. They were 'Some Psychical Consequences of the Anatomical Distinction between the Sexes' (1925); 'Female Sexuality' (1931) and 'Femininity' (1933). The relationship between anatomical sex and the socio-cultural construction of gender was not a straightforward one in Freud's work. He did not understand the concepts of masculine and feminine in anatomical terms, but understood them in terms of three sets of oppositions which included active and passive, subject and object and phallic and castrated.

(Rowley and Grosz 1990: 178)

Whereas the masculine is equivalent to the first of these terms, the feminine is equivalent to the second. As Weedon comments, Freud developed a theory of gender acquisition which made the key to identity the notion of gendered subjectivity. For Freud the acquisition of feminine and masculine subjectivity was located in the origin of 'psychic structures of sexual identity acquired in the early years of childhood' (Weedon 1987: 45).

Simone de Beauvoir in her critique of psychoanalytic theory in *The Second Sex* (1972; originally published in 1949) maintained that Freud's vision was male-centred. She contends that Freud had set up 'a masculine model of individual development and merely adapted this account with slight modification to women' cited in (Rowley and Grosz 1990: 181). Freud insisted that individuals were sexual beings from birth and he further claimed that infants were neither initially feminine nor masculine but were 'polymorphously perverse'. The implication of this was that individuals were capable of developing either normal feminine or masculine identities, or neither. As Weedon (1987: 45) notes, 'the acquisition of psychic femininity or masculinity by the biological female or male involved the repression of those features of the child's initial bisexuality which were incompatible with the sexual identity in question'. As Weedon contends, it is these aspects of Freudian theory, the stress on the initial bisexuality of the child and the precarious nature of the psychic (as opposed to biological) explanation of gender identity, which have interested feminists in their appropriation of psychoanalytic theory. She notes:

the insistence on the psycho-sexual rather than biological structuring of gender identity and on gender acquisition as a precarious process, constantly threatened by the return of the repressed, means that gender identity is not fixed by psycho-analysis in the same way or to the same degree as it is in biological determinism.

(Weedon 1987: 46)

Despite this, Freudian theory gives primacy to anatomical difference in sexual, psychic and symbolic terms. The centrality of the penis acts as a principal signifier of sexual difference, guarantees psychic difference and women's inferiority and can be read in symbolic terms (as a patriarchal signifier). As Weedon (1987: 51) maintains, 'attempts to move away from the centrality of anatomical difference in the acquisition of psychic sexual identity in Freud have prompted some feminists to turn their attention to Jacques Lacan'.

Lacan and feminism

Lacan's work is highly obscure and the ambiguity of his style reinforces the ambiguity of much of the content of his writing and strengthens his claim that unambiguous meaning in language is an illusion. Lacan's style, as well as the content of his writing, has had a great influence on French feminist writing. By repositioning Freud within a new framework of linguistics, Lacan re-established the case for psychoanalysis within feminism. The unconscious and sexuality are not seen by Lacan as natural or biological essences, but as a product of the constitution of the subject in language, i.e. within the imaginary and symbolic orders.

Within the Lacanian model, the child is not born a subject who then acquires appropriate social characteristics. Rather, it becomes a subject through social intervention. At one and the same time it becomes a 'social and speaking subject', i.e. it becomes a Symbolic or social subject only in the process of taking up a masculine or feminine position or identity. Thus, in contradistinction to Freud, the distinction between the sexes is not an effect of nature or anatomy but is a psychical question. The phallus in Lacan is not an organ but a signifier, 'the key signifier of the Symbolic order'.

Lacan removes the question of sexual identity from the realm of biology to place it in the field of signification. In other words, the subject's sexual identity is an effect of its position in the symbolic order. Grosz (1990a: 72) describes the symbolic as 'the domain constituting social law, language and exchange – the domain of the social order'. She goes on to note that this order is governed according to Lacan by 'the Other'. As she states, 'the Other is not a person but a place, a locus from which language emanates and is given meaning'. She further elaborates on the significance of 'the Other' for human experience and maintains that 'the Other is incarnated in human experience in the figure of the Symbolic Father's authority that real fathers invoke to institute the law' (Grosz 1990a: 73). This law is fundamental to

71

patriarchy and, as Grosz maintains, 'the symbolic order is the social field regulated by the law of the father' (*ibid.*).

The notion of the Oedipus complex, so fundamental to Freud, is reframed by Lacan in his notion of the Symbolic. In reworking Freud's paper 'On Narcissism: An Introduction' (1914), where Freud outlines the genesis of the ego through the phenomenon of narcissism, Lacan maintains that the 'ego is the result of the child's narcissistic investment in its corporeal image' (Grosz 1990a: 73). However, like Freud, Lacan concentrates on the boy's Symbolic development, while the complementary processes in the girl remain obscure. Lacan maintains that in abandoning her primary homosexual attachment and transferring her object of desire from the mother to the father, she comes to acquire the traits of femininity. Thus, while Lacan claims to be simply deciphering and interpreting Freud, Lacan's interpretation is a departure from Freud. However, his understanding of femininity is more complex and sophisticated than Freud's. For Lacan, femininity is always in an ambiguous relation to the phallus. As Rowley and Grosz note,

> On the one hand, femininity is defined as the lack (of a phallus). The woman does not have the phallus for which she may compensate by attempting to become the phallus, making the whole of her body into the erotic object of men's desire. Her sexuality and identity are capable of characterization only with reference to the phallic signifier.
>
> (Rowley and Grosz 1990: 187)

On the other hand, Lacan acknowledges that the phallus can in no way adequately contain and capture female sexuality. Lacan contends that there is something in female sexuality which is always outside of the boundaries of the phallus and he puts forward the idea of a feminine *jouissance*. The term *la jouissance* or *jouissance* – meaning orgasmic sexual pleasure, bliss or rapture – appears frequently in French feminist writing, is generally attributed to female pleasure and is represented as a different order of pleasure to that of male pleasure. As Marks and Courtivron (1981: 36–37) note, 'women's jouissance carries with it a kind of potlatch in the world of orgasms, a giving, expending, dispensing of pleasure without concern about ends or closure'.

Psychoanalysis and French feminism

Lacan's reinterpretation of Freud has had enormous influence on French intellectuals. While many French feminists are critical of Lacanian analysis, even those who are critical of Lacan have tended to locate their criticisms within his framework. Particular criticisms concern his position regarding the inevitability of paternal law and the way in which he links the privileging of the phallus to the child's entry into the Symbolic and thus to language.

Grosz notes that

Lacan's work has generated a good deal of controversy in feminist circles. Many French feminists remain unswervingly loyal to his work, arguing that he presents one of the most astute analyses of patriarchal social requirements, and one of the most stringent criticisms of mainstream, logocentric, and phallocentric knowledges (e.g. Clement, Lemaire, Kristeva). Others, while taking his work seriously, remain highly critical, seeing it as a less obvious but equally insidious version of Freud's phallocentrism.

(Grosz 1990a: 78)

Despite the ambivalence shown towards Lacan by different branches of feminism, his work is relevant to contemporary feminist theory in a number of ways. Grosz (1990a: 78) contends that Lacan's reformulation of Freud in terms of language has made psychoanalysis more palatable for feminists. She maintains 'It is no longer a biological account of women's lack or castration, but a socio-historical analysis of the transmission of meanings and values across generations' (*ibid.*). In this context Lacan elaborates the major role that language, metaphor and the play of signification exert in the formation of the unconscious and in the principles governing its interpretation. For Lacan, 'unconscious, desire, and sexuality are not effects of nature, biology, or some human essence, but are consequences of the human subject's constitution in and by the symbolic and the imaginary' (*ibid.*).

Lacan 'decentres' dominant notions of human subjectivity. Grosz (1990a: 79) notes that Lacan 'challenges the presumption of an autonomous, ready-made subject by elaborating his view that the subject is socio-linguistically constituted. The subject is constructed by its necessary dependence on others and on the Other.' As she points out, this is significant for feminist theory for, on the one hand, it provides a critique of the notion of a pre-given or pre-social subject, common to both patriarchal and feminist theory. At the same time, it explains the construction of subjects as masculine/phallic or feminine/castrated, and the possibility for change in these positionings. In this context Lacan's work has been used to provide an account of 'the psychic components of social subjectivity' (*ibid.*).

Grosz shows how Lacan's account of sexuality highlights the crucial role language plays in the construction of personal identity. 'Masculine and feminine identities are not "natural" but products of a *rift* in the natural order, a gap into which language insinuates itself. As the key signifier of the symbolic, the phallus marks male and female bodies and sexualities in different ways' (*ibid.*). The implications of this for feminist theory are important because, as Grosz notes, it highlights 'the end of universalist, or "humanist", sexually neutral models of subjectivity. Such models can be seen as phallocentric, exerting a power of representation and authority to male models' (*ibid.*). Some feminist writers, including Irigaray (1985b) and Gallop (1982), have maintained that Lacan is also representative of these characteristics. However, as Grosz (1990a: 79) maintains, 'his work is still useful for making clear that sexuality is not incidental or contingent, but necessary for the constitution of subjectivity'. Lacan's emphasis is on 'the question of language, law, and symbolic exchange as founding structures of society identities', which, as Grosz notes, points to investments by patriarchal culture. It is this emphasis in Lacan's work that feminists need to understand in order to be able to subvert.

Theories of language: difference/*différance*

Weedon maintains that the basis of much poststructuralist thought can be traced back to a number of theoretical strands, including those of structural linguistics, particularly those of Ferdinand de Saussure. She (1987: 23) notes that 'An understanding of Saussure's theory of the "sign" is fundamental to all poststructuralism. It is Saussure's insistence on a pre-given fixed structuring of language, prior to its realization in speech or writing, which earns his linguistics the title "structural".' These theories, as Kemp (1995: 63) notes, challenge the dominant 'positivist view of language as expressing universal truths linguistically'. He maintains that the 'positivist view of language centres around a referential view of meaning i.e. that words get their meaning by referring to objects in the real world' (*ibid.*). He goes on to note that 'the truth of a linguistic proposition is dependent on whether the objects referred to actually exist in the relations in which they are described' (*ibid.*; see also Weedon 1987: 24).

Saussure undermines this view of language by arguing that the meaning of language is constituted in difference. Weedon points out that, for Saussure,

> meaning is produced within language rather than reflected by language, and that individual signs do not have intrinsic meaning but acquire meaning through the language chain and their difference within it from other signs. These principles are important because they make language truly social and a site of political struggle.
>
> (Weedon 1987: 23)

She states that Saussure conceived of and understood language as a network of signs, each sign containing two parts. The first part is the signifier, which is a written or aural symbol, and 'The second is the signified, which is the component of meaning' (*ibid.*). Saussure maintained that signs gain their meaning, not from any individual's use of language but from being elements in a linguistic network (*ibid.*).

Weedon (1987: 25) notes that Derrida developed Saussure's notion of difference to create a poststructuralist theory. He developed the concepts of *différence* and *différance*: the first concept entails difference, the second deferral. However, as Kemp (1995: 64) notes, because the two words are pronounced the same, the difference can only be understood when the words are written and this reflects Derrida's view that the written word has greater importance than the spoken.

Language, meaning, text

Weedon maintains that Derrida, like Saussure, claims that meaning in language is a product of relations of difference, whereas Saussure argues for a fixed network of meaning. As Weedon notes (1987: 24–25), the 'post-structuralist answer to the problem of the plurality of meaning and change is to question the location of social meaning in fixed signs. It speaks instead of signifiers in which the signified is never fixed once and for all, but is constantly deferred.' Derrida's work expresses this critique most clearly and, as Weedon notes, for 'Derrida there can be no fixed signifieds (concepts), and signifiers (sound or written images), which have identity only in their difference from one another, are subject to an endless process of deferral' (*ibid.*), thus meaning for Derrida can only be fixed temporarily. As Weedon indicates, 'Signifieds are always located in a discursive context and the temporary fixing of meaning in a specific reading of a signifier depends on this discursive context' (*ibid.*). Derrida therefore encourages the free-play of textual meaning, positing the idea of multiple interpretations over fixed interpretations.

In addition, while Derrida remains close to Lacan and Freudian psycho-analysis, as Grosz (1990a: 95) notes, Derrida also attempts 'to deconstruct their logocentric commitments' (Derrida 1978a, 1978b). Despite the fact that structuralism and semiotics are also seen as moments of rupture or subversion, they still remain committed to binary concepts. Thus, in order to designate difference within difference, Derrida coins the term *différance*. As Grosz (1990a: 97) notes, Derrida's deconstruction 'aims to undo the history of logocentrism in order to allow différance its space of free-play'.

While the influence of Derrida's work has been considerable within both French and Anglo-Saxon feminism, it has also aroused, as Grosz states, considerable controversy within feminist circles, especially for his use of the term ' "woman" and "becoming woman" as metaphors for the demise of truth and the play of difference' (*ibid.*).

Derrida and feminism

Derrida's destabilisation of logocentrism and binary logic challenged many of the same targets as feminism. His deconstructive techniques make it clear that if feminist theory is to succeed in its challenge to phallocentric discourses it cannot do so from a position outside of phallocentrism. As Grosz (1990a: 100) notes, 'to remain outside a (logocentric, phallocentric) system is to leave it intact; to remain only within its terms, on the other hand is to risk absorption...' Grosz outlines a number of points where Derrida's work is useful for feminism. She maintains that Derrida's 'deconstructive project' refines and develops the feminist challenge to phallocentrism which is a subcategory of logocentrism. Grosz (1990a: 101) contends that 'Logocentrism is implicitly patriarchal; the very structure of binary oppositions is privileged by the male/non-male (i.e. female) distinction'. Second, Derrida's work provides a 'politically, as well as intellectually, useful trajectory' for the feminist researcher, as it puts stress on the material processes of reading and writing and problematises the very grounds on which various discourses are based.

Deconstructive techniques drawn from Derrida's work have informed the work of a number of French feminist deconstructivists, including Luce Irigaray and Julia Kristeva. Derrida's mode of deconstruction which, instead of creating new truths, aims to unveil the political commitments of various prevailing discourses, has provided Irigaray with a major interpretive technique 'in her critical/lyrical evaluations of texts within psychoanalysis and the history of philosophy (ibid.).[1] Grosz also notes that Derrida's more substantive arguments around the issue of difference inhabiting all identity have inspired Kristeva's analysis of the symbolic and semiotic.

Derrida's concept of difference has come to represent a powerful critical force within feminist theory. While there have been other theorists who have dealt with the concept of difference, his work is probably the most politically motivated. As Grosz (1990a: 101–102) notes, '[he] adds a political dimension to Saussure's concept of pure difference to make it more incisive in challenging metaphysical adherences to identity'. In addition, in 'distinguishing difference from *différance*' (*ibid.*), he opens up a range of other opportunities for feminists.

In spite of Derrida's relevance to feminist theoretical projects, as Grosz comments, even those sympathetic to his work have expressed alarm at his use of 'femininity' as a deconstructive tool. Grosz (1990a: 102) goes on to note that in acknowledging the usefulness of deconstruction as a strategic tool or device for feminist readings, Gayatri Chakravorty Spivak suggests an ambivalent attitude may be the most appropriate one:

> My attitude to deconstruction can now be summarized: first, deconstruction is illuminating as a critique of phallocentrism; second it is convincing as an argument against the founding of a hysterocentric order to counter phallocentric discourse; third as a feminist practice itself, it is caught on the other side of sexual difference.
>
> (Spivak 1983: 184)

Ultimately for feminists Derrida uses women as metaphors of a subversion of truth and order, while not recognising women as subjects and the positions from which they might speak.

The impact of Lacanian psychoanalytic theory and Derrida's theory of deconstruction on French feminism

Weedon claims that French feminists have taken one of two approaches when attempting to make psychoanalytic theory the key to understanding the acquisition of gendered subjectivity. They have either accepted the terms of Freudian discourse, or advocated 'psychoanalytic theory as a way of understanding the structures of masculinity and femininity, under patriarchy, together with the social and cultural forms to which these structures give rise' (Weedon 1987: 43). Weedon considers the significance of psychoanalysis for feminism, maintaining that psychoanalysis offers 'a universal theory of the psychic construction of gender identity based on repression' (*ibid.*). Such analysis gives answers to the question of what constitutes subjectivity and how we acquire gendered subjectivity. Weedon considers Lacan's 'appropriation of Freud', pointing out that Lacan 'stresses the linguistic structure of the unconscious as a site of repressed meanings and the "imaginary" structure of subjectivity acquired...at the point of entry of the individual as speaking subject into the symbolic order of language, laws and social processes and institutions' (Weedon 1987: 51). The symbolic order in Lacanian theory is the social and cultural order which frames gender identity.

In Lacanian theory, as in Saussurean theory, the symbolic order is made up of 'signifiers', but in the Lacanian model signifiers are not linked to fixed signifieds or concepts. Weedon (1987: 52–53) points out that Lacan's theory of language has much 'in common with Jacques Derrida's radical critique of rationalist theories of language, consciousness and the logocentric tradition of metaphysics, which presuppose that the meaning of concepts is fixed prior to their articulation in language'. She shows that meaning for Lacan, as for Derrida, can only occur in specific textual locations. In Lacanian psychoanalysis, it is the mechanisms of desire, rather than the principle of *différance*, that prevent the final fixing of meaning.

Weedon highlights a significant difference in the writings of Derrida and Lacan. For Lacan, meaning and the symbolic order as a whole is fixed in relation to a primary, transcendental signifier, which Lacan calls the 'phallus', the signifier of sexual difference, which guarantees the patriarchal structure of the symbolic order (Weedon 1987: 53). She argues that the phallus signifies power and control in the symbolic order through control of the satisfaction of desire, the primary source of power within psychoanalytic theory. In Lacanian theory the position of the father as 'Other' is primarily symbolic.

The fact that values are illusory, or that men, like women, are produced by and subject to the symbolic order and never in control, does not detract from the social implications of these illusions. As Weedon (1987: 54) maintains, 'men by virtue of their penis can aspire to a position of power and control within the symbolic order'. She goes on to note that women have no position in the symbolic order except in relation to men, 'as mothers, and even the process of mothering is given patriarchal meaning, reduced in Freud, to an effect of penis envy' (*ibid.*).

A number of feminist theorists have considered the significance of psychoanalytic theory for feminism. Jacqueline Rose argues that psychoanalytic theory provided feminist theory with 'a way to identify and fix gender difference through a metanarrative of shared infantile development; it also helped feminists show how the very notion of the "subject" is a masculine prerogative within the terms of culture' (cited in Butler 1990c: 326). Rose's work is based on Lacanian psychoanalytical theory. Butler points out that 'the paternal law which Lacanian psychoanalysis takes to be the basis of all kinship and cultural relations, establishes "male subjects" through a denial of the feminine'. Rose argues psychoanalytic theory gives an account 'of patriarchal culture as a trans-historical and crosscultural force' (*ibid.*). French feminist psychoanalytic theorists have reworked Lacanian theory, the work of Luce Irigaray being seminal in this context.

Psychoanalytic theory and postfeminism: the work of Luce Irigaray

Irigaray studied linguistics and philosophy before becoming a psychoanalyst. She taught in Lacan's Department of Psychoanalysis at the University of Vincennes; however, after she published her book *Speculum of the Other Woman* (1985a), she was dismissed from her position by Lacan. Irigaray is one of the French feminists most interested in the concept of difference: differences between the sexes; differences among women; differences within the single individual woman. Her area of interest is the discursive field of metaphysics and her writing style is literary and creative. Irigaray's work deals with ' "the master-texts of Western philosophy" and her thought engages in an in-depth dialogue with a range of major theories in this field, including Foucault's archaeological/genealogical method, Derrida's metaphysical deconstruction and Deleuze's desiring machines' (Braidotti 1994: 62). Irigaray responds to these theories and adapts them to her project of 'expressing the positivity of sexual difference' (*ibid.*).

One of the central theses in Irigaray's (1977: 71) work is that language and systems of representation cannot express female desire. She studies the language of 'male and female schizophrenics and observes that men have an ability for meta-language (language which talks about language) which women do not have' (Rowley and Grosz 1990: 195). Irigaray contends that this development is not specific to schizophrenia and she maintains that women are 'unable to express their ideas through the language that is imposed upon them when they enter the symbolic order' (*ibid.*). As Braidotti (1994: 63) states: 'How can we speak, think and create within structures that are misogynist and seem to feed off the exclusion and appropriation of the feminine?' Braidotti goes on to reveal how Irigaray confronts this positioning of the feminine in 'a double movement that combines denunciation and creation. [S]he unveils the masculine character of discourse, while positing a new female feminist subject' (*ibid.*).

In *Speculum of the Other Woman* (1985a), Irigaray analyses the history of Western theoretical discourse from Plato to Hegel. In this tradition, to which Freud belongs, Irigaray (1977: 63) states that the feminine is defined as 'nothing other than the complement, the other side or the negative side of the masculine'. In challenging this conception Irigaray is not interested in anatomy, but in its morphology; in other words, in the way it has been represented, conceptualised and articulated in these discourses.

Irigaray's emphasis on heterogeneity and difference in language is influenced by the work of Jacques Derrida. Todd (1983: 237) maintains that, in addition to exploring 'the specific morphological characteristics of the feminine', Irigaray's feminist project is to deconstruct phallogocentric discourse, 'to show that the so-called universal discourse, whether it be philosophic, scientific or literary, is sexualized mainly in a masculine way' (*ibid.*). Thus for Irigaray textual practice cannot be separated from political practice and Irigaray bases her re-evaluation of *écriture féminine* on the feminine multiple plural *jouissance*. As Braidotti (1994: 64) notes, '[h]er 'position on feminism is much more positive than that of the other *écriture féminine* women; Irigaray is the only one to have been involved in feminist actions through the 1970s'. While defending the notion of *différance*, Irigaray subtly combines this with a commitment to collective feminist political action. For Irigaray 'woman does not exist and she will be unable to come into being without women's collective efforts, which empower and symbolize her specific sexuality, jouissance, textual practice and political vision' (*ibid.*).

In another of her texts, *This Sex Which is Not One* (1985b), Irigaray addresses the question of the relationship between equality and difference, and warns against the concept of equality. She states that 'Woman could be man's equal. In this case she would enjoy, in a more or less near future, the same economic, social, political rights as men. She would be a potential man' (Irigaray 1985b: 84). One of Irigaray's most strident criticisms of emancipatory feminism is the danger of its being subsumed within pre-established masculine canons. Braidotti (1994: 65) maintains that Irigaray's 'justification of *écriture féminine* is articulated along with the search for women's unexplored possibilities and potentialities, so that this "other" which is concealed by the masquerade known as femininity may be revealed'.

Irigaray goes beyond Freud and Lacan to produce a radical theory of the feminine libido which is based on, as Weedon (1987: 61) notes, female sexuality and autoeroticism and which celebrates the plurality of female sexual pleasure in separation from men. Weedon indicates that Irigaray extends the Lacanian concept of the phallocentric patriarchal order in arguing that 'the otherness of female sexuality has been repressed by patriarchy which seeks to theorize it within masculine parameters' (*ibid.*: 63).

Irigaray maintains that 'the patriarchal definition of sexuality caused women to lose touch with their essential femininity which is located in the female body; with its capacity for multiple and heterogeneous pleasure(s)' (*ibid.*). Weedon shows how Irigaray argues for an integral relationship between sexuality and language. As in Lacanian psychoanalytic theory, Irigaray shows that 'the acquisition of language produces desire and women's language is motivated by attempts to satisfy desire' (*ibid.*). Irigaray argues that just as women's libido is 'other' to men's, so women's language is necessarily distinct from male language. Weedon highlights the fact that Irigaray offers a theory of the 'female' rather than the feminine. In Irigaray's view, female sexual pleasure is fundamentally autoerotic and plural, while male sexuality is concentrated on the penis, women's has a multiplicity of sexual organs. Irigaray maintains that 'female desire is totally foreign to male desire and the two can only be brought together through a patriarchal repression of the female' (Weedon 1987: 64).

In establishing the interconnection between sexuality and language, Irigaray argues that, when freed from their patriarchal definition and repression of their sexuality, women are assumed to be fundamentally different from men and their use of language is other than the logical language of the symbolic order. In Irigaray's work, 'the male sexuality and desire in the form of the phallus is the organizing principle of the symbolic order and the source of the type of rational language through which social power is exercised' (Weedon 1987: 65). For Irigaray there is no space for resistance within the terms of the symbolic order, and women who do not wish to repress their true femaleness can have no access to it. Irigaray is much more explicit about the link between biology and identity than Lacan:

> The shift of emphasis in Irigaray's work from the 'Oedipus complex' organised around the phallus, the signifier of male desire to female sexual pleasure offers women a positive interpretation of their bodies. They are no longer defined in terms of lack
>
> (Weedon 1987: 65)

Thus Irigaray's commitment to feminist politics is central for the articulation of her theory of difference; it is women's movements which establish 'a separatist space', where women can 'speak their desires and . . . shatter the silence about the exploitation they have undergone; it is the theoretical and political building site for forms of expression and multiple struggles' (Braidotti 1994: 65). Irigaray's approach provides a theoretical basis for an understanding of the transformation of subjectivity in which feminism has played a central role.

While Irigaray's conception of the subject within a system of signification gives her much in common with elements of poststructuralism, 'her aim is the deconstruction of phallogocentrism through the affirmation of another symbolic system, based on female feminine specificity' (Braidotti 1994: 96). As Braidotti observes, for Irigaray, deconstruction is only a dimension in her analytic framework, while it 'constitutes the most critical and most explicitly feminist stage in the rereading of the history of Western philosophy: the heart of her work is about creating an alternative system' (*ibid.*). Ultimately Irigaray's philosophy of sexual difference has at its centre the dissolution of the classical subject of representation to facilitate the possibilities and articulation of 'new non-logocentric ways of thinking' (Braidotti 1994: 67)

Hélène Cixous: and *écriture féminine*

Cixous founded Women's Studies at the University of Vincennes in 1975 and is a keen proponent of 'feminine writing' – texts which subvert dominant phallogocentric logic. She criticises Freudian psychoanalysis for its thesis of a 'natural' anatomical determination of sexual difference, but endorses Freud's belief in the bisexual nature of all individuals. Rowley and Grosz (1990: 198) note that 'Masculine writing is seen by Cixous as systematic, closed, and limited by laws, whereas "feminine writing" comes from the imaginary'. They note that Cixous' famous manifesto for feminine writing called 'The Laugh of the Medusa' (1981a) is a utopian picture of female creative powers. Cixous claims:

> To write. An act which will not only 'realize' the decensored relation of woman to her sexuality, to her womanly being, giving her access to her native strength; it will give her back her goods, her pleasures, her organs, her immense bodily territories which have been kept under seal ...
>
> (Cixous 1981a: 280)

The connection between Lacanian psychoanalysis, feminine and masculine libido, the unconscious and language is also central to 'the work of Hélène Cixous which focuses on the relationship between feminine libido and feminine writing' (Weedon 1987: 66). Weedon goes on to show that 'Like Irigaray, Cixous sees feminine sexuality as rich and plural.' Cixous looks to 'feminine writing for challenge to the patriarchal order'. She maintains that 'masculine sexuality and masculine language are phallocentric and logocentric, seeking to fix meaning through a set of binary oppositions' (Weedon 1987: 66). Cixous points out that patriarchal society accepts 'male libido, male definitions of female libido and male writing as the norm for both women and men' (Marks and de Courtivron 1981: 249, cited in Weedon 1987: 66). Cixous argues that this phallocentric, logocentric order is not unassailable and that feminine writing can challenge it.

Cixous' work is influenced by the anti-essentialism of Derrida's deconstruction and she brings together his notion of logocentrism and phallocentrism. Cixous is relatively optimistic about the possibility of transforming the patriarchal symbolic order through giving women a new sense of themselves. In the struggle to reassert feminine values, feminine writing, which draws on the unconscious, is a key 'site' for bringing about change.

The 'politics' of Julia Kristeva

As well as being a literary theorist and cultural critic, Kristeva was also a practising psychoanalyst. Kristeva's thinking was very much influenced by Lacan but she shifted away from him in her analysis of the 'semiotic'. Rowley and Grosz (1990: 193) note that 'Whereas the symbolic is associated with the paternal – the realm of Lacan's Law of the Father – the semiotic is linked with the maternal. Kristeva sees it as a site of resistance to the symbolic, for it constantly undermines rational discourse.' In linking the semiotic with the maternal, Kristeva is associating this realm with the stage in psychic development when the child experiences the world through the rhythms and gestures of the mother's body. It is not innately female. Thus, as Rowley and Grosz (1990: 194) note, what Kristeva means by 'the feminine' is not something specific to women 'but a psychic position – a realm preserved in the unconscious, a realm marginal to the symbolic'. Kristeva contends that women are not fundamentally different from men, but that 'the semiotic mode is more dominant in the female psyche than in the male psyche' (*ibid.*).

The direction of Kristeva's work is to develop the Lacanian theory of subjectivity by reversing various categories. Rowley and Grosz note that for Kristeva any politics will fail unless it takes the pre-symbolic realm into account. Kristeva contends that 'the subject of a new political practice can only be the subject of a new discursive practice' (cited in Jones 1984: 61).

Kristeva expresses disillusionment with political discourses which, she claims, consistently fail to take account of individuals and subjectivity, and it is for this reason that she advocates political marginality and is critical of feminism as a collective movement. Kristeva's political trajectory, as noted by Rowley and Grosz (1990), mirrors the position taken by the journal *Tel Quel* with which she was closely associated. The political evolution of the journalist is outlined by Dews:

> 1966–8, rapprochement with the *PCF* (Communist Party of France) and strong influence of Althusser; after 1968, the long detour through 'Maoism' ...; 1976, disillusionment with China and beginning of a realignment of theoretical 'pluralism of the text' with political pluralism; 1978, emergence of an ideology of 'dissidence' and discovery that Christianity and literature ... are the true bastions against totalitarianism and 'the political view of the world'.
>
> (Dews 1979: 130)

Ann Rosalind Jones (1984) raises a number of important questions about Kristeva's politics. She asks: 'What is the relationship, exactly between textual and political revolution? Which comes first, a shift in subjectivity or in the social structures that enclose it? Do ruptures in literary discourses have any necessary connection to other social transformations?' (Jones 1984: 61).

'Writing the body' is the focus of attention in the work of Julia Kristeva. She 'uses the Lacanian concept of the symbolic order and the subject to form the basis of the theory of signifying practice which emphasises the disruptive and potentially revolutionary force for subjectivity of the marginal and repressed aspects of language' (Weedon 1987: 68). Kristeva accepts the Lacanian model of the phallocentric symbolic order and concludes that 'woman' in the sense of feminine has no access to language. Weedon indicates that Kristeva's emphasis on feminine and masculine modes of language, rather than on women and men, is integral to her theory of subjectivity, as language is central to the power relations of the social order.

Weedon explores some of the similarities and differences in the work of Cixous and Kristeva. She claims that, like Cixous, 'Kristeva argues that there are feminine forms of signification which cannot be contained by the rational structure of the symbolic order and which threaten its sovereignty' (Weedon 1987: 69). Unlike Cixous, Kristeva does not locate feminine aspects of language in women's female libido. Weedon points out that Kristeva's use of the signifier 'woman' is in the sense that she argues there is no essential womanhood, not even a repressed one, and that feminist practice cannot be directed at recovering some sort of essential state. Kristeva argues that, politically, the notion of being a woman is at best a useful temporary political strategy for organising campaigns on behalf of women's interests as they are currently defined within patriarchy (Weedon 1987: 69).

Weedon claims that, for Kristeva, 'the semiotic, feminine aspects of signification put into question the stability and apparent permanence of economic and social structures' (*ibid.*). It is, as Weedon points out, Kristeva's theory of the 'subject' as unstable which is of most interest to a feminist poststructuralism. As Weedon (1987: 70) notes, 'this view of the subject presents a radical alternative to the humanist view of subjectivity which views the subject as unified and in control and offers the possibility of understanding the contradictory nature of individuals... across a range of subject positions'.

What are the implications for feminism in its intersection with psychoanalysis in both its Freudian and Lacanian forms? Weedon (1987: 71) argues that these models pose a challenge to 'discourses which assume a "unified"... subject of rationality and to theories of innate biologically determined sexual identity'. She concludes that psychoanalysis addresses important concerns (including the structure of the psyche, the importance of desire, the nature of language, representation, sexuality and subjectivity), which all need theorising in a way which is historically and culturally specific and open to change.

French deconstructivist feminists such as Luce Irigaray, Julia Kristeva and Hélène Cixous have employed different strategies to Anglo-American feminists. Butler (1990c) points out that French feminist deconstructivists have established the 'destabilization of the subject' within feminist criticism as a tactic in the exposure of masculine power. Butler claims that 'in some French feminist contexts, the death of the subject spells the release or emancipation of the suppressed feminine sphere,... the condition of *écriture féminine*' (Butler 1990c: 327). The strategy employed of 'reading' and 're-writing' discourses of Western culture breaks with the established distinction between theory and practice. This strategy implies a very different conception of 'theory' from that which informs the Anglo-American tradition. In this tradition, theory is understood in terms of the explanation of categories such as 'women', gender relations or patriarchy. When Irigaray addresses discourses, she is starting from the assumption there is nothing outside cultural systems. In her essay 'The Power of Discourse and the Subordination of the Feminine' (in Irigaray 1985b), Irigaray is concerned with the connection between power and knowledge, i.e. with the power of discourse and how this is dependent upon, and produces, the subordination of the feminine. Irigaray's project is one of disrupting the 'philosophical order of discourse and conceptions of knowledge in the Western philosophical tradition by demonstrating how this order is dependent on the subordination of the feminine' (Game 1991: 13). Game shows how Irigaray is insistent on rigorous readings of specific texts to highlight the ways in which the repression of the feminine is effected in particular discourses and how the conditions are concealed. Irigaray (1985b: 78) claims that her project is one of 'jamming the theoretical machinery'. French feminism has been the major influence in the development of feminist critical strategy.

PSYCHOANALYTIC THEORY AND FEMINIST FILM THEORY

It has become a commonly held view, in contemporary film theory, that the simultaneous development of cinema and psychoanalysis at the end of the nineteenth century was not accidental. Mayne (1994: 56) contends that the affinity between the two has been described in a variety of ways, 'from cinema's obsessive re-enactment of those oedipal crises theorized by psychoanalysis to the cinema as a manifestation of Freud's description of the psychic apparatus'. For feminists the potential usefulness of psychoanalysis for feminists reflects 'a passionate investment in retrieving and affirming women as subjects in the realm of representation, spectatorship, scholarship and production' (Carson *et al.* 1994: 7). However, one of the difficulties for feminists is the tendency of psychoanalysis to draw film discourse into a 'phallocentric orbit and ascribe to identities an aura of universality and inevitability that can lapse into an essentialist view of gender' (*ibid.*).

Mayne (1994) notes that what has made psychoanalysis a controversial subject in feminist film theory is not so much the historical and ideological dimension of the affinity between the two but the fact that contemporary theories of the viewing subject have taken the work of Jacques Lacan as their point of departure. She states that there is an almost

> irresistible fit between the 'mirror stage' and the movie screen, and the relationship between the imaginary and the symbolic has become a grand metaphor for film viewing as simultaneously, regressive and authoritarian. And for cinema, as for Lacanian psychoanalysis, sexual difference is the central determining force.
>
> (Mayne 1994: 56)

Psychoanalytic theorists, particularly those following Lacan, maintain that cinema should be understood through structures of 'the look' that are central to cinematic identification. Feminist film theory which emerged under this influence seemed to offer a new perspective on their potential. Laura Mulvey's (1975, 1989) work is, of course, centrally located in these debates and her work is explored at a later point in the text (see Chapter 8). She examines 'classical narrative cinema', which is collapsed into Hollywood cinema in much of her work, and the possibilities of a new alternative film practice and film theory. Mayne (1994: 50) contends that, whatever connections feminist film theorists have made between a theory of classical cinema and the evaluation of an alternative women's cinema, 'the tension between the two is a persistent feature of feminist work on film'. She maintains that a major task for all feminist critics is to rethink dualism itself: E. Ann Kaplan, in her *Women and Film* (1983: 206), has described this process as the need to move beyond those 'long held cultural and linguistic patterns of oppositions'.

Women and Film is 'pre-postfeminist', but an interesting precursor of the debates that followed, and a 'radical' (for the time) presentation of key filmic concepts and theories including semiology, psychoanalytic theory, realism and the 'male gaze'. Kaplan's objective in the text is to advance and extrapolate on feminist film theory and criticism, particularly feminism's intersection with structuralism, psychoanalysis and semiology. She focuses on the concept of the 'male gaze' which, in terms of the operation of patriarchy, is viewed as dominating and repressing women; it has a controlling power over female discourse and female desire. Kaplan emphasises narrative form and chooses representative examples of female positionings in film while at the same time attempting to maintain historical and filmic specificity. She maintains that dominant film narratives represent women within images that have an eternal status.

Kaplan argues that Lacanian and Freudian psychoanalytic concepts are useful in looking at the construction of women in the classic Hollywood film. She maintains that 'the tools of psychoanalysis and semiology enable women to unlock patriarchal culture as expressed in dominant representations' (Kaplan 1983: 3). Kaplan argues that these theories assist in understanding 'female positionings' and she applies psychoanalytic and semiological concepts and frameworks to the analysis of film.

Kaplan investigates four Hollywood films in depth to reveal the way the dominating male gaze, carrying with it, social, political, economic and sexual power, marginalises women.[2] She shows that women are ultimately refused a voice, a discourse, and their desire is subjected to male desire. Kaplan illustrates her point by giving examples of the strategies that are used, e.g. women live out silently frustrated lives or, if they resist their position, they sacrifice their lives for their daring.

As mentioned above, Kaplan's text is clearly pre-postfeminist in its uncritical use of the concepts patriarchy and oppression. Her approach draws on Symbolic and semiotic models taken from the work of Freud, Christian Metz and Roland Barthes. Metz and Barthes' work is concerned with a semiotics of the cinema. From Barthes' position, film is a sign system which functions largely at the level of myth. Signs function through codes and operate at two levels – *denotative* and *connotative* – denotative reflecting a specific signification and meaning, and connotative a specific cultural/ideological context and meaning. It is at this second level, the level of the connotative, that the cinema operates as 'myth'. Kaplan maintains that in cinema woman (as real woman) is lifted on to the second level of connotation – myth:

she is presented as what she represents for man, not in terms of what she *actually* signifies. Her *discourse* (her meanings, as she might produce them) is suppressed in favour of a discourse structured by patriarchy in which her real signification has been replaced by connotations that serve patriarchy's needs.

(Kaplan 1983: 18)

She contends that our task in looking at Hollywood films is 'to unmask the images, the *sign* of woman, to see how the meanings that underline the codes function'.

Women as film-makers

Mayne (1994) maintains that the development of feminist film theory and criticism in the United States has been shaped by three major forces, all of which are, like feminist film theory, phenomena of the late 1960s and early 1970s. These include the women's movement, independent film-making and academic film studies. She goes on to note that the

new feminist documentaries inspired by independent film-making and the women's movement were also aimed at rejecting stereotyped images of women...Although women's independent film-making was not limited to documentaries, their explicit concern with women's issues marked them as independent films' most decisive influence on feminist film theory and criticism.

(Mayne 1994: 49)

Kaplan (1993) considers three main groups of independent women's film: the formalist, experimental avant-garde film; the realist sociological and political documentary; the avant-garde theory film.

However, the films and film-makers that command the most interest among feminist film critics are those concerned with the problematic fit between cinematic form and female expression. In this context, Kaplan critiques and evaluates realist cinematic strategies and considers the impact of avant-garde film theory that emerged from a critique of realist documentary. Commenting on avant-garde films she maintains that

film makers explore the problem of defining the feminine in a situation where women have no voice, no discourse, no place from which to speak and they examine the mechanisms through which women are relegated to absence, silence and marginality in culture, as well as in classic texts and dominant discourses.

(Kaplan 1983: 10)

Kaplan considers three avant-garde films – Sally Potter's *Thriller* (1979), Laura Mulvey and Peter Wollen's *Amy* (1980) and *Sigmund Freud's Dora* (1979) – and subsequently goes on to consider two films dealing with mothers and daughters – Mulvey and Wollen's *Riddle of the Sphinx* (1976) and Michelle Citron's *Daughter*

Rite (1978). Feminist documentary is of interest in films such as *Daughter Rite*, which challenges the very notion of documentary as truth, and in which Citron alternates 'fake' *cinéma vérité* interviews with two women with home movie footage.[3] Mayne (1994: 60) notes that 'Feminists have been attracted to Laura Mulvey and Peter Wollen's *Riddle of the Sphinx*... for its retelling of the oedipal myth through the questioning voice of the sphinx – the voice located outside established discourse'.[4] In the *Riddle of the Sphinx*, Mulvey and Wollen situate the film in the mother's consciousness and language. Kaplan states that 'Narratively, Mulvey/Wollen's film was new in moving away from the pragmatic/realist level on which motherhood had been treated earlier to a theoretical analysis that combined Lacanian psychoanalysis with Marxist questions' (*ibid.*). It has been suggested by Mayne that *The Riddle of the Sphinx* comes dangerously close to celebrating women's exclusion from patriarchy (*ibid.*).

Sally Potter's *Thriller* illustrates the dilemma. As Mayne notes, the film is

> a rereading of Puccini's *La Bohème* from Mimi's point of view, [and] makes frequent reference to issues of contemporary feminist film theory. At one point... Mimi reads from a collection of writings by Parisian structuralists and bursts into laughter. At the film's conclusion, Mimi and Musetta embrace while the men exit through the window. The final words of the film, spoken by Mimi, suggest that female bonding is what is repressed in a work like *La Bohème*.[5]
>
> (Mayne 1994: 60)

Mayne notes that (as with the other feminist films outlined) there is an ambivalence about *Thriller*, in its simultaneous affirmation of a feminist critique and its recognition of the difficulties involved in such a project. She maintains that the task of feminist criticism is not to resolve the ambivalences but to analyse the nature of the ambivalence. In this context, Kaplan's work is problematic in a number of theoretical and conceptual areas. Her collapsing of feminist and independent women's films leads to an indiscriminate analysis of both classical Hollywood films and independent women's films. More critically, because she has a largely untheorised position, she adopts a psychoanalytic perspective and draws on psychoanalytic concepts in an uncritical way.

Critique of psychoanalytic theory in its application to feminist film analysis

Freudian and Lacanian psychoanalysis became a primary tool for feminist film analysis initially among the editors and writers of the British film journal *Screen* as well as among French film theorists. Byars (1994: 95) notes that, although there was a recognition of a power imbalance inherent in society, these psychoanalytic theorists operated with a model which described the masculine as normative and the feminine as aberrant.

These theories, because of their normative reference points, cannot account for or explain resistance. As Byars (1994: 95) notes, 'they represent, instead, the psychic mechanisms for reinforcing dominant ideologies'. Byars goes on to note that the resulting film theory does explain a remarkable number of Hollywood films, and this can be seen in Kaplan's work, but she notes that 'it fails to explain and 'in fact' misrepresents a significant minority of these texts' (*ibid.*).

Laura Mulvey's work is typical of this theoretical approach which, as Byars (1994: 95) notes, incorporates the totalising notion of a 'classic realist cinema' with the universalising of a male-oriented theory of psychoanalysis which underestimates 'both the complexity and variety of mainstream narratives and the potential for consuming them in ways that challenge patriarchy'. The problematic nature of this perspective for feminist film theory is developed by Byars. She (1994: 97) contends that, within this realm of film theory, 'there is no way to explain resisting, different "voices" that function at both the narrative and the enunciate levels, and there is no way to explain the pleasure of the female spectator without reference to a masculine "norm" '.

Both Freudian and Lacanian theories of psychoanalysis function to naturalise the repression of women, limiting and obscuring 'variant "voices" '. Within a model of Lacanian psychoanalysis, sexuality is produced in and through language and 'language constructs woman as *not* man' (*ibid.*). Further, the tendency to universalise within the Lacanian approach results in a failure to account for 'differences among various patriarchal ideologies, and for any concept of struggle and change in ideology. In addition, Lacan's highly phallocentric theory appears to consign women necessarily and irreversibly to patriarchy' (Byars 1994: 98).

The Lacanian perspective is clearly a difficult one for feminism, and a Lacanian perspective on sexual difference and a feminist one are not coterminous. Mayne (1994: 56) contends that 'Lacan's sexist wit' has made it difficult for many critics to understand what his work can offer feminists. While Mayne recognises the value of 'a critical appropriation of psychoanalysis,' she warns against the danger of 'co-optation' as against 'appropriation' (Mayne 1994: 56). Lesley Stern notes that,

> from a feminist perspective, one would not deny that the patriarchal unconscious is inscribed within cinematic discourse, there is a danger that such an assertion stops at the point of demonstrating the dualities of oppression and seduction and blocks the question of woman's desire: who speaks it, how is it spoken?

(Stern 1979: 222)

The difficulties of drawing on a psychoanalytic model for feminist analysis have been addressed by a number of feminist theorists, from Constance Penley (1977) and Kaja Silverman's (1983) accounts,[6] to the unparalleled work of Teresa de Lauretis (1984, 1994). Penley provides an analysis of the avant-garde, while Silverman provides an account of theories of the subject in semiology and psychoanalysis. In *Alice Doesn't: Feminism, Semiotics, Cinema* (1984), Teresa de

Lauretis draws on psychoanalysis, as well as other theories of subject formation such as semiotics and anthropology. She shows that

> the distinctive and irreducible gap between woman as image – as object of the male subject – and woman as historically defined subjects is most often ignored or suppressed in analyses of difference and representation. The goal of feminist theory in de Lauretis' view, is not some utopian mediation of that gap but, rather, the articulation of its attendant contradictions in the name of women as historical subjects.
>
> (Mayne 1994: 57)

De Lauretis considers the relationship between feminism, semiotics, psycho-analysis and cinema. She traces feminist film theory from its critique of sexist stereotyping of women in film in the late 1960s and early 1970s. This relatively 'early' theorising drew on the Marxist critique of ideology and, as de Lauretis maintains, 'pointed' to the 'sizeable profits' accruing to patriarchy from the accepted view of 'woman as the possessor of an ahistorical eternal feminine essence' (de Lauretis 1984: 4). She notes that the semiotic notion that language and other systems of signification (e.g. visual and iconic systems) produce signs, whose meanings are established by specific codes, was soon seen as relevant to cinema. In particular semiology was seen as capable of explaining how the image of woman was 'constructed by the codes of cinematic representation' (*ibid.*).

De Lauretis sets out two crucial objectives for the text which are central to the analysis of semiology, feminism and representation. The first is to consider theoretical and filmic semiological forms in order to unpack 'the presuppositions and implicit hierarchies of value that are at work in each discourse and each representation of woman' (1984: 6). As she illustrates, in some instances the representation is sharply focused and clearly articulated, and she uses Freud and Lacan's theories of psychoanalysis, the writings of Lévi-Strauss and Alfred Hitchcock's films as examples. De Lauretis shows that in other cases – such as Foucault's *History of Sexuality*, Umberto Eco's semiotics or the films of Nicolas Roeg – 'the representation is excessive, ambiguous, obfuscated or repressed' (*ibid.*).

The second objective, as de Lauretis notes, is to interrogate these texts and discourses with feminist theory. De Lauretis uses a wonderful example to highlight what she means, drawing on Virginia Woolf's metaphor, in *A Room of One's Own* (1929), of woman as the looking glass held up to man: 'Women have served all these centuries as a looking glass possessing the magic and delicious power of reflecting the figure of man at twice his natural size' (Woolf 1929: 39), and shows how this is reformulated 'in Laura Mulvey's film/theoretical metaphor of woman as image and bearer of "the look" and followed through in its implications for female spectators' (de Lauretis 1984: 6).

Developing an early 'postfeminist' model, de Lauretis shows how the work of a range of feminist film cultural and literary critics, including Mulvey and Irigaray, 'rupture the coherence of address, opening up a space of contradiction in which to demonstrate the non coincidence of woman and women' (de Lauretis

1984: 7). That is, postfeminist writers do not simply demystify the whole concept of the representation of women in filmic, literary or art forms; they seek to 'dislocate meaning', to destabilise and finally to alter the meaning of those representations. Postfeminist theories of cultural forms identify 'sites of oppression', but they also actively articulate 'sites of resistance' within different cultural forms.

De Lauretis examines the relationship between (and traces the assumptions behind) classical semiology and Lacanian psychoanalysis to their common heritage in structural linguistics. She argues that, while semiology disregards the questions of sexual difference and subjectivity as not directly relevant to its theoretical field, and while psychoanalysis sees these factors as its primary focus, both theories deny women the status of subjects and producers of culture.

De Lauretis contends that the position of woman in language and in cinema is one of non-coherence. She argues that

> she finds herself in a void of meaning, the empty space between the signs, the place of women spectators in the cinema between the look of the camera and the image on the screen, a place not represented, not symbolized and thus preempted to subject representation.

(de Lauretis 1984: 8)

In the last chapter of her text de Lauretis argues that semiotics has shifted theoretically, from a classification of sign systems 'towards an exploration of the modes of production of signs and meanings, i.e., to the ways in which systems and codes are used, transformed or transgressed in social practice' (de Lauretis 1984: 167). She states that there are two main emphases in current semiotic theory: one is semiotics focused on the subject aspects of signification and strongly influenced by Lacanian psychoanalysis; the other is a semiotics concerned to stress the social aspects of signification, its practical, aesthetic or ideological use in interpersonal communication. De Lauretis argues that the work of Julia Kristeva and Christian Metz is typical of the first area, and the work of Umberto Eco represents the second area.

Teresa de Lauretis' later work takes these debates forward. In her essay 'Rethinking Women's Cinema: Aesthetics and Feminist Theory' (1985) de Lauretis'

> explanation of filmic address, female spectators, and especially representations of difference allows for feminist appropriations of narrative and encourages a more inclusive treatment of feminist interventions. At issue for her are immediate political struggles around the traditionally invisible issues of racial and lesbian difference and the ways multiple narrative viewpoints destabilize the positions of identification available to spectators.

(Carson *et al.* 1994: 9)

CONCLUSION

The impact of psychoanalytic theory on both feminist theory and feminist practice, particularly in the area of feminist writing and film theory, has been profound. The implications of Lacanian psychoanalytic theory and concepts still resonate within feminist theoretical debates. Feminist theory's engagement with dimensions of psychoanalytic theory has had both positive and negative effects. On one level, particularly through the work the French feminists, it has encouraged a more deconstructive and reflexive approach to feminism's critical repertoire, thus encouraging a move in the direction of *postfeminism*. On another level, particularly in the area of feminist film theory, psychoanalytic concepts have been appropriated rather uncritically and have limited the potential of feminist film critics and practitioners for the identification of a 'range of sites of resistance' within different cultural forms.

5

THE 'LANDSCAPE[1] OF POSTFEMINISM'

The intersection of feminism, postmodernism and post-colonialism

INTRODUCTION

Postmodernism as an intellectual movement captured a tendency across a range of disciplines and aesthetic practices for a radical reappraisal of modernist normative structures and representations. Debates emerging from within feminism had already challenged feminism's dichotomous frame of reference around biological and philosophical essentialism and historical reification, which had their origin in modernist discourses. Postmodernism's emphasis on 'deconstruction' and 'difference', and its challenge to the idea of a single epistemological truth, added to the voices of those who had been marginalised by feminism's modernist heritage. Subaltern groups have encouraged both feminism's and post-colonialism's engagement with postmodernist discourses in political, cultural and representational terms. Feminist and post-colonialist theorists have recognised the potential of postmodernism to advance debates around identity, nationality and difference already articulated within these political and cultural movements. The articulation of a 'democratic politics of voice' (Yeatman 1994) and representation has been given greater authority by the intersection of feminism and post-colonialism with postmodernism. This chapter examines the relationship between postmodernism, feminism and post-colonialism for the articulation of a postfeminist politics of resistance.

MODERNISM, POSTMODERNISM AND THE ACADEMY – DOMINANT 'VOICES' IN THE EMERGENCE OF POSTMODERNISM

Seyla Benhabib (1992, 1994), in her essay 'Feminism and the Question of Postmodernism', maintains that 'no other text has marked the contemporary discussion concerning the complex cultural, intellectual, artistic, social and political phenomena which we have come to designate as "postmodernism" as much as Jean François Lyotard's (1984) short treatise on *The Postmodern Condition: A Report on Knowledge*' (Benhabib 1992: 203).

Central to Lyotard's 'postmodern condition' is a recognition and an account of the way in which the 'grand narratives' of Western history, and in particular enlightened modernity, have broken down. Postmodernism tends to claim the abandonment of all metanarratives which could provide legitimate foundations for truth. Waugh (1992), while acknowledging the significance of Lyotard's contribution, maintains that the concepts were already familiar in the thought of Nietzsche, Wittgenstein and Foucault, amongst others. As Waugh (1992: 3) notes, what began to emerge was 'a tendency or mood across a range of disciplines which involved an intense sense of dissatisfaction or loss of faith in the forms of representation, the political and cultural practices associated with Modernism and modernity'.

Postmodernism invented the story of its own genealogy, as Waugh maintains, returning to earlier thinkers such as Nietzsche, Bataille, Artaud and even de Sade as well as more recent theorists such as Barthes, Foucault, Derrida and Lacan. The immediate intellectual context of Lyotard's book (1984) was, as Waugh (1992) notes,

> the demise of structuralism and the development of a poststructuralist critique of systems of knowledge which assume a stable/depth/surface relation such that a hidden 'core' of truth may be archaeologically uncovered with the appropriate tools of excavation and causally related to an apparently contingent surface.
>
> (Waugh 1992: 6)

In Lyotard's work – and in the work of Derrida, Lacan and in Barthes – meaning was shown to be indeterminate, all texts implicated in an endless intertextuality so there could be no space outside the text. As Waugh (1992: 6) elegantly comments, 'History becomes a plurality of "islands of discourse", a series of metaphors which cannot be detached from the institutionally produced languages which we bring to bear on it.'

There are distinct parallels between postmodernism and feminism. As Benhabib (1992: 203) notes, 'viewed from within the intellectual and academic culture of western capitalist democracies, feminism and postmodernism are two leading currents of our time ... each in its own way profoundly critical of the principles and metanarratives of western Enlightenment and modernity'. She maintains that Lyotard is right in highlighting the end of the 'epistemology of representation' and in searching for alternative cognitive and normative options to what has become an increasingly challenged and no longer convincing intellectual paradigm. Benhabib further maintains that feminist friends of postmodernism are correct to note the significant alliances between their own position and postmodernism's critique of Western thought. However, she contends that where Lyotard and postmodern feminists go wrong 'is in their assumption that the end of metanarratives or the death of Man, History and Metaphysics (Jane Flax) allow only one set of conceptual or normative options' (Benhabib 1992: 210). While it is clear that both feminism and postmodernism are theoretical movements growing out of the demise of the modernist epistemology, the real question for feminism is, as Benhabib (1992: 204) notes, '[are] the meta-philosophical premises of the positions referred to as "postmodernism" compatible with the normative content of feminism, not just as a theoretical position but as a theory of women's struggle for emancipation[?]'

THE POSTMODERN CRITICAL ENTERPRISE

By the 1980s, postmodernism was being used in three broad senses: as a term to designate the contemporary cultural epoch 'largely viewed in apocalyptic terms' (Waugh 1992: 3); as an 'aesthetic practice'; and as a development in theoretical thinking which represents a critique of the assumptions of the Enlightenment or the discourses of modernity and 'their foundation in universal reason' (ibid.). Alongside these developments, McRobbie (1994: 6) notes that the 1980s also saw a crisis in the future of Marxism in the context of sociology and cultural studies, and representational politics more generally. She contends that 'Lyotard's critique of the metanarratives of history coincided with the emergence of the post-colonialist critic, the subaltern subject who could not find a comfortable space of identity for herself or himself within the Marxist (class) analysis of history'. The locus of construction of identity shifted from traditional categories of class, work and community to 'other constellations of strong cultural meaning: the body, sexuality, or ethnicity, for example; nationality, style, image, even subculture' (ibid.).

POSTMODERNISM AND POST-COLONIALISM: ISSUES OF COMMONALITY AND DIFFERENCE

The intersection of postmodernism and post-colonialism explores many of the issues around identity, nationality and difference. McRobbie (1994) and Yeatman (1994) both reflect on the interconnections between postmodernism and post-colonialism in understanding both the political and cultural complexity of the contemporary world. Yeatman (1994: 3) contends that 'Acceptance of the reality of the postmodern condition means a relinquishing of a nostalgic holding on to modern(ist) standards of reflection and critique'. Further, she notes that postmodernism's emancipatory politics is 'pragmatic', 'oriented to the con-temporary politics of movements which have adopted and reshaped the modern(ist) imaginary of self-determination' (Yeatman 1994: 6). The parallels between postmodernism and post-colonialism are most clearly demarcated when they operate critically. As Yeatman (1994: 9) notes, the following connotations are brought together: a reformulation of the institutional infrastructure of modern capitalism within a postmodern frame of reference; a rejection of the 'univocalism and monoculturalism' of the modernist rationalist project; and the authorisation of 'a democratic politics of voice and representation' establishing 'creative forms of positive resistance to various types of domination' (ibid.).

The interdisciplinary matrix of cultural studies has provided a framework within which feminist, postmodernist and post-colonialist theoretical debates have coalesced. McRobbie's (1994) work contextualises debates around post-colonialism and postmodernism in the context of cultural studies. She contends that 'culture is a broad site of learning' and recognises that cultural studies represents potentially rich 'sites of opposition' and 'sites of resistance', where disciplinary boundaries are broken down, as well as the barricades between 'the academy and the experiences of everyday life'. Popular cultural forms and practices often claim to be representatively postmodern even though they may be forms and practices which never passed through any recognisable modernist phase. Popular culture has been defined as a 'site of resistance' and 'site of struggle' by many cultural critics and theorists. McRobbie (1994: 66) notes that 'Postcolonialist writing acknowledges the work found in and produced by the intersection of art and popular culture'. However, she goes on to note that if the

> postcolonialist experience shares anything in common with the post-modern experience, then it must be a postmodernism which is much more than an overstylized posture adopted by those who can afford to abandon politics. Instead, it is a way of making out a new set of convergences and divergences round certain critical questions about the society in which we live.
>
> (McRobbie 1994: 66)

Feminist and post-colonialist theorists share this ambition in their engagement with postmodernism.

While all three frames of reference have distinct 'political objectives and ambitions', the 'intensification of theoretical interest' (Ashcroft *et al.* 1995: 117) in them all has led to some confusion and overlap in understanding. All three have challenged earlier epistemologies which 'presupposed a foundation of undislo-catable binaries – centre/margin, self/other, coloniser/colonised' (1995: 86). For example, as Ashcroft *et al.* (1995: 117) note, 'the major project of postmodernism – the deconstruction of the centralised logocentric master narratives of European culture, is very similar to the post-colonial project of dismantling the Centre/Margin binarisms of imperial discourse'.

Similarly postfeminism and post-colonialism share an analysis of oppression in which both have distinct yet parallel theoretical histories and concerns. Ashcroft *et al.* comment:

> Feminist and post-colonial discourses both seek to reinstate the margin-alised in the face of the dominant, and early feminist theory, like early nationalist post-colonial criticism, was concerned with inverting the structures of domination, substituting, for instance, a female tradition or traditions for a male-dominated canon. But like post-colonial criticism, feminist theory has rejected such simple inversions in favour of a more general questioning of forms and modes, and the unmasking of the

95

spuriously author/itative on which such canonical constructions are founded.

(Ashcroft et al. 1995: 249)

The intersection of postfeminist, postmodernist and post-colonialist theoretical debates has challenged existing disciplinary boundaries and paradigms and established a new political and cultural agenda for the 1990s.

POSTMODERNISM, FEMINISM AND REPRESENTATION

The debate around the contextualisation of postmodernism and post-colonialism brings political and aesthetic dimensions together, particularly around the issue of representation. Craig Owens (1983) regards postmodernism as a crisis in Western representation, both in its authority and universal claims; a crisis that Owens states had already been 'voiced' by hitherto marginal or repressed discourses, feminism being the most significant of the discourses. Owens contends that feminism as 'a radical critique of the master narratives of modern man . . . is a political and an epistemological event – political in that it challenges the order of patriarchal society, epistemological in that it questions the structure of its representations . . .' (Foster 1983: xiii). He argues that postmodernism challenges the 'authorization' of these representations, exposing 'the system of power that authorizes certain representations while blocking, prohibiting or invalidating others' (Owens 1983: 59). Women are among those whose representations are denied legitimacy. Michèle Montrelay considers whether, in the sense of producing symbolic representation, psychoanalysis was not articulated precisely in order to repress femininity'.[2] Debates around the issue of representation as raised by postmodernism have been problematic for feminism as it assesses its future direction, located at the juncture of modernism and postmodernism.

MODERNISM, POSTMODERNISM AND FEMINISM

Waugh (1992) argues unequivocally that feminism clearly emerged from Enlightenment modernity, with its conceptions of justice and subjectivity as being 'universal' categories. However, she notes that, in articulating issues of sexual difference, feminist discourses weaken the extremes of universalism in Enlightenment thought. It is in this sense of articulating difference that Waugh argues feminism can be seen as postmodern.

However, as Waugh indicates, feminism recognises a contradiction in its attempt to establish an epistemological base predicted on 'a self-conscious awareness of its own hermeneutic perspectivism' (Waugh 1992: 189); that is, that women look for equality and recognition based on cultural and ideological formations, which feminism seeks to challenge. She charts the emergence of these challenges and cites Julia Kristeva's work 'Women's Time' (1971) as an early move in that direction. However, she notes that feminism cannot sustain itself as an emancipatory movement unless it acknowledges its foundation in the discourses of modernity. Waugh argues that it is possible to draw on the aesthetics of postmodernism without embracing its more negative aspects. The key issues for both postmodernism and feminism are those of 'identity' and 'difference'. She claims that 'Both have assaulted aesthetic or philosophical notions of identity as pure autonomous essence' (Waugh 1992: 190), and both feminism and postmodernism have helped reformulate the issues of agency, personal autonomy and self-determination.

Central to Waugh's argument is the concept of autonomy. The significance of this concept, in Waugh's view, is both its centrality as an Enlightenment concept and its role in the construction of various models of subjectivity. Crucial to both feminism and postmodernism is the deconstruction of liberal individualism. She contends that postmodernism, like feminism, has been concerned with a re-examination of concepts such as subjectivity and autonomous self-determination. Therefore, feminism, like postmodernism, has provided its own critique of essentialist and foundationalist assumptions. However, argues Waugh, as a political practice feminism cannot completely turn its back on 'enlightened modernity' as, to be effective as an emancipatory movement, it must have a belief in an effective 'human agency', in the importance of historical continuity, in formulating identity and in historical progress.

Waugh argues that the deconstruction of 'the other' cannot be accomplished without an accompanying effect of fragmentation of the self. She maintains that 'strong' postmodernism, or the celebration of radical fragmentation, can be seen as an acknowledgement of the impossibility of producing an 'ideal autonomy'. Waugh argues that the concept has functioned in a similar way within aesthetic discourses to suppress the historical and political challenges of cultural and art forms to traditional aesthetics. She maintains that feminism has been engaged in a struggle to reconcile context-specific difference or situatedness with universal political aims. She points to Lyotard's comment on 'emancipatory discourses', where he maintains 'there can no longer be a belief in privileged meta-discourses which transcend local and contingent conditions in order to ground the "truths" of all first order discourses' (Lyotard 1984). From this perspective gender as a category cannot be used cross-culturally to explain the practice of human societies. Waugh makes the important point that 'totalities', such as the concept of political unity, need not mean uniformity, and that Lyotard unnecessarily conflates the concept of totality with that of totalitarianism.

The concept of 'femininity', as developed by some postmodernist 'discourses', is seen by Waugh as problematic. 'Femininity', argues Waugh, has been used to signify an 'otherness' which has effectively been essentialised as the disruption of the legitimate (or the 'Law of the Father'). Waugh argues that the postmodern espousal of decentring as liberatory says little about women as beings in the world, who may continue to find themselves displaced even within a critique of epistemology, which has supposedly deconstructed the centre and

97

done away with the margins. Waugh maintains that postmodern theory increasingly draws on a highly idealised and generalised notion of femininity as 'other' in its search for a space. It rarely talks about women or feminism as a political practice.

Waugh argues that postmodernists' obsessive preoccupation with collapsing frameworks of Western knowledge conceals an unconscious fear of the loss of legitimacy of Western patriarchalism. This fear, argues Waugh, is manifested in different 'cultural forms' within contemporary culture, including: addiction to bodybuilding; violence to women; growth of religious fundamentalism; new forms of pornography; movies which represent women as a threat, e.g. *Fatal Attraction*. Baudrillard's work is seen as the most nihilistic of postmodernist writers and as highly problematic for feminists. However, Waugh points out that many women writers use elements of postmodernism (particularly the emphasis on disruption and deconstruction), while rejecting the more nihilistic elements, for example Angela Carter, Margaret Atwood, Maggie Gee and Fay Weldon.

There are a number of problems with Waugh's critique of feminism's intersection with postmodernism. The first is that she conflates the categories of feminist and women writers and subsumes both categories of writer within an essentialist model of experience, assuming that feminism can be equated with women's experience. Second, her theorisation of the concept of subjectivity and agency draws heavily on the modernist liberal humanist conception of 'the subject'. She argues that 'women' have always experienced themselves in a 'postmodern fashion', decentred, lacking agency, and claims that this was one of the reasons why women felt they had to occupy the centre (and a totalising position) in the early 1970s. Waugh maintains this was why women began to seek 'a subjective sense of agency' and collective identity. She suggests feminist writers may have needed to formulate a sense of identity, history and agency before they could consider deconstructing them.

Waugh goes on to repudiate the postmodern claim that there are no longer any generally legitimated metanarratives. She argues that even within 'a postmodern age' patriarchal metanarratives continue to operate, and the implications for notions of the 'feminine' continue insidiously to function. Habermas, Waugh argues, is part of a critical theory tradition which critiques Enlightenment philosophy because it is too narrowly defined. According to Waugh, however, he seems oblivious, like other thinkers in the same vein, to critiques of modernity raised by feminist theory. She calls for an examination of alternative feminist models of identity which can add to earlier debates which have ignored feminist debates of the last twenty years. She points to psychoanalytic theory as a crucial area in this regard. She claims that her model allows us to think of subjectivity in ways which do not simply repeat the Enlightenment concept of modernity, nor completely dismiss it.

THE 'LANDSCAPE OF POSTFEMINISM': THE INTERSECTION OF FEMINISM AND POSTMODERNISM

Feminism is centrally situated at the intersection of a number of intellectual debates emerging from the dialogue between modernism and postmodernism. Benhabib (1992: 210) notes that, confronted with 'debates about the "end" or "transformation" of philosophy and the emergence of a postmodernist agnostics of language, feminists feel ambivalent...' She maintains that, while feminists want to take advantage of the postmodern intellectual challenge for the development of alternative epistemological positions, they are getting distracted by an engagement with postmodernist debates which sideline 'gender' as a productive category for analysis.

One of the advocates of a postmodern feminism is Linda Nicholson (1990, 1992). She argues against the traditions of an Enlightenment rationalism and teleological character of the 'metanarrative' tradition. In the process of rejecting such a tradition, Nicholson asks whether, in the process, we find ourselves left with a position of total relativism. She points out that one can reject the idea of a general social theory while still retaining the idea of cross-cultural criteria of truth:

> To speak of criteria of truth immanent to the practices which generate them is to focus on the situational elements which make proof possible or not. This approach suggests an alternative mode for interpreting relativism... [Relativism] becomes a life possibility rather than a theoretical position.
>
> (Nicholson 1992: 86)

Nicholson claims that postmodernism does not entail the abandonment of common values and beliefs; nor does it entail abandoning politically useful tools, e.g. categories such as gender, race and oppression. She contends that what is required is a shift in how these categories are used and understood. Nicholson maintains that one of the most important elements of postmodernism is understanding theory as a tool and how social theory is judged in terms of its usefulness. She claims that the postmodernist stance does not necessarily involve a total break with all aspects of modernity. Nicholson argues that the position she is developing is legitimately continuous, with aspects of modernity.[3] Further, she maintains that the 'universalizing thrust of modern social theory' (*ibid.*) (for example in theories like Marxism) has frequently employed such general categories so as to exclude or foreclose genuinely disruptive elements of movements such as feminism, anti-imperialist struggles, anti-racism and gay rights struggles.

Nicholson argues that feminist theorists see their work and the process of theorising as tied to a political movement. As a result, feminists have to address the problem of postmodernism's lack of political strength. Nicholson maintains that feminism, alongside postmodernism, can already be seen to have made critiques of Western philosophy and social theory. However, as the contexts within which the critique emerged were different, feminism's critique has not been identical with that of postmodernism. Feminism's critique of the academy and traditional scholarship has been based on the premise that the bias and limitations of traditional scholarship come from its masculine patriarchal character. Feminists have argued that texts written by women have been overlooked in favour of those written by white Western men. In addition, patterns of thinking and abstraction have reflected 'masculine' modes of thought.

Nicholson argues that feminism has recognised the historical embeddedness of all theoretical perspectives which include feminism. She points out that feminism could hardly criticise other theoretical models without recognising the deficiencies in its own position. However, as she contends, feminism has displayed a casualness about the specific historical context of its claims. She argues that feminism can produce better and politically stronger theory by moving more clearly in a postmodern direction and by abandoning cross-cultural causal models. According to Nicholson, a causal model is not the only means for depicting and explaining cross-cultural pervasive phenomena. She maintains that there is a need to accommodate diversity in terms of a comprehensive explanation of such concepts as sexism.

So what are some of the gains and losses of feminism's intersection with postmodernism. McRobbie (1994: 63) sees 'postmodernity as marking a convergence of a number of discourses each of which opens up new possibilities for positioning the self'. These debates find expression in the work of a number of postmodern feminists, Rosi Braidotti's (1992) work is a case in point, with her rejection of central concepts in the 'modernist armoury', including her rejection of the defence of theoretical reason, the unity of the subject, and of equality, which she defines as 'domination'. As McRobbie (1994: 67) observes, Braidotti defines these 'Enlightenment concepts', as 'part of an apparatus of regulation and subordination hidden under the great achievements of rationality and knowledge'. For postmodern feminists and for subaltern discourses, as McRobbie points out, both the status of thinking and of Western intellectual thought itself is called into question. Braidotti (1992: 181) states that 'Feminists propose that reason does not sum up the totality or even what is best in the human capacity for thinking.'

However, as Benhabib (1992) argues, there are strong and weak versions of the postmodernist conception of 'the death of Man, of History and of Metaphysics'. She notes that, whereas in their weak versions these theses unite critiques from a range of different debates and theorists, in their strong versions they 'undermine the possibility of normative criticism at large. Feminist theory can ally itself with this strong version of postmodernism only at the risk of incoherence and self-contradictoriness' (Benhabib 1992: 213).

Benhabib contends that the feminist counterpoint to the 'Death of Metaphysics' would be 'Feminist Skepticism Toward the Claims of Transcendent Reason', and she argues that for feminist theory 'the most important "knowledge-guiding interest" in Habermas' terms, or disciplinary matrix of truth and power in Foucault's terms are gender relations...' (Benhabib 1992: 213).[4] For some postmodern feminists gender is no longer seen as a credible or legitimate category for analysis and, as Linda Alcoff (1988) has observed, feminist theory is undergoing a 'crisis of identity'. As Benhabib notes, the 'postmodernist position(s) thought through to their conclusions may eliminate not only the specificity of feminist theory, but place in question the very emancipatory ideals of the women's movement' (1992: 213).

A related problematic dimension for postmodern feminism is the issue of subjectivity and gendered identity. Braidotti (1992: 183) contends that the crisis of subjectivity produced by postmodernity 'offers many positive openings', while McRobbie (1994) maintains that postmodernism does not mean that we have to do away with the subject but rather to ask after the process of its construction. Benhabib is less convinced by Flax's (1990b) version of the postmodern 'subject'. Benhabib (1992: 211) distinguishes her own position on the subject from that of Flax, as 'a move toward the radical situatedness and contextualisation of the subject', while situating Flax's position as within 'the French tradition in stipulating the "death of the subject" ' (*ibid.*).

In developing the position more fully, Benhabib (1992: 214) contends that the weak version of the thesis of 'the Death of Man' situates the subject in 'the context of various social, linguistic and discursive practices'. However, as Benhabib notes, in the strong version the subject 'dissolves into the chain of significations of which it was supposed to be the initiator' (*ibid.*), and the strong version of 'the Death of the Subject' thesis is incompatible with the goals of feminism.

The implications of this position for the operation of the concept of gender and 'gender identity' are articulated in the work of Judith Butler (1990a). She is concerned 'to extend the limits of reflexivity in thinking about the self beyond the dichotomy of "sex" and "gender" ' (Benhabib 1992: 215). For Benhabib the logical outcome of Butler's position would mean that the gendered self did not exist, and the self becomes reduced to 'a series of performances'. Butler (1990a: 25) notes, 'there is no gender identity behind the expressions of gender; that identity is performatively constituted by the very "expressions" that are said to be its results'. Benhabib (1992: 215) asks: If we adopt this view of the self, what possibility is there of transforming those 'expressions' which constitute us, as we are 'no more than the sum total of the gendered expressions we perform'? This position has clear implications for the concept of agency and 'undermines the normative vision of feminist politics and theory' (*ibid.*).

Butler (1990a: 143) confronts the relationship between agency, identity and politics. She contends that the concept of agency is contingent on the 'viability of the "subject", where the subject is understood to have some stable existence prior to the cultural field that it negotiated'. This model of the relationship of the subject to discourse and culture understands that there *is* a relationship, but is unspecific about the nature of the relationship and does not understand the subject as constituted by that relationship. Butler claims that this model makes a number of false assumptions about the relationship between agency, discourse and the subject. It presumes that 'agency can only be established through recourse to a prediscursive "I", even if the "I" is found in the midst of a discursive convergence'. In addition, it assumes that 'to be *constituted* by discourse is to be *determined* by discourse', so that the possibility of agency is foreclosed.

Butler attempts to resolve the difficulty by maintaining that 'to be constituted by discourse is not to be determined by discourse' (*ibid.*), and she maintains that 'agency' is located within the possibility of a variation in the repetition of gender performance. However, as Benhabib (1992: 218) observes, where are the resources for that variation to come from? 'What is it that enables the self to "vary" the gender codes? to resist hegemonic discourses.' Butler's argument is unconvincing at the level of the operation of agency, which for both feminist theory and politics is the essential dynamic for the articulation of resistance. Benhabib contends that

> neither the fundamentalist models of inquiry of the tradition, which privilege the reflective I reflecting upon the conditions of its reflective or non-reflective existence, nor the postmodernist decoding of the subject into bodily surfaces 'that are enacted *as* the natural, so [that] these surfaces can become the site of a dissonant and denaturalized performance' (Butler, 1990), will suffice in the task of explaining how the individual can be 'constituted by discourse and yet not be determined by it'.
>
> (Benhabib 1992: 218)

The third dimension of a postmodern feminism which raises problems for a feminist politics is the question of the Death of History. Benhabib (1992: 212) argues that the feminist counterpart to the Death of History would be the 'Engendering of Historical Narrative'. She notes that Western intellectual history has been recorded and narrated as 'his story' and that the philosophies of history which have characterised the Enlightenment 'have forced historical narrative into unity, homogeneity and linearity' (*ibid.*). The consequence of this has been the marginalising or obliterating of the histories of different groups. Benhabib notes that once again there are 'weak' and 'strong' versions of the Death of History. The weak version calls for the end of 'grand narratives' which are essentialist and monocausal. As she notes, 'Politically, the end of such grand narratives would mean rejecting the hegemonical claims of any group or organisation to "represent" the forces of history...' (Benhabib 1992: 219). The 'weak' version of the Death of History defined as the end of 'grand narratives' has found favour with some feminists sympathetic with postmodernist claims. Nancy Fraser and Linda Nicholson (1990) are in the forefront of these debates. They maintain that the practices of feminist theory and politics in the 1980s have produced a new set of pressures which have operated against the construction of metanarratives. They identify changes in the 'class, sexual, racial and ethnic awareness of the movement' as altering the 'preferred conception of theory' (Fraser and Nicholson 1990: 33).

While supporting the 'weak' version of this model, Fraser and Nicholson avoid the implications of the 'strong' version. As Benhabib (1992: 220) notes, the '*strong* version of the thesis...would imply a prima facie rejection of any historical narrative that concerns itself with the long durée and that focuses on macro-rather than on micro-social practices'. Nicholson and Fraser do recognise this 'nominalist' tendency in Lyotard's work, but sidestep the issue. Benhabib maintains that Fraser and Nicholson are arguing more for a neo-pragmatist than a postmodern model. She states that by 'postmodern feminist theory' Fraser and Nicholson mean a theory that ultimately is pragmatic and fallible, that would accommodate a range of categories, 'forswearing the metaphysical comfort of a single feminist method or feminist epistemology' (Benhabib 1992: 221). However, Benhabib contends that the model that Fraser and Nicholson use is not postmodernist and that they are able to reconcile feminist postmodernism with feminist politics because they have replaced 'the "hyper-theoretical" claims of postmodern historiography' (*ibid.*) with a theoretical pragmatism.

THE DISCOURSE OF FEMINIST EMANCIPATORY POLITICS

For feminism, the failure of theories of modernity has been their inability to come to terms with sexual difference and to theorise particularity. Yeatman (1993, 1995a) has argued that the impact of postmodernism and poststructuralism has forced feminism to investigate both 'the genealogy' and 'status of oppression as a category of a modern politics of emancipation' (1995a: 45) within a feminist emancipatory framework. She notes that second wave feminism subscribed to an 'emancipatory politics which made claims to the idea of a universal conception of oppression and "oppressed subject" '. As Yeatman notes, this confirmed second wave feminism's commitment to humanist values of freedom and equality as 'inclusive' of all emancipatory movements. She states that, 'when working-class, feminist and anti-colonial movements are oriented in this way, they subsume the specificity of their struggles within the general project of advancement of humanity' (Yeatman 1995a: 51).

The interpellation of different groupings (e.g. women, the colonised within the modernist discourses of emancipation, freedom and equality) has had implications for emancipatory movements. Yeatman (1995a: 49) notes that struggles by the marginalised for inclusion have resulted in 'a very high degree of formal inclusion'. Discriminatory discourses 'against any subject on the basis of characteristics unrelated to capacities for citizenship: sex, religion, ethnicity, race, age, sexual preference' are no longer tolerated at least within the formal rhetoric of legislation. As Yeatman goes on to note, 'ours is the age of the formal completion of the modern ideal of a universalistic humanity'. The real implications of this are that exclusionary practices still operate but in more subtle ways, so that, while 'dominant modes of social participation have been formally opened to the excluded subjects of modernity', in reality only a minority from marginalised or excluded subject groups find 'a voice'. Yeatman cites the instance of the acclaimed American writer Toni Morrison, who is an 'African-American descendant of a plantation slave'. Yeatman comments that 'Toni Morrison's status is still marked ... in a way which indicates she is not fully included within the dominant subject term: she is constantly referred to as a black woman writer.'

Feminism's recent critique of its own 'genealogy of oppression' is frequently cited as a good reason for the transcendence of the modern paradigm and for the emergence of postmodernism. Many have argued that there appears to be a natural affinity between postmodernism and feminism, based on their shared suspicions about the legacy of the Enlightenment. Jane Flax (1987: 624) characterises feminist theory as a 'type of postmodern philosophy' which joins with other postmodern philosophies to raise 'important meta-theoretical questions about the possible nature and status of theorizing itself'. There are important epistemological and political implications of a postmodern feminism.

THE EPISTEMOLOGICAL POLITICS OF POSTMODERN FEMINISM

The relationship between feminism, postmodernism and epistemology is a complex one. Yeatman (1994: 15) maintains that 'what can be argued is that a postmodern feminism, or one which is refracted through the politics of difference, is a feminism committed to a specific epistemological politics'. She identifies a number of dimensions which characterise such an orientation. These include: a critique of modernism and theoretical traditions emerging around modernism based on a model of deconstruction; an articulation of marginalised or 'minority' voices to resist the universalising aspect of theorising based on a model of the commonality of oppression; a rejection of fixity of 'binary constructions of difference' and a simultaneous emphasis on the fluidity and indeterminacy of such constructions. In addition, Yeatman lists the following dimensions: a theory of knowledge which emphasises relationalism not relativism; a recognition of the historical contingency and specificity of theorising, and a concurrent recognition of the possibility of paradigmatic shifts within theoretical models; the recognition of the role of the theorist in relation to both 'institutionalized intellectual authority and to their actual and prospective audience' and a contingent recognition of their 'embodied subjectivity'. Finally, Yeatman cites a recognition of language as being strategic within theoretical debates; in Grosz's (1988: 100) terms 'a material, active, productive system'.

Yeatman views the epistemological politics of postmodern feminist theorising as 'an emergent politics', which she sees as a product of more wide-ranging political and cultural movements, of which feminism is one. In an earlier analysis of the relationship between feminism, post-colonialism and postmodernism, Yeatman (1990b: 289) contends that postmodernism's identification of the need for a pluralistic conception of subjectivity and agency has been 'shaped' by sociocultural and political movements of the late twentieth century. These have included expressions of revolt against 'the monovocal structures of modern patriarchal possessive individualism' (*ibid.*), including the articulation of a politics of self-determination from post-colonial movements, the wide-ranging and expansive movements around multiculturalism and anti-racism within the context of an urbanised or 'developed' cultural context, and feminist movements: 'All these movements have disrupted the dichotomous structure of subject and other which underpinned the private property relations of modern patriarchal individualism by disestablishing the "other" as a permissible term' (*ibid.*). As Yeatman optimistically contends, postmodernism enjoins a new and qualitatively distinct stage of democratisation. However, she notes that this view is not necessarily one held by those emerging from, and still engaged within, post-colonial and anti-racist struggles. She recognises that, from the position of those who are contesting their status as 'other', 'postmodernism appears as the efforts of the modern imperial, patriarchal master subject to manage the extent and direction of the crisis . . . ' (Yeatman 1994: 27).

Yeatman cites the work of Edward Said and Cornell West who, as post-colonial and anti-racist intellectuals, view postmodernism as lacking the dynamics of an emancipatory politics. As Yeatman (1995a: 51) notes, emancipatory movements are only accepted as authentic to the extent that they accept the leadership of a universalist emancipatory politics. She maintains that, for 'a consciousness of multiple and interlocking oppressions to be possible, the idea of universal human emancipation has to lose legitimacy'. Yeatman contends that this has occurred through post-colonial challenges to 'the assimilationist character of the universal or humanist subject' (*ibid.*).

THE INTERSECTION OF FEMINISM, POST-COLONIALISM AND POSTMODERNISM

This intersection is an interesting one, as all three movements have in common the process of dismantling or subverting dominant hegemonic discourses. In the process all three seek to challenge traditional epistemologies and to re-establish marginal discourses. All three areas have experienced an upsurge of theoretical development in the last two decades and, as Ashcroft *et al.* note, 'it would be true to say that the intensification of theoretical interest in the post-colonial has coincided with the rise of postmodernism in Western society . . . (Ashcroft *et al.* 1995: 117).

The contribution of feminism to post-colonialist and postmodernist debates has given both a more critical edge. As Hutcheon (1995: 130) has noted, while post-colonialism emphasises the relationship between imperialism and subjectivity, and postmodernism stresses the relationship between liberal humanism and subjectivity, 'feminists point to the patriarchal underpinning of both'. In addition, Hutcheon claims that post-colonialism and feminism have 'political agendas and often a theory of agency that allow them to go beyond the post-modern limits of deconstructing existing orthodoxies into the realms of social and political action'.

Spoonley (1995a: 52, n. 2) shows that for some writers 'post-modernity is held to offer little hope for the particularities which arise as a result of localised identity politics'. During (1995: 125) maintains that '...the concept of postmodernity has been constructed in terms which more or less intentionally wipe out the possibility of post-colonial identity'. For During this presents a fundamental incompatibility in the objectives of post-colonialism and post-modernism, as post-colonialism as understood by During is fundamentally about the achievement of 'an identity uncontaminated by universalist or Eurocentric concepts or images' in post-colonial nations. During notes that the desire for a post-colonial identity is strongly allied to nationalism.

There are problems raised by During's model of a post-colonial identity which have been highlighted by both postfeminist and poststructuralist debates around subjectivity and identity. Debates around national identity are increasingly focused on the issue of plural identities. As Bell and McLennan note,

> Not only are there a great many given and inherited cultural identities to take account of in any analysis of political 'subjecthood', increasingly the interchange between these 'local' identities is producing a whole range of *hybrid* forms of consciousness, lifestyle and action.
>
> (Bell and McLennan 1995: 2)

Bell and McLennan also note that nationalism does pose problems for feminist politics, particularly in its more extreme forms. Yeatman (1995b) has highlighted some of the problems inherent in claims for 'national sovereignty'. Bell and McLennan, while noting feminism's challenge to crude 'liberal and "class reductionist" approaches to personal subjecthood', also claim: 'Post-feminist strands of thought have gone further, taking strong issue with any counter-tendency toward "gender reductionism" too' (1995: 3).

The issue of a 'unified' subjectivity or identity is raised by Gunew and Yeatman (1993), who claim that such a model results in a projection of 'the burden of authenticity onto the minority'. They note that 'Even postmodernists who write easily concerning decentred subjectivity and metaphysics of presence in all forms of writing sometimes return to the unified subject when it comes to dealing with the minority or margins' (1993: xviii).

Those whose model of post-colonial identity is characterised by this framework of 'authenticity' are generally critical of parallels between post-colonialism and postmodernism:

Trinh [1993] points out that differences are caught up in the oppositional binary categories of oppressor and oppressed. Authenticity for the latter is thereby demarcated and controlled by the former, a trick which renders oppressed totally dependent on the oppressor. Oppression and repression become commodified into 'codified forms of resistance'.

(Gunew and Yeatman 1993: xviii)

There are clearly major differences in the orientation and discourses of post-colonialism and postmodernism, which, as Hutcheon (1995: 131) notes, 'feminists help to place in the foreground and which must always be kept in mind'. Despite these differences she notes that there are overlaps. However, as Hutcheon observes, 'This does not mean that the two can be conflated unproblematically as many commentators seem to suggest (...Slemon 1988a)'.

POSTMODERNISM, POST-COLONIALISM, ANTI-RACISM AND FEMINISM

The intersection of discourses around postmodernism, post-colonialism, anti-racism and feminism has provided an intellectually vibrant landscape, facilitating a pluralistic model of resistance which Yeatman has described as 'interlocking oppressions'. As a result of critiques posed by feminist and subaltern discourses in the 1980s, she contends (1995a: 53) that it is possible for 'multiple oppressed subjects to claim the multiplicity of their oppressed subject status'. She cites bell hooks as an example of an African-American feminist who, in her critique of second wave feminism, articulated the politics of difference in showing what it means to be black and a woman:

As a group, black women are in an unusual position in this society, for not only are we collectively at the bottom of the occupational ladder, but our overall social status is lower than that of any other group... [We] are the group that has not been socialized to assume to the role of exploiter/oppressor in that we are allowed no institutionalized 'other' that we can exploit or oppress. White women and black men have it both ways. They can act as oppressor or be oppressed. Black men may be victimized by racism, but sexism allows them to act as exploiters and oppressors of women. White women may be victimized by sexism, but racism enables them to act as exploiters and oppressors of black people... As long as these two groups or any group defines liberation as gaining social equality with ruling class men, they have a vested interest in the continued exploitation and oppression of others.

(hooks 1984: 14–15)

Elsewhere hooks (1990) articulates some of the problems integral to the connections between postmodernism, post-colonialism, anti-racism and feminism. She contends that '[since] most of this theory [postmodernism] has been constructed in reaction to and against high modernism there is seldom any mention of black experience or writings by black people...specifically black women' (hooks 1990: 24). She goes on to note that, in more recent work reference is made to Cornell West, the black male scholar who has been a prominent black intellectual engaged with postmodern discourse. While acknowledging that an aspect of black culture may be the subject of postmodernist, critical writing, the works cited will usually be drawn from those of black men.

As a black feminist writer, hooks finds herself on the outside of postmodernist discourse for two reasons: in the first instance because it is a discourse dominated by white male intellectuals, and in the second because of the 'language' of postmodernism. She observes that it is

> ironic that the contemporary discourse which talks the most about heterogeneity, the decentered subject, declaring breakthroughs that allow recognition of otherness, still directs its critical voice primarily to a specialised audience that shares a common language rooted in the very master narratives it claims to challenge.

> (hooks 1990: 25)

The apparent elision of post-colonialism and anti-racism needs to be clarified here. The links being explored by hooks between the radical potential of postmodernism as it relates to post-colonialism and racial domination is reminiscent of the recent work of Stuart Hall.[5] Both argue for a radical postmodernist practice, conceptualised as a 'politics of difference' to incorporate the voices of displaced, marginalised, exploited and oppressed black people.

There are a number of areas where postmodernism can be effective in post-colonialist and anti-racist struggles. hooks contends that radical postmodernism calls attention to its ability to cross boundaries of class, gender and race which can lead to the recognition of common commitments and serve as a basis for solidarity. Cornell West, in his essay 'Black Culture and Postmodernism' (1989: 89), suggests that black intellectuals 'are marginal – usually languishing at the interface of black and white cultures or more thoroughly ensconced in Euro-American settings'. He maintains that black intellectuals lack any 'organic link' with the wider black community and that this diminishes their 'value to Black resistance'. The impact of postmodernism is that many groups within the black community have the potential to share a sense of deep alienation, even if it is not informed by shared circumstances.

A second element in postmodernism seen as useful by post-colonial and anti-racist writers is the critique of essentialism. hooks argues that this is particularly useful for African Americans concerned with reformulating notions of identity. She notes that 'postmodern critiques of essentialism which challenge notions of universality and static over-determined identity within mass culture and mass consciousness can open up new possibilities for the construction of self and the assertion of agency' (hooks 1990: 28). In addition to the affirmation of multiple black identities, hooks also notes that it challenges colonialist/imperialist models of black identity, representing 'blackness' unidimensionally. Resisting essentialist notions of identity would pose a serious challenge to racism, as hooks (1990: 29) states 'coming to terms with the impact of postmodernism for black experience, particularly as it changes our sense of identity, means that we must and can re-articulate the basis of collective bonding'.

The relationship of post-colonialism and feminism with postmodernism is not coterminous. As Yeatman (1994: 28) notes, 'contemporary feminist theorists working within the politics of difference are making postmodernism over to their own agendas'. However, she goes on to contend that post-colonialists and feminist theorists do converge 'in their sustained contestation of how this works to maintain and reproduce domination...' (*ibid.*).

THE 'POLITICAL AMBITIONS' OF POSTFEMINISM AND POST-COLONIALISM

Postfeminism and post-colonialism have both theorised the politics of oppression and repression. As Ashcroft *et al.* (1995: 249) note, 'women, like colonised subjects, have been relegated to the position of "Other", "colonised" by various forms of patriarchal domination'.

They go on to note that, despite the similarities in feminist and post-colonial theoretical discourses, there have been few points of intersection until recently. In the last ten years, both sets of discourses have become more reflexive in terms of their own agendas, and in the process have been more receptive to critical dialogue and interrogation from 'convergent' disciplinary areas. Ashcroft *et al.* (*ibid.*) comment that 'Feminism has highlighted a number of the unexamined assumptions within post-colonial discourse, just as post-colonialism's interrogations of western feminist scholarship have produced timely warnings and led to new directions.'

While the dialogue between post-colonialism and feminism has gained momentum and become more critical theoretically in the 1990s, post-colonial feminists such as Mohanty had raised issues in the 1980s which had impacted on the process of critical self-reflection already under way among Western feminists. In 'Under Western Eyes: Feminist Scholarship and Colonial Discourses' (originally published in 1984), Mohanty critiques the 'totalising' tendencies of 'Western feminist discourse and political practice' (1995: 259). In doing so she seeks to establish a distinction formulated by Teresa de Lauretis (1984), a distinction between 'Woman' and 'women':

> The relationship between 'Woman' – a cultural and ideological composite Other constructed through diverse representational discourses (scientific, literary, juridical, linguistic, cinematic, etc) – and 'women' – real, material subjects of their collective histories – is one of the central questions the practice of feminist scholarship seeks to address.
>
> (Mohanty 1995: 259)

Mohanty goes on to outline the 'colonizing' tendencies of 'Western feminism' and in the process establishes the modernist frame of references within which second wave feminism emerged and operated. She suggests

> that the feminists writings I analyze here discursively colonize the material and historical heterogeneities of the lives of women in the third world. thereby producing/re-presenting a composite, singular 'Third World Woman' – an image which appears arbitrarily constructed, but never-theless carries with it the authorizing signature of Western humanist discourse.
>
> (Mohanty 1995: 260)

The process of colonisation described by Mohanty is identified by Gunew and Yeatman (1993) as 'appropriation' or 'who is permitted to speak on behalf of whom?'. They argue that there is a fine balance between showing solidarity with oppressed groups and assuming a position where one claims to speak on behalf of that group. Liberal feminists frequently fell into the role and, as Gunew and Yeatman (1993: xvii) claim, 'This gesture is of course a profoundly matronizing one and often results in what Trinh has called the nativist line of teaching the "natives" how to be bonafide anti or decolonized others (Trinh 1989: 59)'.

Post-colonial feminist theorising thus had an impact on second wave feminist discourses in terms of critiquing their ethnocentricity and colonising tendencies. Post-colonial discourses also had an impact on feminist theorising in the 1980s through the notion of 'double-colonisation', by showing that women in countries emerging from colonial cultures 'were *doubly* colonised by both imperial and patriarchal ideologies' (Ashcroft *et al.* 1995: 250).

One such theorist is Gayatri Chakravorty Spivak. Her theoretical critique is situated at the 'high end of deconstruction', combining feminist poststructuralist and post-colonialist critiques. McRobbie (1994: 69) notes that 'Spivak works within the discourse of theory but so transforms it as to make it an entirely different kind of practice . . . For Spivak the community of women can only come after the recognition of difference between women'.[6]

The work of Gayatri Chakravorty Spivak (1985a, 1985b) has been fundamentally concerned with the position of the 'doubly oppressed native woman' who is caught 'between the dominations of a native patriarchy and a foreign masculinist-imperialist ideology' (Parry 1995: 36). In Spivak's now famous dictum, 'The subaltern cannot speak', Parry (1995: 37) maintains that Spivak, 'while protesting at the obliteration of the native's subject position in the text of imperialism . . . gives no speaking part to the colonized, effectively writing out the evidence of native agency recorded in India's 200 year, struggle against British conquest and the Raj'. Parry contends that for Spivak the native colludes in their 'own subject(ed) formation as other and voiceless' (*ibid.*).

Parry traces Spivak's positioning of the 'subaltern' within the discourses of English imperialism, which rendered the 'native' generally but the 'native female' in particular, outside its discourses and therefore 'mute'. Parry, in summarising Spivak's view, claims that

> the articulation of the female subject within the emerging norm of feminist individualism during the age of imperialism, necessarily excluded the native female, who was positioned on the boundary between human and animal as the object of imperialism's social-mission or soul-making.
>
> (Parry 1995: 38–39)

Mohanty, in her analysis of the limitations of Western feminism's commentary on 'third world women', argues that 'discourses of representation should not be confused with material realities' (Parry 1995: 37). Mohanty goes on to show that because 'native women' are located at the intersection of multiple discourses – including historical, social and cultural – it is possible 'to locate traces and testimony of women's voice on those sites where women inscribed themselves as healers, ascetics, singers of sacred songs, artisans and artists...' (*ibid.*). This model of multiple subjectivities challenges Spivak's model of the 'silent subaltern'.

The limitations of Spivak's model are addressed by Parry, who claims

> Spivak's deliberated deafness to the native voice where it is to be heard, is at variance with her acute hearing of the unsaid in modes of Western feminist criticism which, while dismantling masculinist constructions, reproduce and foreclose colonialist structures and imperialist axioms...
>
> (Parry 1995: 40)

Spivak's own acknowledgement of the need for a deconstructivist approach to the idea of 'global sisterhood' (Spivak 1986: 226) appears to be limited to white Western feminism and does not include the 'native woman'. Spivak's dismissal of the role of 'nationalist discourses of resistance' (Parry 1995: 37) is highlighted by her emphasis on the role of 'the post-colonial woman intellectual, for it is she who must plot a story, unravel a narrative, and give the subaltern a voice in history...' (*ibid.*).

There appears to be a conflict of interest in the competing tendencies of feminism, poststructuralism and post-colonialism in Spivak's work. The political character of these movements is difficult to reconcile. The political ambitions of feminism and post-colonialism are quite different to those of poststructuralism/ postmodernism. As Hutcheon notes,

> as can be seen by its recuperation (and rejection) by both the Right and the Left post-modernism is politically ambivalent: its critique coexists with an equally real and equally powerful complicity with the cultural dominants within which it inescapably exists.
>
> (Hutcheon 1995: 130)

Despite Spivak's commitment to the deconstructive politics of poststructuralism, and her recognition that 'There is an affinity between the imperialist subject and the subject of humanism' (1988: 202), she seems to stop short at extending this to the 'politics of subjectivity' inherent in her model of post-colonialism. Hutcheon (1995: 131) notes that both feminist and post-colonial discourses 'must work first to assert and affirm a denied or alienated subjectivity: those radical post-modern challenges are in many ways the luxury of the dominant order which can afford to challenge that which it surely possesses'.

POSTMODERN FEMINISM AND THE POLITICS OF RELATIVISM

The problem for both feminist and post-colonial intellectuals is, given this position, how the charge of relativism can be challenged. For critics like McLennan (1992a), as McRobbie notes, relativism is the issue. He raises the question of whether cultural relativism leads to cognitive relativism, encouraging indifference. McRobbie takes issue with McLennan's conclusions and follows Yeatman (1990b: 291–292), who contends that feminists and others who are committed to developing the democratic implications of postmodernism 'need to firmly distinguish their position from those who take postmodernism to imply an anomic relativism'. In this context, Yeatman cites Foucault who, she maintains, achieves 'an intellectual "deregulation" of the democratically oriented culture of individualised agency' (Yeatman 1990b: 292). She contends that, where the notion of a self-reflexive agency is relativised, 'postmodern relativism reveals itself as the last ditch stand of modern patriarchy' (*ibid.*). Yeatman goes on to argue that it is imperative that feminists develop the democratic potential of postmodernism while exposing the 'patriarchalism of relativist deregulation'. In order to do this, Yeatman (1990b: 293) contends that feminists have to reject all 'essentialist tendencies which function to privilege women...and the moral authority which these tendencies accord femaleness'.

Yeatman (1994) groups feminist and post-colonial intellectuals within a category of 'oppositional intellectuals' in that both offer critiques of epistemological foundationalism. She notes:

> Feminist and postcolonial intellectuals...enjoin a *politics* of representation. Central to this politics is the twofold strategic question: whose representations prevail? Whose voice is deprived of authority so that they may prevail? This is a politics of representation which insists on the material effects of discursive power and which contextualises the institutional politics of the Western university within the world historical dynamics of Western capitalist-patriarchal-imperial domination and its contestation.
>
> (Yeatman 1994: 31)

In discussing the role of 'oppositional intellectuals', Yeatman (1994: 30) maintains that feminist and post-colonial intellectuals 'proceed beyond cultural relativism in their insistence on contested representations within what are putatively singular or common cultures. They refuse to accord a discursive formation coherence through any other effects than those of power.' Yeatman argues that feminist theorists have carried this over into accounts of their subject positioning. She contends that in the process feminist and post-colonial intellectuals are 'attempting to open up contested epistemological spaces' (Yeatman 1994: 31). This is evident in the work of feminist and post-colonialist writers such as Trinh T. Minh-ha (1989), Homi Bhabha (1990a) and Gayatri Chakravorty Spivak (1992). As McRobbie (1994: 64) notes, their writings 'appear unruly and truculent and poetically disrespectful of the boundaries which have guarded and guaranteed the old rules of academia'. The question remains to what extent postfeminist discourses emerging from the intersection of these 'interlocking oppressions' articulate a politics of voice and representation which challenge dominant representational politics.

CONCLUSION

What are the implications for feminism of its intersection with postmodernism and post-colonialism? McRobbie is an enthusiast for 'the new feminist theory'. She argues that the 'value' of the contribution lies in its rejection of the idea of 'one voice'; in its willingness to explore 'the relatively unnavigated political continent which lies "beyond equality and difference" '; in its 'engagement with the politics of difference'; and in its 'abandonment of the search for the "real me" ' (1994: 64). However, as Yeatman (1994: 31) notes, there should be no illusion that 'just because the dominant epistemological order is subject to contest, the material force of this dominant order will not prevail', nor should it be assumed that 'multivocalism' means that all voices are equally represented. hooks (1990: 24) considers Meaghan Morris's discussion of postmodernism in her text *The Pirate's Fiancée: Feminism and Postmodernism* (1988), and observes that Morris provides a bibliography of works by women, identifying them as important contributions to a discourse on postmodernism that offer new insight, as well as challenging male theoretical hegemony. However, she notes that there are no references to works by black women writers. The identification of feminism and postmodernism as conceptual and political allies is viewed by Benhabib (1992) among others as highly problematic. She states that a strong postmodernism denies those dimensions which frame feminism as politically dynamic. These include: the denial of a history where women are centrally positioned; the denial of women's agency; and a denial of gender as a significant category. While postfeminist and post-colonial theorists have recognised the potential of postmodernism to advance a 'cultural politics of difference', Edward Said (1989: 213) warns against 'the fetishization and relentless celebration of "difference" and "otherness" [which] can...be seen as an ominous trend'. However, as Gunew and Yeatman (1993: xxiv) contend, 'there is no question that the ability to deal with difference is at the centre of feminism's survival as a movement for social change'.

Part III

POSTFEMINISM AND CULTURAL FORMS

6

POSTFEMINISMS AND CULTURAL POLITICS

Feminism, cultural difference and the cultural politics of the academy

INTRODUCTION

Feminism and postmodernism are recognised as two leading intellectual critiques of 'epistemological foundationalism' emerging from the liberal humanism of the Western Enlightenment which has framed academic culture's modernist discourse. However, it is apparent that there is an overwhelming monopolisation of these debates by male theorists and critics, and a marginalisation of feminist writers and issues within these debates. Despite the limitations of second wave feminist interventions, the challenges posed to dominant academic discourses through the emergence of Women's Studies opened up a number of 'sites of resistance' for feminist discourses. The positioning of Women's Studies within the academy established 'a voice', facilitated 'a space' and encouraged an intellectually dynamic forum for the articulation of contested theoretical debates emerging from within feminist theorising. The unsettling of the intellectual discipline of feminism by theoretical challenges from its 'margins', from subaltern discourses, both within and outside feminism has forced feminist debates within the academy to be increasingly responsive to these 'politico-ethical challenges' (Yeatman 1994). Significant for this area of debate has been the intersection of feminism and post-colonialism (see Chapter 5), which has enhanced postfeminist discourses in terms of both resistance and contestation within the intellectual enterprise. This chapter highlights the impact of feminism's intersection with modernist, postmodernist and post-colonialist discourses for the articulation of postfeminist discourses within the academy.

THE CULTURAL POLITICS OF THE ACADEMY: MODERNISM AND THE ABSENCE OF GENDERED VOICES

What becomes apparent in reflecting on the theorists and critics of modernism and postmodernism is that there is an overwhelming monopolisation of the debate by male writers and an attendant marginalisation of feminist writers and issues within these debates. Examples of the absence or marginalisation of feminism's contribution to modernism's project, as Marshall (1994) notes, can be seen in the fact that writings by feminists such as Mary Wollstonecraft and Harriet Martineau were virtually ignored by classical social theorists. The absence of feminist issues and gender-related issues more generally is apparent in the work of more contemporary theorists such as Habermas. As Marshall (1994: 22) notes, Habermas' model 'suffers from his lack of attention to ... gender relations as organizing principles in the modern age, which leads to questions arising about his relevance to feminist theory'. Fraser (1989) also points out that Habermas neglected the gendered character of modernity. Benhabib criticises Habermas for his failure in restricting 'the ideal of autonomy' to the standpoint of 'the generalized other'. She states that

> This results in a corresponding inability to treat human needs, desires, and emotions in any other way than by abstracting away from them and by condemning them to silence ... Institutional justice is thus seen as representing a higher stage of moral development than interpersonal responsibility, care, love and solidarity; the respect of rights and duties is regarded as prior to care and concern about another's need; moral cognition precedes moral affect; the mind, we may summarize, is the sovereign of the body, and reason, the judge of inner nature.
>
> (Benhabib 1986: 342)

Benhabib's critique of Habermas' model highlights some of the limitations which feminists have identified in the modernist paradigm: notably the privileging of reason over affectivity which is implied in models of individuated autonomous subjectivity, and the valorisation of the generalised, universal other as against particularity. Benhabib's critique emphasises 'inter-subjectivity' and she seeks to 're-orient Habermas's disembodied autonomous ego to recognition of the concrete and particular' (Marshall 1994: 103). Benhabib's critique of Habermas conveys gaps in the modernist analytical framework more generally. As Marshall (1994: 24) notes, from a feminist perspective, the failure of these theories 'has been their inability to come to terms with sexual difference – to theorise particularity' in a way that does not ignore, obscure or marginalise issues of gender and feminist critiques.

The emergence of the Women's Movement in the 1960s and 1970s brought forward a range of women and feminist writers offering a critical voice to discourses in literature, art, politics and social theory. These voices served to highlight the absence of gender-related issues and feminist debates in modernist discourses; however, not all women writers set out to critique the lack of a gendered reference point. In fact many critics, particularly in the US, ignored both feminism and postmodernism. The work of one American writer and cultural critic represents many of these tendencies and, while somewhat atypical, provides an interesting example.

Susan Sontag is valorising of high modernism and, as McRobbie (1994: 80) notes, as America's best-known woman intellectual, one has to be curious in 'so singular an intellectual project as Sontag's, and [her] unswerving lack of interest, ... in all [the] debates which have fuelled the establishment of feminist criticism ... ' Sontag has little or no interest in feminist debates or more generally in questions of gender. McRobbie (1994: 79) contends that this distance between Sontag's work and questions of gender is related to the lack of a gendered frame of reference for the period of 'high or late European modernism', which is the area in which Sontag has written. McRobbie states that 'there was no critical place for women unless they demonstrably transcended gender. There was no available space to speak as a woman' (*ibid.*). Sontag has maintained her distance from concurrent feminist debates, critiques and issues. Stylistically she has seemingly had no interest in critical feminist discourses and practices and, as McRobbie notes, her own critical style of writing is modernist:

> This puts her in the same kind of relationship to those figures who remain in her canon ... [Walter Benjamin, Roland Barthes] ... as feminist art critics like Janet Wolf ... or Griselda Pollock are to feminist artists like Barbara Kruger or Nancy Spiro in the USA.
>
> (McRobbie 1994: 80)

The work of many literary and cultural critics can be contextualised within a broader analysis of the modernism/postmodernism debate as it emerged in the US. Andreas Huyssen's work *After the Great Divide* (1986) attempts to map the cultural transformation of Western society through examining the relationship between modernism and postmodernism. Huyssen (1986: 181), an American cultural critic, describes the 'cultural climate' of postmodernism as 'defining sensibilities, practices and discourse formations' which, he maintains, 'distinguishes a postmodern set of assumptions, experiences and propositions from that of a preceding period'. He goes on to ask whether this cultural transformation has generated new aesthetic forms or whether it is mainly recycling modernist strategies and techniques, 'reinscribing them into an altered cultural context'. While Huyssen sees the process of transformation as establishing a new cultural milieu, his understanding of postmodernism is very much an 'aesthetics'-related one, and the philosophical implications of postmodernism are not significantly engaged with.

He maintains that the attempts to contextualise postmodernism, as either distinct from modernism or as directly continuous with it, are inadequate. As Huyssen (1986: 182–183) notes, to 'have questioned the validity of such dichotomous thought patterns is of course one of the major achievements of Derridean deconstruction. But the poststructuralist notion of endless textuality cripples any meaningful historical reflection on temporal units ... ' Huyssen attempts to locate postmodernism in terms of its relational nature, 'mapping', 'several territories ... on which the various postmodern artistic and critical practices could find their aesthetic and political place' (*ibid.*). By using the concept of 'mapping' Huyssen is drawing on both Derrida and Foucault as conceptual reference points. In fact, as with many American writers in the area of cultural politics, Huyssen conflates postmodernism and poststructuralism, conceptually and analytically.

In this process of 'mapping postmodernism' through a range of disciplines, Huyssen (1986: 184) notes that, while 'the postmodern break with classical modernism was fairly visible in architecture and the visual arts, the notion of a postmodern rupture in literature has been much harder to ascertain'. He maintains that postmodernism 'migrated' to Europe in the 1970s, appearing in the work of Kristeva and Lyotard in France and Habermas in Germany. He also notes that paralleling this geographic migration was a disciplinary migration from the arts to social theory. Huyssen comments that by 'the early 1980s the modernism/postmodernism constellation in the arts and the modernity/postmodernity constellation in social theory had become one of the most contested terrains in the intellectual life of Western societies' (ibid.).

In discussing the development of postmodernism and poststructuralism since the 1970s in the US, Huyssen argues that a consensus has emerged that if postmodernism represents contemporary thinking in the arts, poststructuralism must be its equivalent in 'critical theory'. He also notes that in both France and the US, poststructuralism is seen as much closer to modernism than is postmodernism. In the process of contextualising the debate within the US, Huyssen (1986: 208) maintains that 'it is no coincidence that the politically weakest body of French writing (Derrida and Barthes) has been privileged in American literature departments over the more politically intended projects of Foucault, Baudrillard, Kristeva and Lyotard'. Huyssen maintains, that Barthes has become a major figure, as has his significant work *The Pleasure of the Text*, for many American literary critics. Huyssen (1986: 211) argues that Barthes 'positions himself safely within high culture and the modernist canon, maintaining equal distance from the reactionary right which champions anti-intellectual pleasures and the pleasure of anti-intellectualism, and the boring left which favours knowledge, commitment, combat and disdains hedonism'.

It is in this context that Sontag's work can be understood – at least in part. Sontag is a spokesperson for high modernism like many of the male writers whom she has spent most of her time researching and being influenced by, e.g. Walter Benjamin, Roland Barthes, Elias Canetti. As McRobbie (1994: 83) notes, Sontag's work is characterised by a 'defence of high modernism as a defence of the role of the intellectual in a world which seems dangerously anti-intellectual'. In addition her work can be see as 'shying away from those notions of a politically engaged art which emerged throughout the 1970s'. Sontag represents for McRobbie 'the image of a woman writer, for whom distance has been central, but whose distance from the intellectual community of the last twenty years, including the community of feminist intellectuals, cannot be construed as anything other than a loss' (ibid.).

While much feminist writing, particularly in the area of feminist literary criticism, has pursued a very different course, 'looking to non-canonical works,

120

and by developing a critical language aimed at understanding their meaning, rather than assessing their value' (McRobbie 1994: 81), Sontag has developed both stylistically and substantively, as McRobbie (1994: 81) comments, a diametrically opposed approach to that of feminist critical practice. In most of her writing the 'sensibility of literary modernity which Sontag explores, enters into and shapes her own critical style of writing...' (McRobbie 1994: 84). As McRobbie observes, there is little trace of her own personal voice, or of gender; 'Sontag's modernity is stripped bare' (*ibid.*).

Sontag has operated at the interface of modernism and postmodernism, a position which she shared with writers such as Benjamin and Barthes. Her writing is uninfluenced by many of the movements in art and culture which reflected a range of aesthetic sociocultural movements by feminist and subaltern groups. McRobbie contends that, against the

> decanonization of art by literary theorists, the relativism of cultural values by a new generation of black intellectuals, and the rediscovery of a huge stock of women's art and women's writing by feminist intellectuals, Sontag holds out in favour of what she perceives as the great, the good and the (seriously) terrible.
>
> (McRobbie 1994: 83)

Despite Sontag's commitment to European high modernism which released her from any obligation to engage with feminist discourses or 'voices', Sontag has not occupied the intellectual high ground within the academy in the same way as her male counterparts in the area of cultural criticism, e.g. Walter Benjamin and Andreas Huyssen. While gaining access to the privileged world of the American academy, unlike many feminist cultural critics whose voices remain marginalised, her contribution to cultural commentary and criticism has not been recognised as original, substantial or profound as feminist writers of equal intellectual stature such as Simone de Beauvoir and Gayatri Chakravorty Spivak. Unlike these writers, Sontag has 'spurned the personal and the feminine as the objects of study' (McRobbie 1994: 950). However, as McRobbie points out, 'history, art and culture have moved far beyond that moment when women had to forget gender to be taken seriously' (*ibid.*).

EARLY ATTEMPTS AT FINDING 'A VOICE': FEMINIST INTERVENTIONS

At virtually the same time as the male hegemony of the modernist literary canon was being valorised by some writers, a number of feminist writers and literary critics (in both the US and Europe) were establishing a range of feminist interventionist strategies. The growth of the Women's Movement and Women's Studies in the US and Europe in the 1960s and 1970s, and the publication of books such as Betty Friedan's *The Feminine Mystique* (1963) through to Kate Millett's *Sexual Politics* (1972) in the US, heralded the emergence of feminist discourses within the academy. While subsequently criticised by debates from within the feminist movement from women of colour, Third World women and lesbian feminists, these texts and the ensuing debates nevertheless established a number of 'sites of resistance' for feminists working within and outside the academy.

These second wave feminist interventions, while retaining a model of binary opposition, nevertheless opened up debates in the area of literary criticism and women's writing. Millett's (1972) text explored the way sex and sexuality was represented in the work of a number of male writers and considered the power relations involved in such representations. Millett presented an analysis of the portrayals of the sexual act in the writings of Henry Miller, Norman Mailer, D.H. Lawrence and Jean Genet. She highlighted the importance of male power and female subordination, showing how consent is manufactured and male domination maintained. She established the fact that sexual relations were political ones and 'patriarchy', 'gender' and 'oppression' emerged as key concepts in second wave feminism and the women's liberation movement. Pringle (1995: 201) comments that these 'theorists assumed the existence of patriarchy based on relations of domination and subordination between two fundamentally opposed categories of people, men and women'.

Women's Studies was a product of the demands for 'a space' and 'a voice' by the second wave of the feminist movement at the end of the 1960s. Yeatman (1994) contends that the establishment of Women's Studies within a distinct and separate sphere within the academy opened up a real opportunity and space for feminist intellectual labour. At the same time, she notes that 'the way in which women's studies is institutionalized ensures that it is sequestered and ghettoized in relation to what is regarded as the mainstream aspects of the university' (Yeatman 1994: 43). Yeatman also notes that Women's Studies frequently contributes to its own ghettoisation by 'adopting an insular and even separatist attitude to its intellectual enterprise, while simultaneously depending upon the very mainstream values and practices of the university it lambastes as patriarchal' (ibid.).

The development of Women's Studies as an intellectually dynamic area has reflected many of the theoretical debates and conflicts which have preoccupied feminism increasingly in the 1970s, 1980s and 1990s. The critiques posed to a largely white, middle-class feminist movement by non-Western women and women of colour resulting from a neglect of what Yeatman (1995a) has called 'interlocking oppressions' based on class, race, ethnicity and sexuality by the feminist movement, has, as Yeatman (1994: 46) notes, 'unsettled the normal certainties of this movement-oriented intellectual discipline and propelled it into its own distinctive sociology of knowledge'.

DECONSTRUCTING 'BINARY OPPOSITIONS': REDEFINING FEMINISM AND CREATING CULTURAL SPACE – THE WORK OF JULIA KRISTEVA

At the same time as Women's Studies was emerging from the Women's Movement in the US and the UK in the 1960s and early 1970s, the feminist movement in Europe and particularly France was being influenced by debates emerging from the strong tradition of psychoanalysis, psychoanalytic theory and poststructuralism (see Chapter 4).

Toril Moi (1985a) states that it does not take long to discover that French feminist theory has contributed powerfully to the debate about the nature of women's oppression, the construction of sexual difference and the specificity of women's relations to language and writing. She claims that Julia Kristeva's work is central in this process. Kristeva's main preoccupation, '(her desire to theorise a social revolution based on class as well as gender, her emphasis on the construction of femininity), have much more in common with Beauvoir's views than with Hélène Cixous' romanticised versions of the female body as the site of women's writing.' (Moi 1985a: 98).

Kristeva drew on Freudian and Lacanian psychoanalytic theory. She turned to 'Freud's narrative of the socialisation of the child through the early drives of infantile sexuality which produces the unconscious' (Jones 1984: 57). divided adult psyche. She also drew on 'Lacan's emphasis on the role of language in psychic formation, through which the child is separated from its primary relationship to its mother and placed in a network of gendered Symbolic systems centred upon the father as the representative of power.' (*ibid*). It is Lacan's concept of entry into the symbolic order which is the takeoff point for Kristeva's theory of the speaking and writing subject.

Kristeva goes further than Lacan; she associates psychic repression with the actual structures of language, which she takes as the basis for culture. Jones (1984) claims that 'Kristeva goes on to associate the Symbolic with the various discourses that organise public life: religion, economics, tribal and national groupings, law, politics, metaphysics' – and she links the dominant logic and the power base of each with paternity and masculinity. Jones states that in Kristeva's work

> The Symbolic Order is a man's world, it dominates the primary pleasures of the body and senses, suppresses non reproductive sexuality and any physical and psychic expenditure not aimed at profit and accumulation. Kristeva, that is, identifies the Symbolic with patriarchy, understood as the totality of culture.
>
> (Jones 1984: 58)

Jones goes on to note that 'Given Kristeva's global theorisation of culture as constraint, it is understandable that Kristeva wanted to discover sites of resistance to the Symbolic'. She looked for it, as Jones indicates, by returning to the pre-Oedipal stage using research into early childhood language acquisition. Jones points out that Kristeva concentrated on the infant's early closeness to its mother, its explorations of her body and its own, and she used the term 'semiotic' to categorise these pre-verbal activities, 'censored by the Symbolic order but never entirely lost...Kristeva uses the term "jouissance" to sum up the delights of this pre-genital, pre-symbolic stage' (Jones 1984: 59). The 'semiotic' enters into an adversarial relationship with the Symbolic, as Jones states, 'persistently pushing against rational discourse but never dissolving it into pure (psychotic) nonsense' (ibid.). Jones goes on to explain Kristeva's understanding of the 'signifying process' and 'signification'. She maintains that

> The interplay of semiotic and Symbolic produces a 'signifying process' *(significance)* rather than a fixed univocal meaning *(signification)*; and the place where the signifying practice occurs is a 'text', a site in which the energies of the unconscious simultaneously attack the formal conventions of language and are supported by them.
>
> (Jones 1984: 59)

Kristeva maintains that the only way of producing interesting results from such texts is to take the whole of the text as one's object, which means studying its ideological, political and psychological articulations, its relations with society, with the psyche and with other texts. As Moi (1985a: 60) indicates, 'Kristeva has coined the concept of intertextuality to indicate how one or more systems of signs are transposed into others'. Moi goes on to explain the concept of intertextuality as used in Kristeva's work. She maintains that

> political and power related interests...intersect in the sign. The meaning of the sign is thrown open – the sign becomes 'polysemic' rather than 'univocal' – and though it is true to say that the dominant power group at any given time will dominate the intertextual production of meaning, this is not to suggest that the opposition has been reduced to total silence. The power struggle intersects in the sign.
>
> (Moi 1985a: 158)

However, as Jones maintains, Kristeva's claim for the revolutionary effects of the semiotic depends on leaving major questions unanswered. Her focus on the text, he argues (1984: 60), 'blinds her to issues of literary context and reception'.

FEMININITY AS MARGINALITY

The French feminists maintain that it is a masculine rationality which has always privileged reason, order, and unity, and that it has done so by excluding and silencing the irrationality, chaos and fragmentation which they argue has come to represent femininity. Kristeva therefore refuses to define 'woman', as she maintains 'To believe that one "is a woman" is almost as absurd and obscurantist as to believe that one "is a man".' She states, 'I therefore understand by "woman"... that which cannot be represented, that which is not spoken, that which remains outside naming and ideologies' (Kristeva, cited in Moi 1985a: 163). As Moi indicates, patriarchy defines women and oppresses them accordingly, making it necessary to campaign in the name of women. Moi paraphrasing Kristeva states that 'it is important to recognize that in this struggle a woman cannot be: she can only exist negatively...' (Moi 1985a: 163).

Kristeva's image of 'woman' has parallels with Irigaray's. However, unlike Irigaray, Kristeva sees her 'definition' as strategic. Her deep suspicion of identity leads her to reject any idea of écriture féminine that would be inherently feminine or female. Thus, as Moi (1985a: 165) observes, 'Kristeva does not have a theory of "femininity" and even less of "femaleness". What she does have is a theory of marginality, subversion and dissidence.' In so far as women are defined as marginal by patriarchy, their struggle can be theorised in the same way as any other struggle against a centralised power structure. Moi proceeds to draw parallels in Kristeva's work between 'femininity' and the semiotic. She argues that they 'have one thing in common; their marginality. As the feminine is defined as marginal under patriarchy, so the semiotic is marginal to language' (Moi 1985a: 166). Moi's analysis of Kristeva's work is considered and powerful as she maintains

> To posit all women as necessarily feminine and all men as necessarily masculine is precisely the move that enables patriarchal powers to define not femininity but all women as marginal to the symbolic order and society... Kristeva's emphasis on marginality allows us to view this repression of the feminine in terms of positionality rather than of essences.
>
> (Moi 1985a: 166)

Kristeva refuses to define 'femininity' and prefers to see it as 'a position' which is related to the concept of 'marginality'. As Moi (1989a: 126) elucidates, 'if femininity can be said to have any definition at all in Kristevian terms it is simply as that which is marginalised by the patriarchal symbolic order'. Moi states that from a patriarchal perspective, as women are seen to occupy a marginal position, they are seen as the 'border line' of that order. Moi (1989a: 127) goes on to point out that from 'a phallocentric point of view, women will then come to represent the necessary frontier between man and chaos'. The problem with Kristeva's 'positional perspective' is that it does not address the political questions feminism raises. As Moi (ibid.) argues, 'if we have deconstructed the female out of existence, it would seem that the very foundations of the feminist struggle have disappeared'.

Moi then considers how Kristeva's deconstructive approach to sexual difference is developed in her essay 'Women's Time'. Belsey and Moore (1989) state that the essay

> 'begins by arguing that people can be thought of as belonging to national units on the one hand, or to transnational or international groupings on

the other (young people, for instance, or women). These distinct ways of classifying people correspond to two ways of thinking about time: one historical and linear, and the other cyclical (repetitive, according to the rhythms of nature) or monumental (eternal, timeless, mythic). The second of these ways of thinking, the cyclical or monumental, has been associated specifically with women, but this association, common to many cultures and especially to mystical ones, is not fundamentally incompatible with masculine values'.

(Belsey and Moore 1989: 240).

Kristeva argues that the feminist struggle must be seen historically and politically as a three-tiered struggle. In the first phase, women demand equal access to the resources of society (Symbolic order) and this phase is represented in liberal feminism. In the second phase, women reject the male Symbolic order and assert the concept of difference; this second phase is characterised by radical feminism. The third phase, the position held by Kristeva, is one that has 'deconstructed the opposition between masculinity and femininity and therefore challenges the very notion of identity' (Moi 1989a: 128).

Moi sums up Kristeva's contribution to feminism and feminist theory. She maintains that 'Kristeva's deconstructed form of feminism' in one sense leaves things unchanged in relation to feminist politics. However, as Moi (1989a: 129) notes, in another sense it radically transforms our awareness of the nature of the struggle: 'A feminist appropriation of deconstruction is therefore both possible and politically productive as long as it does not lead us to repress the necessity of incorporating Kristeva's two first stages into our perspective.'

POSTFEMINISM AND CULTURAL POLITICS IN KRISTEVA'S WORK

Kristeva's work can in no way be characterised as primarily feminist, as it is not even consistently political in its approach. Even in her early, more feminist work, Kristeva does not try to speak from or for 'the feminine'. For Kristeva to 'speak as a woman' would in any case be meaningless, since she argues that woman, as such, does not exist. Instead of an exclusive emphasis on the gender of the speaker, she recommends an analysis of the many discourses that together construct the individual.

Jones outlines some of the political (feminist) problems in Kristeva's work:

...her refusal to assign women any specificity beyond a widely shared position outside the symbolic implies a peculiar politics. Her position reinforces a long term mainstream tendency in Western thought to exclude women along with madmen and slaves from cultural centrality; she stays within the Symbolic by affirming the gender logic that locates women outside it, with the implication: 'if we are called the Dark Continent let us by all means be the Dark Continent'. And she effaces the historical reality of women, past and present, who have taken political action to change both the conceptual and social position of women in the worlds they inhabit (Barrett and Coward 1982).

(Jones 1984: 62)

Kristeva's literary studies reveal her lack of interest in women as 'agents in culture' rather than as objects of men's cultural representation. As Jones shows,

she reproduces the omission of women from the literary canon by omitting them from detailed consideration in her own analyses and by judging them according to a single masculine standard of value. Typically she is contemptuous of women's writing which she assesses according to standards she derives from male modernism.

(Jones 1984: 63)

Kristeva does deal with three modernist women writers in her book *Des Chinoises* (1974), but she emphasises their fragility rather than their textual adventurousness. According to Jones, Kristeva maintains that Virginia Woolf, Marina Tsvetaeva and Sylvia Plath found the challenge they made to 'the Symbolic' so threatening that their experimental writing drove them to suicide. However, as Jones notes, there were clearly other reasons and Kristeva's conclusions were overstated. Jones (1984: 64) maintains Kristeva 'bases her notion of women's cultural insecurity on her persistent assumption that culture is immovably and exclusively masculine'. Jones links Kristeva's view with her analysis of pre-Oedipal identity, as she states,

In this psychic and cultural economy, Kristeva assumes women lose more: because their identification with the father is also an identification with Father, the master figure of the Symbolic, they cannot afford to lose their psychic and cultural identity by returning via unconscious memory to the jouissance of their early bonds with their mothers.

(Jones 1984: 64)

Jones describes Kristeva's work as characterised by an anti-feminist logic and her (Kristeva's) increasingly sharp criticisms of feminism, Jones maintains, are highlighted in her essay 'Women's Time'. Jones is not alone in her critique of Kristeva's work. Moi states that

many women have objected to Kristeva's highly intellectual style of discourse on the grounds that as a woman and a feminist committed to the critique of all systems of power, she ought not to present herself as yet another 'master thinker'.

(Moi 1985a: 169)

Despite Jones's critique of Kristeva's work and Moi's reservations, the contribution of her work within the academy in France should not be devalued. As Moi comments,

Her commitment to thorough theoretical investigation of the problems of marginality and subversion, her radical deconstruction of the identity of the subject, her often extensive consideration of the material and historical contexts of the works of art she studies, have opened up new perspectives for further feminist enquiry. Her theory of language and its disrupted subject (*sujet en procès*) allows us to examine both women's and men's writing from an anti-humanist, anti-essentialist perspective.

(Moi 1985a: 172)

CULTURAL POLITICS AND THE ACADEMY

Contemporary debates within feminist theorising have been reflected within the academy through the medium of Women's Studies. Yeatman (1994: 42) observes that the position of Women's Studies within 'the contemporary university has to do with making institutionalized knowledge accountable and responsive to contemporary politico-ethical challenges'. As such, it is 'the site of a radical critique of modern western epistemology' (*ibid.*).

The intersection of feminism with poststructuralist and postmodernist discourses has encouraged a greater level of reflexivity around feminist epistemological debates and about its positioning within the academy. Morris (1988: 8) notes that Foucault's conception of the 'specific intellectual' has been very useful for feminist theory and critique in allowing institutional struggles to occupy a 'politics of everyday life' rather than being confined to academic debates relegated to an 'ivory tower'. As Morris goes on to note, feminism has both benefited from and been actively engaged with 'this kind of reconceptualization of academic politics' (*ibid.*). Yeatman (1994: 48) maintains that Women's Studies, and more particularly feminist theory, is making a significant contribution to the

new wave of theorizing in the humanities and the social sciences... This new body is both supremely skeptical and democratic in relation to the values which are also embedded in knowledge... This kind of analysis creates a space for those who have been 'othered' in discourse.

(Yeatman 1994: 48)

However, there have been concerns raised about the remoteness of contemporary feminist theorising from the reality of and operation of power in the academy. Paul Smith in an essay entitled 'Men in Feminism' (1987) contends that poststructuralist feminist theory 'however "feminist" it may be, and howsoever "feminist" is construed – does not exist outside the academy' (Smith 1987: 34, 267, n. 2). However, Smith does indicate in a note that he is referring only to what is known 'in the academic vernacular' as poststructuralist feminist theory.

Meaghan Morris comments on the significance of recent theoretical debates within feminism for the creation of 'sites of resistance' within the academy. She states that intellectual work needs to go through a process of self-reflection in order to transform itself politically. However she notes that

> one of the most important consequences of the notion of the 'specific intellectual' is not to translate 'specificity' as 'confinement', but rather to begin to accept firstly that work produced in an academic context...can be used and rewritten in unpredictable ways...elsewhere: and secondly that this movement can run the other way: academic theorization can and should transform its practices by learning from the experiences, the concepts, and the methodologies developed by people in broader social and political movements.
>
> (Morris 1988: 10)

Morris notes that the 'intensity' of feminist theoretical debate, which has emerged from feminism's intersection with poststructuralism and postmodernism, has corresponded with the emergence of feminism as a significant 'presence' in the academy. It has also reflected feminism's engagement with a number of wider 'political struggles' around race, ethnicity, class and nationality. Additionally Morris maintains that it has run concurrently with a weakening of feminism as a significant social force.

Despite the growth in the importance of feminist theoretical debates in the academy, Morris comments on the absence of references to feminist writers within many of the discourses around postmodernism and poststructuralism. She raises the question of why the 'critically associated work of Catherine Clément, Hélène Cixous, Luce Irigaray, Shoshana Felman, Jane Gallop, Sarah Kofman, Alice Jardine, Michèle Le Doueff, Gayatri Chakravorty Spivak, or Jacqueline Rose' (Morris 1988: 10) is not referred to in the same way as many of the male literary and cultural critics. She goes on to note that if we add to this list those who have been concerned with theorising modernism/postmodernism we can add 'Janet Bergstrom, Mary Ann Doane, Elizabeth Grosz, Barbara Johnson, Donna Haraway, Teresa de Lauretis, Angela McRobbie, Patricia Mellencamp, Tania Modleski, Nancy K Miller, Naomi Shor, Kaja Silverman, Judith Williamson' (ibid.). Further, Morris states that if we consider writers and theorists who have investigated the 'politics' of postmodernism, then 'the works of Nancy Hartsock, Carol Pateman, Juliet Mitchell or Chantal Mouffe' (ibid.) should be added. The work of Anna Yeatman, Michèle Barrett, Patricia Waugh, Nancy Fraser, Linda Nicholson, Susan Bordo, Judith Butler, Christine di Stefano, Joan Scott, Seyla Benhabib and many more can also be added to the list. In addition Morris (ibid.) observes that the 'new theorizations of politics by writers differently placed in histories of racism and colonialism' has produced an area of writing vibrant in its interweaving of cultural criticism and politics. This includes writers such as Geeta Kapur, Trinh T. Minh-ha, bell hooks, Sneja Gunew, Rey Chow, Angela Davis and Gloria Anzaldúa.

Morris also raises the related issue of the way women artists and feminist theorists have been portrayed by male cultural critics. She points to the work of

Andreas Huyssen (1986) and Craig Owens (1983), who, she contends, identify postmodern women artists and feminist theorists 'as objects of commentary' but as not 'engaging' in a debate with postmodernism. As Morris (1988: 14) ponders, 'Doesn't this distinction return us precisely to that division between a (feminized) object-language and a (masculine) meta-language that feminist thought has taught us to question for its political function, rather than for its epistemological validity?'. She goes on to question how Huyssen (1986) can confirm Owen's view that feminism has not been fully engaged with debates around postmodernism, while at the same time 'conceding that crucial aspects of postmodernism ... - would be "unthinkable" [Huyssen 1986: 220] without the impact of feminist thought' (*ibid.*). It is Huyssen himself, who in his essay 'Mass Culture as Woman: Modernism's Other', comments that the preoccupation of 'male authors' with imaginary femininity 'can easily go hand in hand with the exclusion of real women from the literary enterprise [Huyssen 1986: 45]' (Morris 1988: 14). It is hardly surprising then, as Morris goes on to comment, that if we follow Huyssen, a postmodernism dominated by male 'authors' 'could be seen as renewing one of the inaugural gestures (in Lyotard's sense) of modernism: inscribing its "bafflement" by an imaginary, "absent", silent femininity, while erasing and silencing the work of real women in the history and practice of the theoretical enterprise' (*ibid.*).

POSTFEMINIST DISCOURSES, CULTURAL POLITICS AND THE ACADEMY: DECONSTRUCTION AND 'THE POLITICS OF DIFFERENCE'

The intervention of feminism within the academy has been strengthened by the developments in the 1980s and 1990s of a greater degree of feminist pluralism, particularly as a result of debates emerging from non-Western women and women of colour. As indicated earlier, women of colour have challenged the uncritical use of concepts such as 'oppression' and 'patriarchy' and questioned the assumptions on which second wave feminism was based. bell hooks (1984: 18) has shown that such assumptions tacitly presuppose shared class, race and ethnic group status with dominant group men. As hooks points out, it clearly does not make sense for women who are racially, economically and ethnically exploited to seek equality with their male peers. As hooks notes,

> Knowing that men in their groups do not have social, political and economic power, they could not deem it liberatory to share their social status. While they are aware that sexism enables men in their respective groups to have privileges denied them, they are more likely to see exaggerated expressions of male chauvinism among their peers as stemming from the male's sense of himself as powerless and ineffectual

in relation to ruling male groups rather than an expression of an overall privileged social status.

(hooks 1984: 18)

Women's Studies and feminist theorising have responded to the criticisms emerging from within feminism by the development of a number of critical strategies. Yeatman (1994: 47) outlines some of these developments, the first of which she defines as 'feminism as critique' and identifies the work of Judith Butler (1990a), Denise Riley (1988) and Elizabeth Grosz (1990a) as representative of this position. Yeatman (1994: 47) contends that 'feminism as critique' confirms the very ground it seeks to challenge by reproducing and confirming the 'binarisms of a patriarchal gender division of labour, and, paradoxically, becomes complicit with that order'. A second response, identified by Yeatman, has been the development of a theory based on the intersection of different bases of oppression such as class, gender, ethnicity, race and sexuality. These intersecting bases, it is argued, should be treated analytically, separately, and then examined in their historical specificity. A third response is developed from this and looks at what has become defined as 'the politics of difference', based on articulation of a 'politics of voice and representation' emerging from 'women who regard themselves as differently positioned in terms of ethnicity, race, class and sexuality' (Yeatman 1994: 48). As Yeatman notes, these challenges have brought out 'the neglect of class, racist and ethnic oppression by the feminist movement with its tendency to concentrate on gender issues' (1994: 46). The value of the work of feminist writers and theorists, as McRobbie notes, lies in their interrogation

> of the ground rules, the boundaries and the barriers which define feminist theory and politics and which simultaneously have to be broken, have to be trespassed upon ... The riposte to white feminists that they were not speaking and could not speak on behalf of 'all women', has prompted a reassessment of the feminist self and who she is, and is speaking to and about. At the same time this particular fragmentation of the feminist subject is confirmed through the global and postmodern critique of the European Enlightenment.
>
> (McRobbie 1994: 72)

It is to these issues, and to the emergence of a significant literature within feminist theoretical debates around 'the politics of difference', that we now turn.

'MARGINALISED VOICES' AND 'THE POLITICS OF DIFFERENCE'

Feminism has been confronted by debates emanating from its 'margins' and from the theoretical challenges raised by postmodernism, poststructuralism and post-colonialism. A major area of debate for second wave feminism has been its ability to deal with differences among women, without losing the impetus that derives from a unified and coherent movement for social change. Postmodernism and poststructuralism have assisted feminist debates by providing a conceptual repertoire centred on 'deconstruction', 'difference' and 'identity'. Within this wide frame of reference all knowledges are defined as 'situated ones' (Haraway 1991).

Sneja Gunew and Anna Yeatman (1993: xiii) show how post-colonialism 'loosely defined as a body of theories which offer a place to speak for those who have been excluded from Western metaphysics', together with poststructuralism, gives us 'the tools to deconstruct these homogenizing categories so that it is possible to admit difference, not simply as the self confirming other, but as the admission and recognition of incommensurabilities'. Elsewhere Yeatman (1995a) notes that these challenges have emerged, in the post-colonial era, to what she describes as 'the assimilationist character of the universal or humanist subject' (1995a: 51). A 'politics of difference' does not articulate pluralism *per se* but rather 'implies incommensurable differences which cannot be subsumed under one universal category' (*ibid.*). As Yeatman (1995a: 52) explains, in order to understand how this kind of difference can develop, one has to understand the fundamental challenge that is posed to the idea of a unitary national identity or human subject.

The emerging postfeminism or 'feminist pluralism' of the 1990s not only demonstrates that both the universal subject and the national community is 'internally fractured', but understands that this 'fracturing applies also to feminism's own identity, as representing the interests of women' (Yeatman 1995a: 52). The nature of a humanist emancipatory politics meant, as Yeatman (1995a: 53) notes, that 'a subject could be positioned as both black, for example and woman, but this meant she had to subscribe to the most heavily marked of these identities and its politics'. As Yeatman goes on to argue, this is meant for a black woman or a working-class woman subscribing to either a black or working-class status and to its 'contestation'. In each case, 'the feminine subject within the oppressed race or class was asked to subordinate her own distinctive claims to what would further the well being and good of the whole race or class' (*ibid.*). The implications of these 'positionings' for a feminism dominated by white, middle-class women were clear: they were the only group 'whose subject status threw into relief the condition of women as a marked term and oppressed group' (*ibid.*).

The type of politics emerging from this latter perspective is a politics which valorises 'separatism'; a kind of 'separatism' which 'advances an identity claim on behalf of a group in a way which denies reciprocity of respect for its others' (Yeatman 1995b: 197). Yeatman contends that this type of 'separatist' or 'identity politics' can be identified in both feminist and bicultural movements. An example of biculturalism, despite the contested nature of the territory, can be applied to the concept of cultural difference in New Zealand and the relations between Maori and Pakeha. Margaret Wilson and Anna Yeatman, in their text

Justice and Identity Antipodean Practices (1995), claim that 'Maori and Pakeha constantly run the risk of overlooking both New Zealanders who fall outside this binary and the complexities within these two identities' (1995: viii). They also raise the question of how adequate a bicultural policy and practice can be without being part of 'a multi-cultural policy and practice'.

Within a framework of feminist or Maori separatism, there are claims to the privilege of sovereign selfhood, as Yeatman (1995b: 97) comments, 'in the same way as those who have had privileged subject status have done'. It is not the claims to territorial integrity which are at issue within any questioning of a separatist identity politics. What is at issue, and what is problematic about such a politics, as Yeatman contends, 'is the claim to sovereign selfhood which is often made in ways which appear to deny reciprocal respect for that same claim on behalf of others' (*ibid.*). She goes on to show how a separatist politics operates in the case of feminism and Maori: 'Feminist separatists who have designed a moral universe that excludes men operate in such a way as to deny justice. The same occurs when Maori separatists make identity claims that seem to deny the historical fact of Maori co-existence with Pakeha' (*ibid.*).

The conception of selfhood that emerges from these 'separatist' positions has been problematised by contemporary feminist and post-colonial theorists who have posited a conception of selfhood which is 'contradictory, incoherent and multiple' (Yeatman 1995b: 207). Both cases offer a conception of selfhood which is characterised by what Bartky (1990) calls an ethical ambiguity. Yeatman (1995b: 208) claims that, while feminist and post-colonial theorists of difference reject the concept of the unified sovereign self in favour of 'a selfhood that is contradictory, hybridised and disjunctive, they do not abandon the claim to sovereign selfhood for the post-colonial or feminist self'. The concept of self that emerges is a contested one, 'contesting the oppressed subject positioning that specifies the terms of the selfhood' (*ibid.*). The challenges posed to the claims to sovereign selfhood that are raised by post-colonial and feminist theorists of difference change the conception of 'modern sovereign selfhood' by their abandonment of 'the premise of indivisibility' (Yeatman 1995b: 209).

The 'politics of difference', as outlined by Gunew and Yeatman (1993), is one which challenges strict binary oppositional logic. Larner (1993), in her analysis of bicultural politics in New Zealand, suggests that New Zealand needs to move beyond the bicultural model of Maori–Pakeha differences. Trinh T. Minh-ha deconstructs the Western model of 'individuated subjectivity', which posits a conception of the 'self' in opposition to and in a hierarchical relation to 'other'. Trinh (1989) suggests that, 'In a society where they remain constantly at odds on occupied territories, women can only situate their social spaces precariously in the interstices of diverse systems of ownership.' She goes to state that women need to cut across borders rather than fetishising them 'into a spectacle of difference' which in the end 'disavows difference'.

FEMINIST AND POST-COLONIAL INTELLECTUALS AND THE CULTURAL POLITICS OF THE ACADEMY

This 'insistence on the ambiguous nature of the border which constitutes differences' is identified elsewhere by Yeatman (1994: 17) as an aspect of the 'epistemological politics of a postmodern feminism'. As she explains, postmodern feminist models of differentiation dispense with 'binary hierarchical models of differentiation' and 'substitute multiple hierarchies of differentiation' (*ibid.*) around race, ethnicity, gender and class. She sees feminist and post-colonial intellectuals as playing a crucial role in the process of change in the academy in their critique of epistemological foundationalism. Yeatman (1994: 30) asserts that feminist and post-colonial intellectuals refuse to be assimilated into the mainstream and 'place themselves in a contestatory relationship to the authority of modern foundationalist science'. They are strategically placed for establishing a range of 'sites of resistance' and 'sites of opposition' within the academy. As Yeatman (1994: 31) contends, 'Theirs is a narrative which is ordered by metaphors of struggle, contest, forced closure, strategic interventions and contingent opening of public spaces for epistemological politics.'

CONCLUSION

The challenge to the epistemological foundationalism of the academy through 'the politics of difference' is a challenge to the representational politics of the academy. As Yeatman (1994: 32) notes, 'By disrupting the we-ness of the community of knowers and locating all knowledge claims within the politics of contested domination, the epistemological force of the politics of difference is to refuse any vantage point for knowledge outside or beyond this field of contested domination.'

7

POSTFEMINISM AND POPULAR CULTURE

Representations and resistance

INTRODUCTION

Many popular cultural forms and practices have a claim to be representatively postmodern even though they may be forms and practices which never passed through any recognisable modernist phase. Popular culture has been defined as 'a site of struggle' where many of these issues and meanings are determined and debated. However, contemporary cultural critics have been mainly male (Hoggart, Williams, Barthes, Huyssen, West, Hall, Grossberg and CCCS [Centre for Contemporary Cultural Studies, Birmingham University]). Feminism in its intersection with dimensions of cultural studies and cultural theory, particularly postmodernism, has re-evaluated popular culture forms – music, style, dance, social rituals – from a feminist/postfeminist position. This chapter will focus on the re-evaluation of popular cultural forms as 'sites of struggle' for feminist and postfeminist writers.

MODERNISM, POSTMODERNISM AND POPULAR CULTURE

One of the now classic texts which charts the positioning of mass culture or popular culture within the nexus of the modernism/postmodernism debate is Andreas Huyssen's *After the Great Divide* (1986), in which he draws attention to 'the structuralist preference for the works of high modernism, especially the writing of James Joyce or Mallarmé' (McRobbie 1994: 13) and comments on the fact that 'the classical modernists' occupy a central position in the development of critical theory. He cites the examples of 'Flaubert ... in Barthes ... Mallarmé and Artaud in Derrida, Magritte ... in Foucault ... Joyce and Artaud in Kristeva ...' (Huyssen 1984: 39).

Huyssen (1986) looks at some of the ways in which postmodernist developments have challenged what he calls 'the modernist dogma' of the 1940s and 1950s. He considers how 'pop art' can be seen as a 'postmodernist cultural form' challenging many of the traditional distinctions made between high and mass culture. He contends that 'Pop in the broadest sense was the context in which a notion of the postmodern first took shape, and from the beginning until today, the most significant trends within postmodernism have challenged modernism's relentless hostility to mass culture' (Huyssen 1986: 188).

Huyssen charts what he considers to be a shift in the cultural reference points of postmodernism as it emerged in the US from the postmodernism characteristic of the 1960s and 1970s to that of the 1980s. He contends that the postmodernism of the 1960s 'tried to revitalize the heritage of the European avant-garde and to give it an American form' (*ibid.*). He goes on to note that by the 1970s the 'avantgardist postmodernism of the 1960s had...exhausted its potential, even though some of its manifestations continued well into the new decade' (*ibid.*). Huyssen's main point is that the cultural statements of the 1960s did not reject modernism, but rebelled against the socio-cultural articulation of a society driven by the politico-economic military complex. As Huyssen (1986: 191) comments, 'neither the variations on modernism of the 1950s nor the struggle of the 1960s for alternative democratic and socialist cultural traditions could have possibly been construed as *post-modern*'. He also makes the point that the emergence of postmodernism in France in the 1960s did not imply the same break with modernism as was the case in the US.

For Huyssen the significance of the avant-garde is of paramount importance in establishing a dialogue with the cultural establishment and in creating a 'climate' within which postmodernism could emerge. He maintains that

> it was [the]...specific radicalism of the avant-garde, directed against the institutionalization of high art as a discourse of hegemony and a machinery of meaning, that recommended itself as a source of energy and inspiration to the American postmodernists of the 1960s.
>
> (Huyssen 1986: 193)

POSTMODERNISM IN THE 1970S AND 1980S

Huyssen claims that postmodernism as a concept only gained currency in the 1970s, although he maintains that the critical element within postmodernism can only be fully understood if the 1950s are seen as the starting point of the 'mapping of the postmodern'. He maintains that the general atmosphere of political and economic disillusionment of the 1970s led to an 'emerging cultural scene which seemed much more amorphous and scattered than that of the 1960s' (Huyssen 1986: 196). Huyssen describes this period as characterised by a mixing of mass culture and modernism set against the challenges raised by a number of social movements demanding 'a voice'. In powerful summary of the cultural climate, Huyssen notes that

> It was especially the art, writing, film-making and criticism of women and minority artists with their recuperation of buried and mutilated traditions, their emphasis on exploring forms of gender- and race-based subjectivity in aesthetic productions and experiences, and their refusal to be limited to

136

standard canonizations, which added a whole new dimension to the critique of high modernism and to the emergence of alternative forms of culture ... Women's criticism has shed some new light on the modernist canon itself from a variety of different feminist perspectives. Without succumbing to the kind of feminine essentialism which is one of the more problematic sides of the feminist enterprise, it just seems obvious that were it not for the critical gaze of feminist criticism, the male determinations and obsessions of Italian futurism, Vorticism, Russian constructivism, Neue Sachlichkeit or surrealism would probably still be blocked from our view ...

(Huyssen 1986: 198)

While acknowledging the integral role of women's art, literature and criticism to the emergence of a postmodern culture in the 1970s and 1980s, Huyssen comments on the absence of feminist critics within the modernism/postmodernism debate. Morris (1988) has commented on the limitations of Huyssen's perspective, and in a somewhat dismissive commentary on Huyssen, she (1988: 12) contends that the real question is not whether feminists have or have not written about postmodernism but rather 'under what conditions women's work *can* "figure" current in such a debate'.

Huyssen's (1986: 214) engagement with feminist 'interventions' is limited to Julia Kristeva's work. He maintains that for Kristeva the question of postmodernism is the question of how anything can be written in the twentieth century and how we can talk about this writing. Kristeva argues that postmodernism is 'that literature which writes itself with the more or less conscious intention of expanding the signifiable and thus the human realm'.[1] Huyssen (1986: 214) notes that Kristeva's is a 'fascinating and novel approach to the question of modernist literature and one that understands itself as a political intervention. But it does not yield much for an exploration of the differences between modernity and postmodernity.'

He goes on to argue that postmodernism cannot be regarded simply as a sequel to modernism. He maintains that postmodernism is different from modernism in that it raises the question of cultural tradition 'in the most fundamental way as an aesthetic and a political issue' (Huyssen 1986: 216). However, he notes that 'postmodernism is far from making modernism obsolete'. On the contrary, Huyssen claims that postmodernism casts new light on modernism and 'appropriates many of its aesthetic strategies and techniques, inserting them and making them work in new constellations' (*ibid.*).

Huyssen comments that modernism's critique of mass culture and 'the avant-garde's attack on high art as a support system of cultural hegemony always took place on the pedestal of high art itself' (Huyssen 1986: 218). He goes on to note that neither high art nor high culture occupies the privileged space that it used to. He makes the point that the more diffuse and fragmented nature of culture has made it 'harder to contain [culture] in safe categories or stable institutions such as the academy, the museum or even the established gallery network' (Huyssen 1986: 219).

Despite the limitations of his analysis of feminist interventions into postmodernism, Huyssen makes a number of interesting points which anticipate some of the issues raised by post-colonial and feminist critics espousing 'the politics of difference' in the 1980s and 1990s. He maintains that the emergent postmodernism will 'have to be a postmodernism of resistance'. He goes on to comment that this resistance 'will always have to be specific and contingent upon the cultural field within which it operates' (Huyssen 1986: 220–221).

In his essay 'Mass Culture as Woman: Modernism's Other' (1986), Huyssen explores the notion, which he argues gained ground during the nineteenth century, that 'mass culture' is somehow associated with 'woman', while real authentic culture remains the prerogative of men. Huyssen cites Stuart Hall in his observation that the hidden subject of the mass culture debate is 'the masses'.[2] However, Huyssen goes further in developing the point made by Hall to argue that there was yet another hidden subject in the debate. As Huyssen (1986: 47) notes, in the age of socialism and the growth of the first major women's movement in Europe, the masses were not simply the working class, they were also women challenging the bastions of male-dominated culture:

> It is indeed striking to observe how the political, psychological and aesthetic discourse around the turn of the century consistently and obsessively genders mass culture and the masses as feminine, while high culture, whether traditional or modern clearly remains the privileged realm of male activities.
>
> (Huyssen 1986: 47)

Huyssen notes that the conceptual and ideological shift away from the term 'mass culture' to concepts such as 'the culture industry' as developed by the Frankfurt School reflects changes in critical thinking, and he notes that 'mass culture' theories have largely abandoned 'the explicit gendering of mass culture as feminine' (Huyssen 1986: 48).[3]

He explores the idea of women as representative of mass culture in relation to dominant trends within modernism, and claims that the gendering of an inferior mass culture as feminine is linked with the emergence of 'a male mystique in modernism (especially in painting)' (*ibid.*). Huyssen (1986: 49) argues that this was manifested in 'the powerful masculinist and misogynist current within the trajectory of modernism, a current which time and again openly states its contempt for women and for the masses and which had Nietzsche as its most eloquent and influential representative'. He contends that attempts to theorise modernist writing as feminine ignore this fact, and criticises developments within French critical theorising and writing to 'claim the space of modernist and avant-garde writing as predominantly feminine'. Such a 'deconstructivist' approach, embodied in the work of Julia Kristeva, is highly problematic, as Huyssen notes, because it threatens to 'render invisible a whole tradition of women's writing'.

138

Huyssen cites the work of Teresa de Lauretis (1985), who he claims has criticised 'this Derridean appropriation of the feminine by arguing that the position of woman from which Nietzsche and Derrida speak is vacant in the first place, and cannot be claimed by women' (Huyssen 1986: 49).[4]

Huyssen goes on to consider the relationship of postmodernism to mass culture and its gender inscriptions. He argues that one of the few widely agreed upon features of postmodernism is 'its attempt to negotiate forms of high art with certain forms and genres of mass culture and the culture of everyday life' (Huyssen 1986: 59). He maintains that it is probably no coincidence that such merger attempts occurred more or less simultaneously with the emergence of feminism and women as major forces in the arts, and with 'the concomitant reevaluation of formerly devalued forms and genres of cultural expression (e.g., the decorative arts, autobiographic texts, letters, etc.)'.

THE ESSENTIALISING OF A 'FEMININE OTHER': MODERNISM, POSTMODERNISM AND 'THE FEMININE'

A number of feminist theorists and writers have commented on Huyssen's work. Probyn (1987: 353) claims that Huyssen's argument is framed around a range of binary oppositions such as high/low and masculine/feminine. Within this framework 'Mass culture is conceived of solely as the denigrated as is the feminine reader in her affinity with the former.' Probyn describes this 'positioning' of the feminine within postmodernism as the 'essentializing of a "feminine other" ' (*ibid.*), and she notes that this 'particular articulation of "woman-as-other" to postmodernist concerns frequently places women as the last frontier at the end of history' (Probyn 1987: 350).

Morris links the debate more specifically with issues around popular culture. She makes the point that, given

> the persistence of the figure of woman as mass culture (the irony of modernism), it is no accident that a debate about a presumed silence and absence of women has already taken place in relation to the work on popular culture that is in turn a component of postmodernism.
>
> (Morris 1988: 14)

She also questions 'the myth of a postmodernism still waiting for its women' and makes the point that, as 'feminism has acted as one of the enabling conditions of discourse *about* postmodernism' (Morris 1988: 16), it is imperative that postmodernism is framed within feminist discourses and not the other way around.

One feminist whose work is at the intersection of feminism, postmodernism and popular culture is Tania Modleski (1986a, 1986b). Her earlier work (1983) showed a tendency to oversimplify women's positioning within mass culture. Probyn argues that her later work incorporates a 'threefold project to bring together the mass, the popular and the postmodern through the passage of the feminine' (1987: 354). This involves 'a recuperation of mass culture and its pleasures in the pejorative sense through a celebration of the pleasure inherent in the "feminization of American culture" [Modleski 1986b: 163]' (Probyn 1986a: 354).

Elsewhere Modleski draws on the work of another postmodernist writer, Jean Baudrillard, claiming that 'Baudrillard himself is justifying the masses on account of their putative femininity' (1986a: 49). However Probyn (1987: 354) maintains that, because Modleski appears to ignore Baudrillard's (1983: 22) earlier statement that 'the masses are no longer an authority to which one might refer as one formerly referred to class or the people', she (Modleski) ignores alternative 'sites' for an investigation of the feminine in the postmodern. Probyn notes that Baudrillard can be read positively from a feminist perspective 'as having raised one of the key disruptions that characterise postmodernist thought: the dissolution of patriarchal chains of reference' (Probyn 1987: 354). As Probyn observes, if class analysis is no longer viable and the masses no longer authoritative, at least as regards a more formal Marxist metanarrative, 'then gender, freed of the modernist series of oppositions becomes one of the more interesting lines of analysis within the postmodern' (ibid.).

POSTMODERNISM, POLITICS AND POPULAR CULTURE

The intersection of postmodernism with popular culture, which some have dismissed as trivialising serious political debate, is profoundly political – if by 'political' it is meant an engagement with the 'politics of everyday life'. The terrain of popular culture articulated in a range of cultural forms and expressed in a range of cultural styles is fundamentally about such a politics. As McRobbie comments,

> This landscape of the present, with its embracing of pastiche, its small defiant pleasure in being dressed up or 'casual', its exploration of fragmented subjectivity – all of this articulates more precisely with the wider conditions of present 'reality': with unemployment, with education, with the 'aestheticization of culture' and with the coming into being of those whose voices were historically drowned out by the (modernist) meta-narratives of mastery which were in turn both patriarchal and imperialist.
>
> (McRobbie 1994: 15)

It is in this sense that McRobbie (1986: 2) describes the meaning of living 'along the fault-lines of the postmodern condition' as 'engaging with questions, dilemmas and difference which were on the surface and no longer "hidden from history" (Rowbotham, 1973)'. The shift of emphasis within cultural criticism has been articulated as a move away from 'the search for meaning in the text towards the sociological play between images and between different cultural forms and institutions' (McRobbie 1986: 3–4).

POPULAR CULTURE AS A 'SITE OF RESISTANCE': SOCIAL MOVEMENTS, RESISTANCE AND SUBCULTURAL IDENTITIES

The distinctions between high/low culture and serious/popular culture within a modernist frame of reference have been increasingly broken down by the emergence of cultural studies. Sheridan (1995: 89) describes cultural studies as a wide-ranging area of enquiry which includes media studies and popular culture, and which incorporates 'everyday practices and cultural habits as well as texts and institutions'. As she goes on to note, 'cultural "representations" . . . have to be understood as including not only the images or textualisations of modern social experience but also the processes of their production, circulation and consumption' (ibid.).

In this respect the early emphasis within feminism on the study of media representations of gender has shifted to more broadly conceived questions about the status of these representations within the context of cultural difference and diversity. As Sheridan notes, these questions 'go beyond the modernist dichotomy between serious and popular culture and its gendered associations' (ibid.). They raise questions not just about media representations per se but whose interests they serve, how these representations are constructed and circulated, and (in this context) how social subjectivities are constructed.

The shift in emphasis in cultural studies, has been charted elsewhere (Tester 1994; During 1993a; Grossberg 1993). Grossberg (1993: 22) claims that cultural studies has always been a contested terrain, within which 'the boundaries of the tradition are themselves unstable and changing, sites of contestation and debate'. He goes on to note that the contestation within cultural studies was not only around competing theories of cultural politics, but also around competing theories about 'the nature of cultural and historical specificity' (Grossberg 1993: 23).

Cornell West, in his essay 'The New Cultural Politics of Difference' (1993), calls this new direction within 'the politics of culture' the 'culture of difference'. He defines it as a global movement made up of a range of different social movements. As During (1993a: 13) notes, these cultural theorists were interested in studying culture and theory in culturally and historically specific terms, within fragmented models of culture and society. The emphasis of cultural studies shifted from one which positioned a reading of culture 'oppositionally' in terms of the hegemonic state to one which affirmed concepts of 'otherness'. New expressions and modes of resistance emerged from feminist, ethnic and women's groups 'committed to maintaining and elaborating autonomous values, identities, and ethics' (During 1993a: 15).

The work of the Centre for Contemporary Cultural Studies (Birmingham, England) was representative of this new focus in cultural studies. The emphasis of the Centre's work was on the development of a positive engagement with mass-mediated popular culture, complicating earlier models of cultural politics based around class with the politics of race and ethnicity. Sheridan maintains that in theoretical terms

> they rejected not only the liberal humanist idea of culture as the expression of the 'human spirit' but also the economistic Marxist model of culture as the reflection of ruling class interests and 'mass culture' as the sedative pap designed to be consumed by the workers.
>
> (Sheridan 1995: 92)

The emphasis of the '*new*' cultural studies was on agency, that is on the agency of ordinary people in contesting and producing cultural meaning. Meaghan Morris powerfully expresses this concept of agency as follows:

> This means studying not how people *are* in a passively inherited culture ('tradition') but what they *do* with the cultural commodities that they encounter and use in everyday life ('practice') and thus what they *make* as 'culture'. Inflected by post-structuralist theories of reading as well as by empirical audience research . . . this shift enabled a crucial redefinition of popular culture not as a stratum (the 'low') one of aesthetic practice but as a social 'zone of contestation', in Hall's famous phrase – the ground in and over which different interests struggle for hegemony.
>
> (Morris 1992: 10, cited in Sheridan 1995: 92)

Sheridan contends that two senses of 'agency' emerge from this approach. In the first instance there is 'the sense of people producing meaning rather than passively consuming it, through their exchanges with cultural commodities' (Sheridan 1995: 92). Second, there is a concept of political agency implied in 'notions of struggle and contestation, *resistance* and *subversion*' (*ibid.*). As Tester contends, drawing on the work of Bennett (1980, 1981a, 1981b, 1986) and Hall (1980, 1992a), cultural studies 'became a means and a training centre for the new cultural politics of the resistances and constructions of hegemony' (Tester 1994: 21). He cites Hall's assertion that 'we are trying to find an institutional practice in cultural studies that might produce an organic intellectual' (Hall 1992a: 281).

The concept of the 'organic intellectual' was introduced by the Italian neo-Marxist Antonio Gramsci. 'Organic intellectuals' were seen by Gramsci as the vanguard of the attempt to construct new hegemonies, and would be at the forefront of struggles to speak for and on behalf of different interests. Tester states that Hall uses Gramsci's concept of the organic intellectual to validate what Hall sees as two important dimensions of cultural studies: first, that cultural studies should be 'at the very forefront of intellectual theoretical work' (*ibid.*); and second, that cultural studies has a political role outside the purely academic sphere in that it has, as Tester (1994: 21) claims, a 'responsibility to become a force to be reckoned with in the material world of day to day relationships, day to day oppression and the lived experiences of struggles of hegemony'.

The problem with Hall's analysis of the role of the organic intellectual is that he does not explain who the organic intellectuals are 'organic' to, for or with. Bennett attempts to resolve the problem by claiming that they have a responsibility towards 'the people'. The definition and constituency of 'the people' is as 'a group and an identity which is only constructed in and through the struggles and strategies of popular culture' (Tester 1994: 23).

Feminist theorisation of the notion of 'resistance' within identifiable subcultural contexts has clarified and grounded some of the more abstracted theoretical debates initiated by male cultural theorists. McRobbie claims that as

> class no longer underwrites the critical project of cultural analysis and ideology seems too monolithic a category, too focused on social passivity and conformity to be usefully alert to the more micrological level of dispute and contestation, we can scale down the field of study and abandon claims on unity or totality in favour of pursuing what Laclau has called the 'dignity of the specific'.
>
> (McRobbie 1994: 159)

She shows how this operates within a traditional model of subcultural analysis, maintaining that to subcultural theorists patterns of participation and consumption represent 'only the moment of diffusion, the point at which the oppositional force is incorporated or "recuperated" back into society through the processes of commodification' (*ibid.*). The process of commodification into a mass market depoliticises the potential within the subculture for contestation and as a result makes it more viable for popular consumption. McRobbie maintains elsewhere that this class-based and genderised subcultural model is less relevant for an analysis of patterns of 'resistance' within a model of 'cultural production'. She contends that subcultures are less significant to working-class girls than 'the intimate world of magazines' which they can use 'as a means of creating their own space in the school, the youth club or even in the home' (McRobbie 1991: xvii). Sheridan (1995: 93) maintains that girls and women are more likely to construct their own imaginary social space from these cultural commodities rather than 'a material subculture'.

Understanding femininity and its relationship to feminism is now more complex. McRobbie maintains there is a greater degree of fluidity about what femininity means and how exactly it is represented in social reality. She states that as a result there is 'a greater degree of uncertainty in society as a whole about what it is to be a woman, and this filters down to how young women exist within this new *habitus* of gender relations (Bourdieu, 1984)' (McRobbie 1994: 157).[5]

One area of popular culture which highlights the shift away from the traditional inscription of gender relations is romance. McRobbie (1994: 167) notes that while feminist academics (Radway 1984; Modleski 1982) have done a great deal to restore the status of romance by reclaiming it as a hidden pleasure of femininity, it is now no longer a situation of those with the cultural capital 'who know (feminist academics) and those are the "victims" of ideology (girls and women)'. Charlotte Brunsdon (1991/1992: 4) has argued that there has been quite a dramatic realignment between feminism and the lived experience of femininity (and its textual representation).

McRobbie uses the examples of TV series such as *Heathers* and *Twin Peaks* to suggest that young women may prefer 'the quirky postmodern subjectivities' offered in these narratives. As she contends, 'while the TV series deployed an intensely heightened sexuality in its cast of exceptionally beautiful female characters and good looking men, it was sex, danger, terror and "strangeness" rather than love or romance which held the fragmented structures of the episodes together' (McRobbie 1994: 167). She goes on to note that femininity is no longer the 'other' of feminism and that femininity is constructed as the product of less stable, emergent subject positions which tally with the more fluid subjectivities of postmodernism.

Feminism has been enormously instrumental in the reformation of the 'new' cultural studies. As Grossberg (1993: 26) notes, 'it is fair to say that there is no cultural studies which is not "post-feminist", not in the sense of having moved beyond it but rather in the sense of having opened itself to the radical critique and implications of feminist theory and politics'. The negation of metatheory and narratives together with the affirmation of otherness in cultural studies can also be linked to the emergence of the 'new cultural politics of difference' (West 1993), in part a product of the globalising of cultural production and distribution from the 1970s onwards. As During (1993a: 17) notes, globalisation meant that the role that subcultures and the working class occupied in earlier approaches within cultural studies began to be replaced and transformed by communities and movements outside the west or 'internal migrant (or "diasporic") communities'. Such developments involved new theoretical and political problems.

REPRESENTATIONS AND RESISTANCE: SUBCULTURAL IDENTITIES

Race and ethnicity: black formations and representations

Lawrence Grossberg (1993: 23), in identifying 'formations of cultural studies', identifies 'a specific [cultural] formation around the biographical figure of Stuart Hall and intellectual and political commitments of Marxism'. Hall's role in the development of cultural studies can be seen in terms of Gramsci's 'organic intellectual' or Foucault's 'specific intellectual'. Hall's article 'Cultural Studies: Two Paradigms' (1980) attempts, as Grossberg (1993: 43) notes, 'to reinterpret the debate between humanism and structuralism, from a third cultural studies perspective', by attempting to combine elements of resistance and domination. Hall's work has been increasingly influenced by postmodernism and by a postmodern cultural studies attempt to 'rearticulate the increasingly transnational context of (post)modernity' (Grossberg 1993: 58). Hall sees potential within a postmodern fragmentation, McRobbie notes, of producing a 'decentring of consciousness' which allows him as a black person to emerge 'divided but more fully foregrounded'. Hall claims, 'Now that, in the postmodern age, you all feel so dispersed I become centred. What I've thought of as dispersed and fragmented comes paradoxically, to be the representative modern condition! This is coming home with a vengeance' (Hall 1987, cited in McRobbie 1994: 27).

It is the position of Hall and other black intellectuals that West (1993) recognises as so strategic for the new cultural politics of difference. As West states,

> The new cultural politics of difference are neither simply oppositional in contesting the mainstream (or *male*stream) for inclusion, nor transgressive in the avant-gardist sense of shocking conventional bourgeois audiences. Rather, they are distinct articulations of talented (and usually privileged) contributors to culture who desire to align themselves with demoralized, demobilized, depoliticized, and disorganized people in order to empower and enable social action and, if possible, to enlist collective insurgency for the expansion of freedom, democracy and individuality. This perspective impels these cultural critics and artists to reveal, as an integral component of their production, the very operations of power within their immediate work contexts (i.e., academy, museum, gallery, mass media).
>
> (West 1993: 204)

One of the crucial challenges facing the new cultural politics of difference is the intellectual challenge of how to think about the issue of representational practices in terms of the wider framework of history, culture and society. West contends,

> The modern Black diaspora problematic of invisibility and namelessness can be understood as the condition of relative lack of Black power to present themselves to themselves and others as complex human beings, and thereby to contest the bombardment of negative degrading stereotypes put forward by White supremacist ideologies.
>
> (West 1993: 210)

West goes on to note that the initial response from the black diaspora was 'a mode of resistance' which took the form of a fight for representation and recognition which highlighted issues regarding 'Black "positive" images over and against White supremacist stereotypes' (*ibid.*). Hall has identified these responses within the context of what he has called the 'relations of representation'.

Despite the prominence of figures such as Hall and West in these debates, West himself notes that in First World countries the critique emerged not from the black male component of the left but more specifically from the black women's movement. As West (1993: 212) comments, 'The decisive push of postmodern Black intellectuals toward a new cultural politics of difference has been made by the powerful critiques and constructive explorations of Black diaspora women (e.g., Toni Morrison)'.

Black feminist cultural critics such as Michele Wallace (1993: 654) have recognised that, while the role of the black intellectual is an important one in challenging racist stereotypes, 'the inadequate representations of "race" currently sponsored by both blacks and non-blacks in both "high" and "low" culture" also needs to be contested'. Wallace argues for a radical black feminist perspective which she comments could build upon the work of Trinh T. Minh-ha, Gayatri Chakravorty Spivak, Hazel Carby and bell hooks. The strength of such a perspective would be its ability to investigate 'the interplay of "gender", "race" and class in Anglo-American and Afro-American culture as they may shape the "production of knowledge", the structure, content and "circulation" of the "text", as well as the "audience of consumption" ' (Wallace 1993: 655).

It is the potential within such a black feminist perspective based on the intersection of gender, race and class for the establishment of a range of 'sites of resistance' and 'sites of oppression' that makes such a perspective so powerful. In this regard West (1993: 212) notes that 'the Black diaspora womanist critique has had a greater impact than the critiques that highlight exclusively class, empire, age, sexual orientation or nature'.

Wallace advocates a radical black feminist perspective informed by postmodernist, poststructuralist and psychoanalytic theoretical debates. Such a 'theoretically engaged stance' for black feminist cultural theory Wallace (1993: 659) sees as challenging the 'more cautious and skeptical tendencies within African-American literary theory'. In this respect she is critical of the work of the Afro-American literary critic Henry Louis Gates, who she contends 'fails to portray Afro-American writing as a "minority" literature hotly engaged in an antagonistic dialogue with a majority "white" culture in order to transcend and/ or transform it' (Wallace 1993: 660). She goes on to make the point that the failure is particularly disappointing in relation to contemporary Afro-American literature written by women. Wallace contends that 'In feminist terms, it is just as important to have a way of talking about *The Color Purple*'s impact on how racism or sexism is perceived in contemporary culture, as it is to talk about [Alice Walker's] *The Color Purple* as a symbolic (literary) resolution of racism's concrete irresolvability' (*ibid.*). She maintains that Alice Walker's novel provides a perfect example of what was initially a text which proposed 'a complex rereading' of Afro-American history and literature but which, in the context of being a bestselling novel and blockbuster movie became something entirely different. While black women's writing over the last few years has clearly been very successful, it does not present an opposition around either dominant literary canons or dominant representations. Wallace points out that Toni Morrison's novel *Beloved* was met with wide critical acclaim in 1987. However, she notes there were no commensurate changes in the status or condition of black women in general. Wallace (1993: 662) comments, 'It is not enough merely to address the dilemma posed by the black female condition in the US or the world as an object of misery and pathos. Black feminism must insist upon a critical oppositional representation of the black female subject.'

The incorporation of deconstruction into any model of oppositional black politics is recognised by Afro-American literary and cultural critics alike. Gates claims:

> And, if only for the record, let me state clearly here that only a black person alienated from black language-use could fail to understand that we have been deconstructing white people's languages and discourse since that dreadful day in 1619 when we were marched off the boat in Virginia. Derrida did not invent deconstruction, *we* did! That is what the blues and signifying are all about. Ours must be a signifying, vernacular criticism, related to other critical theories, yet indelibly black, a critical theory of our own.
>
> (Gates 1987: 38)

West claims that the main aim of theorists working within the new cultural politics of difference is not simply about access to representation in order to produce more positive images, nor is the primary goal that of contesting stereotypes regardless of the fact that contestation is still significant around the issue of stereotyping. West states:

> Following the model of the Black diaspora traditions of music, athletics and rhetoric, Black cultural workers must constitute and sustain discursive and institutional networks that deconstruct earlier modern Black strategies for identity formation, demystify power relations that incorporate class, patriarchal, and homophobic biases, and construct more multivalent and multidimensional responses that articulate the complexity and diversity of Black practices in the modern and postmodern world.
>
> (West 1993: 212)

Madonna, pleasure and 'cultural populism'

The location of popular culture at the intersection of debates around modernism and postmodernism can be seen to coalesce around a number of themes, including representational politics, (subcultural) identities and cultural theory. Centrally placed in many of these debates has been the popular cultural phenomenon of Madonna, which can act as a valuable case study framing a particular moment in cultural studies and more particularly feminist/postfeminist inflections of it.

The work of the cultural theorist and critic John Fiske (1987a, 1987b, 1889a, 1989b) has been influential both in his contribution to the significance of popular culture generally and more specifically in his analysis of the representational politics around Madonna. Fiske's definition of popular culture is quite different to that of other cultural theorists such as Stuart Hall or Tony Bennett. Fiske, as Tester (1994: 25) notes, is more concerned to emphasise those aspects of popular culture which make certain products and activities pleasurable. Despite the

147

importance of this definition of popular culture in Fiske's work, he does not ignore the political dimensions of cultural studies. Fiske (1989a: 43) notes that 'popular culture is always formed in reaction to, and never as part of, the forces of domination'. Elsewhere Fiske, clearly influenced by postmodernist and poststructuralist interventions into popular culture, claims that 'The differences that I call popular are produced by and for the various formations of the people: they oppose and disrupt the organized disciplined individualities produced by the mechanisms of surveillance, examination and information' (Fiske 1992: 161).

Fiske's (1987b: 239) emphasis on popular culture as providing 'pleasure in the processes of making meanings' draws on the work of Roland Barthes, who maintained in his later work that 'markedly polysemous texts generate particular intense and liberating pleasures' (During 1993a: 18). Fiske, in writing about Madonna as a popular cultural form, maintains that she offered her fans 'her own form of feminist ideology-critique' (1987a: 275). He claims that Madonna 'calls into question binary oppositions as a way of conceptualizing women', and maintains that Madonna offers young girls the opportunity to find independent meanings of their own feminine sexuality.

However, there are a number of problems with Fiske's analysis. Kaplan claims that one of the problems involves a shift

> from the level of discourse analysis (how girls are constituted by male adolescent culture or what female images are in circulation) to the level of lived psychological or social 'development' as if such development were not always already discursively constituted.
>
> (Kaplan 1993: 154)

A second problem which emerges is the issue of what During (1993a: 18) calls 'cultural populism' and to what extent this passes over the question of co-option.[6] He claims that Madonna's later work in particular has been very much aligned with the 'needs of capital'. During (1993a: 18) points out that Madonna the 'material girl' subtly (in some cases, not so subtly) draws from the 'iconography of sexuality (including "perverse" sex like S and M)' as part of her repertoire, extending to new and larger markets, the representational industry around Madonna. Thus Madonna, at the same time as claiming subversion and transgression, is also promotional of market forces. However, During does recognise that 'a cultural populism' which can celebrate Madonna can also be a positive one. He comments:

> This is not to say that Madonna is not an important agent in breaking down the barriers which organised the relation between the popular and the sexual as well as the popular and femininity, nor is it to say that entering cultural markets means co-option in any rigid or formal way... cultural populism requires a very nuanced account of these relations between cultural markets and cultural products, and between culture and politics, in order convincingly to celebrate (some) popular culture as progressive.
>
> (During 1993: 18)

The representation of Madonna as a postfeminist cultural phenomenon

In recent years much has been written about what is seen by some writers as a 'site of struggle' within popular culture – the representation of Madonna as a postmodernist postfeminist cultural phenomenon. The following analysis considers some of the debates around Madonna positioned at the interface of postfeminism and popular culture. A collection of essays which focuses on some of the key issues raised by these debates is contained in *The Madonna Connection*, edited by Cathy Schwichtenberg (1993).

Madonna and her work are used as a paradigm case in the book, which documents 'cultural struggle', based around 'the political effectivity of Madonna's multifaceted representations' (Schwichtenberg 1993: 3). Schwichtenberg argues that Madonna's performances integrate symbolic aspects that reference different subcultural groups including African Americans, Hispanics, gay men, lesbians, feminists and others who represent minority or subordinate positions. Issues of subjectivity and identity figure largely here and, as Schwichtenberg maintains, 'Madonna's subculturally evocative texts may very well present the conditions for the coalescence and mobilization of identities yet to be pacified by commodity culture' (*ibid.*). As Schwichtenberg notes, Madonna has inscribed herself on the public consciousness in multiple and contradictory ways. She argues that, in drawing on Madonna as situated at the interface of postfeminism and popular culture, we are following Edward Said's directive 'to that intersection of politics and popular culture where as cultural critics and theorists we make connections between culture as it is lived and culture as it is theorized' (Schwichtenberg 1993: 4). Schwichtenberg's book, using Madonna as a 'multifaceted site of contestation', sets out to achieve Said's directive.

Madonna as 'a site of subversion'

The relationship between Madonna's representational politics and feminist theory is a complicated one. A number of theorists have attempted to investigate the problem of representational politics by engaging with different dimensions of the 'Madonna paradigm as an equivocal challenge to feminism as it is both lived and theorized within patriarchal culture' (Schwichtenberg 1993: 8).

E. Ann Kaplan's (1993) essay 'Madonna Politics: Perversion, Repression or Subversion? Or Masks and/as Master-y' provides a wide-ranging analysis of the various cultural discourses within which Madonna has been constructed. She draws on Mikhail Bakhtin's theory of the mask, which locates differing conceptions of the mask in history.[7] Kaplan wishes to use the concept of the mask in a Foucauldian sense in representing the fact that there is no stable identity (Foucault 1981a).[8] She investigates Bakhtinian theories of the mask in relation to strategies of subversion, and uses the concept of the mask to investigate resistance to the 'patriarchal feminine'. Kaplan has not rejected concepts such as patriarchy and does not claim a postfeminist position. In this context she cautions against an over-optimistic interpretation of Madonna's work, particularly the claim that her work 'celebrates a girl culture' which is resistive to patriarchy. At the same time, Kaplan presents a 'compelling argument for the subversive potential of Madonna's masks that eschew any inherent notion of identity' (Schwichtenberg 1993: 8).

Kaplan maintains that there are three dominant stances to what she describes as the 'Madonna phenomenon': the first she identifies as 'perversion', which she defines as the somewhat censorial attitude to Madonna by a number of countries including the US; the second is identified as 'repression'; and the third as subversion. Many of Madonna's videos and performances have been censored, sometimes even by the conglomerates which paid for the advertisement. Kaplan cites the case of the video/advertisement *Like a Prayer*, for which Madonna had been paid US$5 million which was subsequently censored by Pepsi-Cola. In addition, the video *Justify My Love* was censored by MTV and the *Blond Ambition Tour* was censored in some US cities. As Kaplan (1993: 152) notes, the responses present Madonna 'as a cheap exhibitionist at best, a pervert at worst' and the media generally seem 'unaware of the level of fantasy within which Madonna explicitly works'.

The second response to Madonna is 'repression'. In this category Kaplan frames the 'Madonna phenomenon' within a wider discussion of psychoanalytic theory. Kaplan draws on the work of Freud, Lacan and Laura Mulvey (1975, 1991), to explain the implications of this concept. She cites Mulvey's (1991) essay 'Xala and Fetishism' to show how an abstracted quality '(eroticism, status, power) is added to a material thing (the object to be consumed)' and combines this with an analysis of Freud's concept of fetishism. Kaplan (1993: 152) maintains that this partly explains 'the attraction of icons like Madonna who cover over or stand in for castration anxiety'.

Kaplan outlines the concept of 'fetishism' as developed in Mulvey's (1975) work:

> Freud's theory of the fetish was the most semiotic of the perversions because the fetishist focuses on the sign (the shoe, the fur collar) that replaces the actual object... Within the Lacanian framework, men and women alike, if for different reasons, desire the phallus. Stars like Madonna fill this space of desire – this gap that constitutes the subject in desire for an object...
>
> (Kaplan 1993: 152)

The third dimension, and one which has resonance in the context of the debate around Madonna as a potential 'site of resistance', is 'subversion'. One of the problems inherent in the concept of subversion is that it keeps 'binarisms intact'. Kaplan (1993: 156) points out that the 'approach leaves untouched the notion of individual subjects. It entails deciding... if Madonna subverts the patriarchal feminine by unmasking it or whether she ultimately reinscribes the patriarchal feminine by allowing her body to be recuperated for voyeurism.'

A second approach to understanding Madonna's subversive potential can be found in Judith Butler's (1990a) theory of 'parodic performance'. As Kaplan notes,

> Butler's notion of challenging binary constructs through parodic play with gender stereotypes in gay, trans-sexual and carnivalesque reversals is attractive. In many ways Madonna would seem to precisely embody what Butler believes is the most useful future strategy to avoid oppressive binary 'engendering'.
>
> (Kaplan 1993: 156)

Butler works through a number of possibilities for subverting and displacing 'naturalized and reified notions of gender that support masculine hegemony and heterosexist power, to make gender trouble' (Butler 1990a: 33–34). In order to do this Butler suggests a process of 'mobilization, subversive confusion and proliferation of precisely those constitutive categories that seek to keep gender in its place' (*ibid.*). One of the limitations of Butler's approach is that, as with many feminist theorists interested to 'unpack' issues of identity and subjectivity, she does not engage with cultural texts. However Kaplan contends that many of Madonna's videos can be seen within the context of Butler's mobilisation of strategies of subversion of 'constitutive categories of gender' (*ibid.*).

Kaplan provides a range of examples from Madonna's work which she claims force the viewer to question and challenge gender constructions. She notes that

> The cross-dressing in videos like *Express Yourself*, the shocking violation of conventional sexual representations on prime-time television in *Justify My Love*... the constant parody through exaggeration of pornographic symbols in *Open Your Heart* and then throughout the *Blond Ambition* performance – these are just some of the ways in which Madonna has increasingly subverted dominant gender categories.
>
> (Kaplan 1993: 157)

Butler's model of subversion is framed within a 'politics of the signifier', which, as Kaplan (1993: 159) points out, sees agency as meaningful only within specific 'gender sign systems'; Butler's subject is only 'a surface constituted through signs'. Kaplan points out that Butler's theories tend 'to mesh ... with the concept of the mask in ancient folklore'.

Drawing on the two theories of the mask, Kaplan shows how they are useful in distinguishing 'two "subversion" themes' in relation to Madonna's texts: first, 'Madonna as resisting "a patriarchal feminine" in offering alternative female identification (the patriarchal mask can be abandoned and the "real" woman can step forth)' (Kaplan 1993: 150); and second, Madonna as problematising 'the bourgeois illusion of "real" individual gendered selves'.

Kaplan uses the concept of the mask to highlight three main issues relating to theories of subjectivity in relation to Madonna's work. First, argues Kaplan, there is the theory that the Madonna image

> adopts one mask after another to expose the fact that there is no 'essential' self and therefore no essential feminine but only cultural constructions – that is, the mask as *mastery*, as play with the given gender sign system, as, in Freudian terms, deployment and exposure of the oppressive processes of the fetish that rests on fear of castration. Secondly there is the theory that the Madonna image self consciously uses the mask to reproduce patriarchal modes and fantasies – the mask as *deception*. Finally there is the notion that the Madonna image offers a positive role model for young women in refusing the passive patriarchal feminine, unmasking it and replacing it with strong, autonomous female images.
>
> (Kaplan 1993: 160)

However, Kaplan goes on to note that what none of these positions offer is an analysis of Madonna as commodity and how this interacts with an oppositional politics. Kaplan argues that there is a need to understand how issues of 'commodification' intersect with issues of subjectivity and gender.

She draws on Butler (1990a) to show 'that positing a strong or autonomous female subject leaves intact gender bi-polarities and institutional structures that given gender positions sustain' (Kaplan 1993: 159). As Kaplan notes, these binarisms in turn marginalise gay and lesbian sexual practices. Kaplan comments that, despite Madonna's consistent support for gay and lesbian sex, it is argued her videos are predominantly heterosexist and even the video *Justify My Love* has been seen as 'masking the lesbian scene or (making) it a spectacle for the male gaze – in the text' (Kaplan 1993: 161).

Kaplan concludes in maintaining that Madonna may well construct herself as merely making use of 'consumption economies' that she neither created nor can be held responsible for. However, Madonna has never addressed the process of commodification or the material level of stardom in anything other than a casual way.

Madonna and the politics of postmodernism: 'material girl' and the politics of consumer culture

Madonna's high measure of success as 'a postmodern phenomenon' highlights the interplay between postmodernism and consumerism, and her transformative identity can be understood at the level of materiality and simulation. At a material level Madonna's ability to market herself and to accommodate the 'late capitalist marketplace' (Schwichtenberg 1993: 9) addresses the needs of 'the media, beauty and music industries' demand for flexibility in its requirements for an 'inauthentic and reinventionist' response to marketing strategies. Tetzlaff (1993) outlines the 'metatextual' narrative of the 'material girl' which explores how power is a 'material issue' and is linked to Madonna's success. Tetzlaff's is an 'ideological critique' of Madonna's material reality: her popularity confirms his model of the way in which popular culture has been incorporated into late capitalist values and thus cannot act as a site of resistance to patriarchal and capitalist domination.

The issue of simulation within the conceptualisation of Madonna as 'a postmodern phenomenon' is explored by Pribram (1993) in her analysis of Madonna's 'performance documentary' *Truth or Dare*. Pribram sets out to 'deconstruct the simple binary framework of truth and illusion' which has characterised commentary on the film in the popular press. In this context Pribram explores feminist critics' challenge to the 'subject/object' dichotomy within which Madonna has been framed and from which position she has been seen as both 'inauthentic' and 'as object' (Schwichtenberg 1993: 9).

Pribram draws on the postmodernist concepts of 'simulation' and 'seduction' as developed in the work of Jean Baudrillard (1983, 1988, 1990). She challenges the materiality of the 'realist' critiques of Madonna and claims that Madonna's use of 'simulated seductive techniques' reveals a 'large measure of control over her own images' (*ibid.*). While cautious in her conclusions, Pribram suggests that postmodernism and feminism may not be antithetical and further that this model may be seen as a 'point of departure' for the development of a postmodern feminism.

This is not a view shared by Roseann Mandzuik, in her essay 'Feminist Politics and Postmodern Seductions: Madonna and the Struggle for Political Articulation' (1993). Mandzuik critically assesses the viability of postmodern theory for feminist theory and politics. She holds a feminist realist position and examines a number of Madonna texts, including the '*Nightline* interview, and the videos *Rock the Vote* and *Vogue* to illustrate the political dangers inherent in mistaking individual play for social intervention' (Schwichtenberg 1993: 8). Mandzuik's critique of what postmodernism has to offer feminism is based on what she sees as inauthentic and 'ephemeral promises of liberation'. She claims that postmodernism denies women any real position from which to speak. Mandzuik, while critical of feminist 'identity politics', advocates a more reflective reworking of such politics and she warns against a postmodern feminist politics as exemplified by Madonna. From Mandzuik's feminist realist position, to adopt a postmodernist feminist position is simply to deny women 'as real subjects' a voice and a position from which to speak, and involves relinquishing real politics. As Mandzuik comments, this is tantamount to 'sleeping with the enemy'.

Mandzuik argues that Madonna's texts constantly equate pleasure with power and sexuality with control. She notes that Madonna's assertion that personal freedom and sexuality are inextricably linked is part of a larger debate over political articulation in contemporary feminist theory. Mandzuik (1993: 168) claims that 'Madonna is a fitting representation of feminism's theoretical struggle to come to terms with the intersection of cultural images and political practices.'

She notes that, for feminism, 'the postmodern holds out a theoretical enticement to leave the public sphere of reason for the private, localized regions of pleasure' (Mandzuik 1993: 169). Mandzuik asks whether feminism's enticement by the postmodern has resulted in feminism 'relinquishing something too precious by celebrating the political potential of images like those projected by Madonna' (*ibid.*). She expresses a deep concern with feminism's 'enticement' by postmodernism. She argues that to move from an analysis of Madonna texts to the interrogation of the interchange between feminism and postmodernism entails a large step from praxis back to theory.

Mandzuik investigates three of 'Madonna's texts' and central to all texts is Madonna's insistence on the individual ownership of her sexuality, and the 'conflation of sexual expression and political freedom within her discourse' (Mandzuik 1993: 170). She considers first Madonna's appearance on *Nightline*, which she argues stands as Madonna's most fiercely 'modernist' appearance on television.

Madonna's defence against some of the charges made by feminists about her work is to assert 'authorial intentionality' and 'unified identity'. As Mandzuik (1993: 172) argues, Madonna's appearance on *Nightline* was framed in terms of a 'feminist realist epistemology' which argues for 'a direct relationship between public images and public responsibility as the grounds for feminist politics'. In assessing Madonna's performance on *Nightline* Mandzuik (1993: 173) comments that 'Feminist politics conceived as cultural intervention in the name of woman seems hopelessly bound up with the discourse of essentialism and epistemology, domination and subjugation.'

Mandzuik's summary of Madonna's *Rock the Vote* video 'underscores questions of feminist realist epistemology and its alternatives' (Mandzuik 1993: 175)[9] and leads Mandzuik to comment that 'It is a particularly good example of a text where representational politics engages and exposes the liberal pluralist belief in the transparency of images and the serious facade of interventionist politics' (*ibid.*). Mandzuik notes that Madonna, as a signifier of both femaleness and Americanness, operates at a number of discursive levels and challenges the politics of feminist realist epistemology. The 'theoretical boundaries that view representation as an unproblematic process' (*ibid.*) are as a result challenged. The deficits of the realist model thus make a theoretical move in the direction of postmodernism more attractive.

The multiplicity characteristic of the alternative definition of politics in postmodernism is a feature of Madonna's 1990 video *Vogue*. As Mandzuik (1993: 178–179) notes, 'the content of the lyrics and the discourse of posing that constitute this video offer the perfect textualization of the postmodern dream of a politics in which subjectivities constantly traverse different forms'. The shooting of the video in black and white adds to the sense of timelessness of the setting. Further, Mandzuik notes that the men in *Vogue*, as in *Rock the Vote*, are 'coded as gay' and 'the act of voguing is traceable to the gay subculture in which various personas and identities are enacted in dance and drag as a form of subversion of and opposition to the dominant heterosexual culture' (Mandzuik 1993: 179). Mandzuik notes the postmodern vision of politics is as problematic as the politics of feminist realist epistemology, for it 'refuses responsibility for itself while reinforcing the very power structures and boundaries it promises to violate' (Mandzuik 1993: 180). The problem for feminism of postmodernism is that, 'when feminism accepts the dehistoricizing tendency of the postmodern, it loses its specificity as a discourse different from and in opposition to the historicized power of patriarchal narratives' (Mandzuik 1993: 181).

Mandzuik (1993: 181) maintains that postmodern feminism involves the abandonment of 'feminism's ability to retain its status as a theoretical enterprise motivated by critique'. Christine di Stefano (1990: 73) argues that the abandonment of categories within postmodern feminism produces what she calls 'the postfeminist tendency', that is, 'a refusal to privilege any particular form of difference or identity against the hegemonic mainstream'. As Mandzuik comments, regardless of how much fun Madonna's notion of 'voguing' may be, 'posturing' cannot be allowed to replace politics. She contends that 'If feminism relinquishes the authority of identity in favour of an elided distinction between politics and pleasures, we have gained nothing but an invitation to participate in the endless dance of non commitment' (Mandzuik 1993: 182). Thus, for Mandzuik the postmodern feminist politics as represented by Madonna's texts involves the replacing of intervention or resistance with the 'discourse of style'.

Popular culture and the 'postmodern body'

The intersection of postmodernism, popular culture and political economy can be seen to coalesce around the issue of consumer culture, where, as Schwichtenberg (1993: 9) notes, 'star packaging and targeted audiences are critical for profitability'. Susan Bordo's essay 'Material Girl: The Effacements of Postmodern Culture' (1993b) considers those aspects of the materiality of 'the postmodern body' exemplified by Madonna. They include discourses that promote 'plastic surgery, body building, liposuction, exercise regimens and other bodily enhancements that contribute to "plasticity" as a postmodern paradigm' (Schwichenberg 1993: 10). Schwichtenberg shows how, within a broad debate around the promotion of beauty and diet regimes, Bordo situates 'the physical reconstruction of Madonna, who has come to represent the perfect postmodern body in both theoretical and popular discourse' (ibid.). Bordo puts forward a feminist critique of Madonna's bodily transformations as representative of postmodernism's tendency 'to efface women's physical differences, in accordance with a plastic standard of beauty' (ibid.). Bordo's essay, as Schwichtenberg observes, warns against the political dangers of a postmodern feminism, particularly in its conjunction with contemporary capitalism, and draws on 'Madonna's physical iconography' to emphasize how 'commercial imperatives inform a "plastic aesthetics of the body" ' (ibid.).

Bordo shows how postmodernism's intersection with capitalism has, through the currents of consumerism, led to 'a new "postmodern" imagination of human freedom from bodily determination ... In place of ... materiality we now have what I call "cultural plastic" ' (Bordo 1993b: 265). Bordo outlines the emphasis on fitness, beauty, diet, and what she claims medical science has designated as 'polysurgical addicts' who undergo surgical operations in pursuit of the perfect body. She sees the pursuit of the 'sculpted body' as an expression of the process of 'normalisation'. Bordo draws on the term 'disciplinary' as used in a Foucauldian sense, which points to practices which do not merely transform but 'normalise' the subject. Illustrating her point, Bordo draws on two examples of normalising feminine practice which highlight issues of race as well as gender. She cites Bo Derek's hair in corn rows (in the film *10*) and Oprah Winfrey's admission on her show that she has always wanted 'hair that swings from side to side', as examples of the power of racial, as well as gender, normalisation. As Bordo states (1993b: 273), 'normalisation not only to "femininity" but to the Caucasian standards of beauty that still dominate on television, in movies, in popular magazines'.

She correctly identifies the dark side of the transformative process, including damaging, sometimes fatal operations, exercise addictions and eating disorders. Further, Bordo notes that these normalising images are 'suffused with the dominance of gender, racial, class, and other cultural iconography' (*ibid.*). In addition she maintains that

> they reproduce on the level of discourse and interpretation the same conditions which postmodern bodies enact on the level of cultural practice: a construction of life as plastic possibility and weightless choice, undetermined by history, social location or even individual biography.
>
> (Bordo 1993b: 270)

Bordo discusses the impact of postmodernism and capitalism in terms of consumerism, power and popular culture. She draws on Foucault's use of the term 'power' and the 'postmodern misappropriation of Foucault' as shown in John Fiske (1987b). Foucault does not conceive of power as the possession of individuals or groups, but is concerned with the operation of power 'though multiple "processes of different origin and scattered location", regulating and normalising the most intimate and minute elements of the construction of time, space, desire embodiment' (Bordo 1993b: 278). The crucial issue here is 'resistance'. Foucault describes the instability of modern power relations and the fact that resistance is 'unpredictable and hegemony precarious' (Bordo 1993b: 278). However, Fiske (1987b) transforms the Foucauldian concept of discourse into 'a notion of resistance as jouissance', 'a creative and pleasurable eruption of cultural "difference" through the "seams" of the text' (Bordo 1993b: 278). Bordo argues that, whereas Fiske talks about 'the power of being different' as an act of creative interpretation, she interprets it as an ongoing political struggle. She notes that for Foucault the 'metaphorical terrain of resistance is explicitly that of "the battle"; the "points of confrontation" may be "innumerable" and "unstable" but they involve a serious often deadly struggle of embodied (that is historically situated and shaped) forces' (Bordo 1993b: 280).

Bordo considers the representation of the black woman's body and draws on an example of the magazine *Essence*, which she maintains has consciously and systematically tried to promote positive images of 'black strength, beauty and self acceptance'. She notes that despite this, advertisers 'continually elicit and perpetuate consumers' feelings of inadequacy and insecurity over their racial bodies' (Bordo 1993b: 281).

Pursuing the concept of resistance in relation to Madonna, Bordo references the work of Susan Rubin Suleiman (1986) who advises moving beyond the valorisation of historically and culturally constructed and suppressed values towards 'endless complication'. Suleiman draws on Derrida's metaphor of 'incalculable choreographies' to 'capture the dancing, elusive continually changing subject that she envisions, a subjectivity without gender, without history, without location' (*ibid.*). Bordo relates this to the body and Madonna's representations as she states:

> the truly resistant female body is not the body that wages war against feminine sexualisation and objectification, but the body as Cathy Schwichtenberg has put it that 'uses simulation strategically in ways that challenge the stable notion of gender as the edifice of sexual difference . . . an erotic politics in which the female body can be refashioned in the flux of identities that speak in plural styles'.
>
> (Bordo 1993b: 282)

Bordo maintains that the new postmodern heroine of this exotic politics is Madonna.

Bordo charts the significance and relevance of Madonna's representations for the politics of feminist resistance. She maintains that until recently 'Madonna's resistance has been seen along "Body as Battleground" lines deriving from her refusal to allow herself to be constructed as an object of patriarchal desire' (Bordo 1993b: 282). As she notes, Madonna presented a model of female heterosexuality that was independent of patriarchal control, 'a sexuality that defined rather than rejected the male gaze, teasing it with her own gaze deliberately trashy and vulgar, challenging anyone to call her a whore . . .' (Bordo 1993b: 282). Bordo goes on to note that this is no longer the Madonna body type and that during 1990–1991 Madonna went on a strenuous reducing and exercise programme, running several miles a day. As Bordo (1993b: 284) notes, Madonna 'has developed in obedience to dominant contemporary norms, a tight, slender, muscular body'. As Bordo indicates,

> in terms of Madonna's own former lexicon of meanings within which feminine voluptuousness and the choice to be round in a culture of the lean was clearly connected to spontaneity, self definition and defiance of the cultural gaze – the terms set by the gaze have now triumphed.
>
> (Bordo 1993b: 284)

Bordo argues that this type of critique of Madonna's obsessive preoccupation with 'body praxis' does not appear to challenge the representation of Madonna as postmodern heroine. For both Madonna and those that emulate her, Madonna is 'in control of her image not trapped by it'. Madonna herself maintains that 'Everything I do is meant to have several meanings, to be ambiguous'. As Bordo notes, she resists an overinterpretation of her work in terms of 'artistic intent'. In an interview with *Cosmopolitan* magazine, Madonna said that 'she favours irony and ambiguity to "entertain myself" and (as she told *Vanity Fair*) out of "rebelliousness and a desire to fuck with people" ' (Bordo 1993b: 286).[10]

Bordo goes on to highlight the significance of the 'new' Madonna body as displayed in her work and its implications. Using the video *Open Your Heart*, Bordo states that, as is the case with 'all rock videos, the female body is offered to the viewer purely as a spectacle, an object of sight, a visual commodity to be consumed' (Bordo 1993b: 287). As Bordo (1993b: 287) states, 'Many men and women may experience the primary reality of the video as the elicitation of desire for that perfect body; women however may also be gripped by the desire...of becoming that perfect body.' As Bordo (1993b: 288) concludes, despite the 'internal' ambiguities it contains, the 'video's postmodern conceits...facilitate rather than deconstruct the presentation of Madonna's body as an object on display'.

Probyn, in her essay 'Bodies and Anti-Bodies: Feminism and the Postmodern' (1987), investigates the concept of the 'postmodern body' and, like Bordo, is critical of the political implications for the place of 'the feminine body in mass and everyday culture'. In this context she claims that 'the question is much too difficult to impose any postmodernist closure on these sites' (Probyn 1987: 356). In developing the relationship between postmodernism, popular culture and the body, Probyn (1987: 356) argues that the way 'the popular' is articulated and 'lived in the shadow of postmodernist theorizing' needs to be investigated as well as the implications of this for 'the death of the social'. As Probyn notes, the multiple subjectivities that have 'emerged' from postmodernist and poststructuralist critiques means that 'our bodies are more actively articulated and that a surface is only one way of reading' (*ibid.*). While cautious of the implications of postmodernism for feminism, Probyn recognises the *potential* of postmodernism for feminism. Drawing on the work of Mikhail Bakhtin (1968), she argues that feminism in the postmodern must search for interconnections between bodies and memories which can point to 'all that prolongs the body and links it to other bodies or to the world outside' (Bakhtin 1968: 317). She warns against feminism's tendency towards essentialising around subject positioning, and recognises that 'bodies and memory in the postmodern can be seen defining epistemological lines which articulate subjectivities and practices' (Probyn 1987: 357).

An example of the interpenetration of bodies, memories and subjectivities with the politics of everyday life can be seen in the work of Angela McRobbie (1982a, 1982b, 1986). Probyn (1987: 357), drawing on McRobbie's (1986) work, shows how she entwines memory, fantasy, dance, biographical references and extracts from others' lives through the meanings of 'adolescent femininity'.

Probyn shows how 'McRobbie articulates the memories of school dances, [the films] *Fame* and *Flashdance*, Camden Palace [London] and families, not to valorize them, but to bring out their specificity' (*ibid.*).

The extremes of the postmodern body have been outlined by Donna Haraway in 'A Manifesto for Cyborgs' (1985). Probyn (1987: 355) contends that 'In the truly postmodern sphere of "cyborgs" there is no longer a self ("one is too few, but two is too many" [1985: 96]) and the gendered bounded body is past...' As Probyn notes in what Haraway calls the 'post-information age', 'cyborg politics' boils down to 'the struggle for language and the struggle against perfect communication (1985: 95)' (*ibid.*). Probyn warns that the implications of Haraway's politics framed within her 'techno-emancipation' are unstable and obscure. She argues for a theory of articulation to problematise and politicise 'unyielding' hegemonic and patriarchal sites, central among which is sexuality.

Postfeminism and representational politics

Schwichtenberg (1993) explores the issue of gay and lesbian representational politics around Madonna within the context of the broader theoretical debate around a postmodern feminism.[11] As Schwichtenberg (1993: 7) contends, 'Madonna's postmodern interventions prey open a space in the mainstream to provide sexual minorities with visibility and confirmation'. She notes that much of Madonna's later work – *Express Yourself, Vogue, Justify My Love*, the *Blond Ambition Tour* and *Truth or Dare*, for example – 'deals explicitly with representations of sexuality that have particular resonance for gay and lesbian audiences but are typically misread or ignored by the mainstream' (Schwichtenberg 1993: 6). Schwichtenberg goes on to argue that 'The Madonna paradigm provides the impetus to shift the margins to the center and thus it highlights the complexities of gay and lesbian politics and pleasures as they are lived, constructed and contested' (*ibid.*).

In her essay 'Madonna's Postmodern Feminism: Bringing the Margins to the Centre', Schwichtenberg argues from a postmodern feminist perspective and cites Madonna's later music videos (*Express Yourself* and *Justify My Love*) within the context of the ongoing feminist/postmodernist debate to illustrate how 'Madonna's postmodern representational strategies challenge the foundational "truths" of sex and gender' (Schwichtenberg 1993: 7). She contends that the use of deconstruction and sexual multiplicity in Madonna's texts address marginal groups (such as gay men and lesbians) 'while at the same time provoking feminism to rethink its own lines, limits and boundaries' (*ibid.*). She argues that Madonna's multiple video incarnations have been described as a postmodern challenge to aesthetic boundaries, and refers to Kaplan's (1987: 126) view that Madonna's 'postmodern feminism' is part of a larger postmodern phenomenon in her blurring of boundaries such as male/female, high/popular art, fiction/ reality, private/public.

Schwichtenberg notes that Madonna's postmodernism is of particular concern for feminists, who see postmodernism's lack of authenticity, unity and stable categories as challenging the modernist foundational tenets of feminism. She considers the debate around the intersection of feminism and postmodernism and notes that, while 'feminists have willingly subordinated philosophy to social criticism, philosophy as a male preserve has continued to subordinate questions of feminism' (Schwichtenberg 1993: 130). She goes on to discuss postmodernism's neglect of generalised aspects of modernist social theory, citing both Christine di Stefano (1990) and Kate Soper (1990), who maintain that 'postmodernism with its emphasis on fragmented identities runs the risk of destroying or subverting a feminism that, as gender politics, is based on a unified conception of women as social subjects' (Schwichtenberg 1993: 131).

In the debate surrounding the relevance of postmodernism for feminism, Schwichtenberg notes that postmodernism may not be a political liability for feminism. She draws on the concept of simulation, the key concept of Jean Baudrillard's (1983) postmodern theory, which she points out is often overlooked in feminist debates. She states that 'simulation which stresses the artificial as "dress-ups", "put-ons" and "make-overs" is not a political liability for a postmodern feminism intent on reclaiming simulation for the "other" ' (Schwichtenberg 1993: 132). Schwichtenberg argues that this is relevant for 'Madonna's political stylistics' and their appeal for lesbian feminists who she argues have long been 'the other' in feminism.

Schwichtenberg contextualises Madonna within Baudrillard's theory and notes that 'simulation is the pivotal term for a postmodern feminism that addresses differences between and among women' (Schwichtenberg 1993: 132). She argues (1993: 133) that Madonna uses simulation strategically to challenge the stable notion of gender as sexual difference, and, although Baudrillard's postmodernism may appear to have nothing in it for feminism, she argues that the concept of simulation challenges the *binary* opposition of male/female, which she maintains 'buttressed the edifice of heterosexuality, ostensibly excluding all "others" who did not accede to the male/female couplet (de Lauretis 1986, 1987)'.Using the concept of simulation, Schwichtenberg shows how constructions of gender, such as femininity, can be regarded as artifice or masquerade. She cites the work of psychoanalyst Joan Riviere (1926), who notes that 'women who wish for masculinity may put on a mask of womanliness to avert anxiety and retribution feared from men'. However, Schwichtenberg notes that although Riviere contends that 'femininity is *used* as a masquerade in the form of "protective coloration" she is unwilling to assert that all femininity is put on' (cited in Schwichtenberg 1993: 133).

Schwichtenberg goes on to consider drag as a second form of representational strategy used by Madonna. She maintains that

> in Madonna's video *Express Yourself*, drag is a deconstructive performance staged against the futuristic intertextual backdrop of Fritz Lang's *Metropolis*. This revitalised postmodern backdrop provides a pastiche of sexually

loaded signifiers that reference everything from S/M to gay male pornography thereby setting the stage for a suited Madonna (Curry, 1990).

(Schwichtenberg 1993: 135)

Schwichtenberg cites Dempster in stating that Madonna's drag dance resonates with postmodern dance 'which directs attention away from any specific image of the body and towards the process of constructing all bodies' (Dempster 1988: 48).

Schwichtenberg develops her argument further to maintain that, if for postmodern feminism the category of gender has collapsed, then the next stage is to deconstruct sex as the basis of identity. She asserts that

> ... it is time for a break – a radical break from the impoverished script of univocal sexuality. Here the postmodern proliferation of bodies, pleasures and knowledges advocated by Michel Foucault (1980) deregulates the univocal aim of sexual agency, thereby calling into question the fundamental categories of sex and gender as the basis for a 'unified identity'.

(Schwichtenberg 1993: 136)

Schwichtenberg notes that a range of charges have been brought against Madonna's *Justify My Love*, including nudity, bisexuality, sadomasochism and multiple partners (group sex), which she argues is judged by a single sexual standard.

Schwichtenberg draws on Judith Butler's work on the deconstruction of sex as the basis of identity. Butler's article 'The Force of Fantasy: Feminism, Mapplethorpe, and Discursive Excess' (1990b: 110) argues that 'Fantasy enacts a splitting or fragmentation or perhaps better a multiplication or proliferation of identifications that puts the very locatability of identity into question.' Butler draws on the Foucauldian strategy of proliferation which combats the attack on sexual pluralism by displacing 'the binary structures of gay and straight as discursively uncontrollable' (*ibid.*).

Drawing on Madonna's video *Justify My Love* and others, Schwichtenberg argues that, rather than drawing clearer boundaries between feminism and postmodernism, movement should be in the direction of 'the postmodern possibilities of multifaceted alliances'. As Schwichtenberg (1993: 140) notes, Madonna's popularity 'traverses the ranks of cross-dressers, drag queens, "Dykes for Madonna" and various gay and lesbian sex radicals, [which] brings the margins to the center of feminist debate through representational strategies'. Schwichtenberg contends that feminism inflected by postmodernism may be more radical in its range of possibilities and potential sites of resistance. She notes that gay men and lesbians have been in the forefront of political movements challenging notions of identity. Schwichtenberg (1993: 140) argues that 'postmodern sex and gender representations as practiced within the gay community and popularised by Madonna can fracture the notion of "an identity" with a motley pastiche of interests, alignments and identities that intersect at decisive moments'.

Schwichtenberg maintains that Madonna's videos, through the use of strategies of simulation, through masquerade, fantasy and drag, 'fissure the destabilized sex identity' and advance a sexual pluralism. Drawing on the relationship between the deconstruction of identity and the deconstruction of politics, Butler (1990a: 148) argues that the two are not the same and the former 'establishes as political the very terms through which identity is articulated'. Schwichtenberg concludes that postmodernism's inauguration of regulation and fragmented identities need not be the cause of political pessimism, 'especially in regard to "others" who have lived in the shadows of realist epistemology and sex and gender essentialism' (Schwichtenberg 1993: 141).

CONCLUSION

The intersection of postfeminist debates with popular culture and popular cultural forms is potentially a rich one for investigating representational politics and issues of identity. These elements are central for encapsulating the concept of feminist pluralism in its engagement with cultural theory, particularly postmodernism. This chapter has considered postfeminism's redefinition and re-evaluation of popular culture, as an area of political and representational contestation. These debates can be seen to have coalesced around Madonna as a popular cultural icon. The intersection of postfeminist debates around Madonna can be seen as representative of a particular moment in feminism's intervention into cultural studies.

8

POSTFEMINIST VARIATIONS WITHIN MEDIA AND FILM THEORY

INTRODUCTION

Postfeminist interventions into the arena of media and film theory are an outgrowth and development from feminism's involvement with both filmic and media discourses. Feminists have long been engaged in the development of a feminist practice in the areas of film production and scholarship. They have in the process interrogated the language of film with a view to demystifying the assumptions on which much media and film theory has operated. Second wave feminist interventions sought to investigate the way in which patriarchal ideology and the social formation of patriarchal society was sustained through media and filmic discourses. Feminist theorists and practitioners have been interested in the tensions between classical Hollywood cinema and independent cinema; in the intersection of debates in the area of feminism and psychoanalytic theory and in the potential for challenges to traditional dominant discourses in the areas of filmic texts and spectatorship, particularly in the context of viewing pleasures and 'resisting' pleasures. The emergence of a feminist scholarship around media and film theory has challenged traditional film canons and modes of production. In addition, the intersection of feminism with post-colonialism and anti-racism has posed challenges to feminism's use of models from psychoanalytic theory as well as to mainstream analysis of popular cultural texts, and has established multiple voices in feminist film criticism and practice.

PSYCHOANALYTIC THEORY AND FEMINIST FILM THEORY

The emerging feminist film criticism of the 1960s and 1970s was confronted by the Marxist critique of realism[1] and by developments in film theory such as semiology and psychoanalysis. Feminist film criticism shifted in emphasis from an earlier sociological emphasis on 'content' to an emphasis on the production of meaning, where stress was put on the processes of interaction between psychoanalysis and cinema. Mulvey (1993) notes that feminist politics, as it emerged in the late 1960s and early 1970s, played a significant part in putting

Freud on the political agenda, alongside Marx. As she notes, 'In these polemics, the influence of Brecht met psychoanalysis and modernist semiotics' (Mulvey 1993: 3).

Mulvey notes that semiotics and psychoanalytic theory were centrally important in the conceptual liberation of feminist aesthetics, by introducing concepts that highlighted gaps between images and the objects they claimed to represent, thus establishing a fluidity and instability of meaning in representations. Mulvey claims the theoretical implications of feminism's engagement with semiotics and psychoanalytic theory went further than this, 'not only opening up a gap in signification but also offering a theory that could decipher the language of displacements that separated a given signifier from its apparent signified' (ibid.).

In what are now seen as classic contributions to the analysis of psychoanalytic theory within feminist film theory, the work of Laura Mulvey (1981, 1989, 1992 [1975], 1993) and Mary Ann Doane (1982, 1987, 1991) have both drawn on psychoanalytic concepts and frames of reference to explore their relevance for feminist film theory.

LAURA MULVEY AND CLASSICAL NARRATIVE CINEMA

Mulvey's now seminal article 'Visual Pleasure and Narrative Cinema' (1975) examines classical narrative cinema (realist film), which she understands as exemplified by Hollywood cinema. Mulvey (1989: 14) critiques classical narrative cinema as an expression of 'the way the unconscious of patriarchal society has structured film form'. She proposes a demystification of the assumptions of classical narrative cinema and concludes that the goal of feminist cinema, and presumably feminist film theory, is to destroy the forms of pleasure associated with classic Hollywood cinema. One of the key elements of Mulvey's article is the way 'pleasure' is constructed by mainstream (Hollywood) cinema and the significance of such pleasure for different spectators.

Mulvey sets out to establish the significance of psychoanalysis for an analysis of film, within film theory generally but more specifically within feminist film analysis. In drawing on psychoanalysis, Mulvey intends to show how filmic pleasures reinforce patterns of subjectivity and social formations which already exist in the individual subject and in society. She sets out to establish how film reflects and cultivates interpretations of sexual difference already 'normalized' and which control representations and 'erotic ways of looking'. Mulvey clearly sees psychoanalysis as a useful political weapon for feminism, which she maintains can demonstrate and surface 'the unconscious of patriarchal society'. Mulvey's usage of 'patriarchy' and 'phallocentrism' is typical of pre-postfeminist writers, and both terms are used unproblematically.

For Mulvey, from a phallocentric perspective the dominant image is that of 'the castrated woman'. As she comments, 'An idea of woman stands as linchpin to the system: it is her lack that produces the phallus as a symbolic presence, it is her desire to make good that lack that the phallus signifies' (Mulvey 1992: 158). As Mulvey indicates, this model establishes women's desire as subjugated to her image, i.e. one which is 'castrated' and which she (woman) is unable to rise above. Mulvey (1992: 159) notes that, within patriarchal culture, woman stands 'as a signifier for the male other bound by a symbolic order in which man can live out his fantasies and obsessions through linguistic command by imposing them on the silent image of woman still tied to her place as bearer not maker of meaning'. The issue of differentiation within the concept of 'woman' is not at this point an issue for Mulvey, and she operates within a model of simple 'binary opposition'. This is shown in Mulvey's unproblematic use of the concept of 'oppression' and her use of psychoanalysis which 'faces us with the ultimate challenge, how to fight the unconscious structured like a language...while still caught within the language of patriarchy?' (*ibid.*).

Mulvey shows how psychoanalysis and the concept of the unconscious can be used to theorise concepts of 'pleasure' and 'the look'. She notes: 'As an advanced representation system, the cinema poses questions about the ways the unconscious (formed by the dominant order) structures ways of seeing and pleasure in looking' (Mulvey 1992: 159). This system of representation reaches its apotheosis in the Hollywood film: as Mulvey (1992: 160) comments, 'mainstream film coded the erotic into the language of the dominant patriarchal order'. The aim of Mulvey's analysis is not simply 'to challenge dominant forms and erotic pleasure which has women at its centre but to negate the relationship between pleasure and the narrative fiction film in order to conceive a new language of desire' (*ibid.*).

Drawing on Freudian and Lacanian psychoanalysis, Mulvey examines the pleasures that classic Hollywood cinema offers the spectator. She uses the concepts of 'scopophilia' and 'narcissism' as mechanisms through which to examine pleasures. In psychoanalytic theory, 'scopophilia' is defined as a basic human sexual drive to look at other human beings in such a way that the process of looking arouses sexual stimulation and objectifies the person looked at. As van Zoonen (1994: 89) comments, the feelings of lust and satisfaction that result are not directly related to erotogenic zones. Scopophilia can be further divided into fetishism and voyeurism (these are explored more fully below). The second concept is narcissism,[2] which Mulvey describes as a process of identification with the image on the screen.

Mulvey develops the concept of voyeurism around the way the cinema is structured. Kaplan maintains that voyeurism 'is linked to the scopophilic instinct (i.e., the male pleasure in his own sexual organ transferred to pleasure in watching other people having sex)' (Kaplan 1983: 30).[3] Mulvey maintains that scopophilia, pleasure in looking, is one of a number of possible pleasures offered by cinema. As she (1992: 160) indicates, 'there are circumstances in which looking itself is a source of pleasure, just as...there is pleasure itself in being looked at...' Mulvey refers to scopophilia as used in Freud's 'Three Essays on Sexuality', 'where he associated scopophilia with taking other people as objects subjecting them to a controlling and curious gaze' (*ibid.*). Despite further development of the concept of scopophilia in Freud's later work,[4] Mulvey argues that it continues to exist as the erotic basis for pleasure in looking at another person as an object. She goes on to note that, 'at the extreme, it can become fixated into a perversion, producing obsessive voyeurs and peeping toms whose only sexual satisfaction can come from watching in an active controlling sense, an objectified other' (Mulvey 1992: 161). Mulvey indicates that the cinematic 'experience' (the contrast of the darkness of the auditorium and the shifting patterns of light and shade) serves to heighten and enhance the 'illusion of voyeuristic separation'. As she notes, the circumstances and conditions in which cinema is experienced, combined with the narrative conventions, locate the spectator in an illusory situation where it appears they are looking in on a private world.

Mulvey establishes the link between scopophilia and narcissism and the construction of the ego, which she shows comes from identification with the image seen:

> Thus in film terms, one [scopophilia] implies a separation of the erotic identity of the subject from the object on the screen (active scopophilia), the other [narcissism] demands identification of the ego with the object on the screen through the spectator's fascination with and recognition of his like. The first is a function of the sexual instincts, the second of ego libido.
>
> (Mulvey 1992: 162)

She goes on to consider 'woman' as the object of the male gaze and man as 'the bearer of the look'. As Mulvey (1992: 162) notes, 'Woman displayed as sexual object is the leitmotif of erotic spectacle from pin ups to strip-tease from Ziegfeld to Busby Berkeley, she holds the look, and plays to and signifies male desire.' However, the position of the male figure is very differently located in terms of narrative structure. The man controls the film fantasy and the narrative dynamic. The film, as Mulvey points out, is structured around the main controlling figure with whom the spectator identifies:

> As the spectator identifies with the main male protagonist, he projects his look onto that of his like, his screen surrogate, so that the power of the male protagonist as he controls events coincides with the active power of the erotic look both giving a satisfying sense of omnipotence.
>
> (Mulvey 1992: 163)

Van Zoonen (1994: 88–89) maintains that the mechanisms of pleasure identified by Mulvey, voyeurism and identification, appear to be incompatible and not immediately reconcilable with a single 'unitary cinematic experience'. However, 'the conflict between what Freud called libido (scopophilia) and ego (identification) is resolved by the cinematic display of women as objects of the male gaze' (*ibid.*). Mulvey explains 'the reconciliation of the two contradictory, but constitutive pleasures of narrative cinema' by positing a distinction in male and female pleasures of looking. She contends that the patriarchal structuring of mainstream film establishes 'looking as a male activity', and being looked at as 'a female passivity'. As van Zoonen claims, in classic Hollywood films, 'women function simultaneously as erotic objects for the male audience who can derive scopophilic pleasure from their presence, and as erotic objects for the male protagonists with whom the male audience can identify' (1994: 88–89). The driving force in this process of binary opposition are the narrative conventions of Hollywood cinema. Mulvey contends that the organisation of the narrative is patriarchal and Hollywood cinema constructs the male protagonist as the active agent propelling the story forward. As Mahoney (1994: 69) comments, Mulvey 'identifies the "look" of the camera as well as the "gaze" of both spectator and protagonist as male'.

However, within the psychoanalytic framework, male viewing pleasures are not unproblematic. As van Zoonen (1994: 90) notes, 'To the patriarchal unconscious, "woman" signifies sexual difference and more particularly she connotes the lack of a penis which evokes fear of castration and "unpleasure"...' The only way in which male viewing pleasure can be rendered unproblematic is if the castration threat that women pose is removed. This can be achieved through the 'scopophilic order of narrative Hollywood cinema' in two ways (*ibid.*): first, by taking control of the woman's body visually and narratively; and second, by denying the castration of the woman through 'substituting her lack with a fetish object – high heels, long hair or earrings for instance – or turning her into a fetish object herself, exaggerating, stylizing and fragmenting female beauty into a reassuring object of the gaze' (*ibid.*). Mulvey draws on the films of Hitchcock and von Sternberg as representative of voyeurism and fetishism respectively.

The second major concept used by Mulvey (the first being voyeurism) is fetishism.[5] This is a process where cinema (unconsciously) fetishises the female form, representing it in a phallus-like way, thus undermining the threat posed by women. As Mulvey (1992: 164) notes, men turn 'the represented figure itself into a fetish so that it becomes reassuring rather than dangerous (hence over-evaluation, the cult of the female star)'. She uses the concept of 'fetishistic scopophilia' to describe a process whereby the physical beauty of the object is built up transforming it into 'something satisfying in itself' (*ibid.*).

Mulvey (1992) explains the structure of the cinema around three male looks or gazes: the look of the camera; the look of the audience; and the look of the (male) characters within the narrative. As she (1992: 165) notes, the conventions of narrative film 'deny the first two or subordinate them to the third, the conscious aim being always to eliminate intrusive camera presence, and present a distancing awareness in the audience'. However, as Mulvey (1992: 166) argues, in this reading the very 'structure of looking in narrative fiction contains a contradiction in its own premises: the female image as a castration threat'. She goes on to say that... 'the look of the audience is denied an intrinsic force: as soon as fetishistic representation of the female image threatens to break the spell of illusion . . . ' (*ibid.*).

Mulvey's article was part of a political project which had the aim of destroying the gendered pleasures of mainstream Hollywood cinema. Mulvey extended her theoretical project into the area of film-making (see Chapter 4), producing 'avant-garde' films in conjunction with Peter Wollen. In films such as *Bad Sister* and *Riddle of the Sphinx*, Mulvey illustrates the issues raised in her article, breaking with 'naturalistic techniques' in film-making which she maintained produced the 'libidinous and ego drives in mainstream narrative film' (van Zoonen 1994: 90).

Mulvey's work has been criticised from a number of different perspectives, and her project has been accused of being 'overly successful in destroying the pleasure of looking' (*ibid.*). Her work has also been criticised by feminist critics and non-critics for being inaccessible and elitist, and for drawing on concepts which marginalise feminist film theory and the role of the female spectator. Some of these critiques are explored below.

THE IMPACT OF MULVEY'S WORK ON FEMINIST FILM THEORY

Mulvey's analysis of some key concepts in the area of psychoanalytic theory provoked a significant growth in feminist scholarship in the area of feminism and psychoanalysis. Many of the texts which appeared subsequently have become classic contributions to the debate in their own right. They include: E. Ann Kaplan (1983) *Women and Film*; Teresa de Lauretis (1984) *Alice Doesn't: Feminism, Semiotics, Cinema*; Mary Ann Doane (1987) *The Desire to Desire: The Women's Film of the 1940s*; and Tania Modleski (1988) *The Women Who Knew Too Much: Hitchcock and Feminist Theory.* Many of these texts raised some 'early' concerns within the feminist community about the limitations of Mulvey's use of psychoanalytic concepts, and about psychoanalytic theory more generally. Mulvey did not directly address the issue of female pleasure. Mahoney (1994: 68) maintains that this is because the psychoanalytic analysis of cinema is problematic because 'it is theorised predominantly from a perspective of masculinity and its constructions'. Gledhill (1988: 65), drawing on the work of Mulvey and others, contends that 'early cine-psychoanalysis found it difficult to theorise the feminine as anything other than "lack", "absence", "otherness" '. Thus, while female pleasure in looking is inconceivable within the frame of reference used by Mulvey, there is an implicit argument within her article which, as van Zoonen (1994: 90) notes, suggests that 'within patriarchal culture a reversal of the structure of looking – facilitating concurrent female scopophilia and identification – is out of the question'.

This issue was also raised by Kaplan, who asked whether the gaze is necessarily male. In raising this question Kaplan (1983: 25) maintains that it is only 'through asking such questions within the psychoanalytic frame-work . . . [that we can] . . . begin to find the gaps and fissures through which we can insert woman in a historical discourse that has hitherto been male dominated and has excluded women'. She contends that psychoanalysis is a useful mechanism to deconstruct Hollywood films, thereby exposing the operation of patriarchal discourses and myths on which Hollywood film is based and through which women are constructed as 'other'.

Kaplan argues that in the dominant Hollywood genres women are marginalised and the only Hollywood genre where women and women's issues occupy a central space is that of the family melodrama. Kaplan outlines the centrality of Oedipal issues in the classic framing of Hollywood melodrama. She shows, however, that it can be approached in a different way, as Laura Mulvey's work has shown. Mulvey, while viewing melodrama as concerned with Oedipal issues, sees it as a potential 'space' for women, 'primarily as a female form, acting as a corrective to the main genres that celebrate male action' (Kaplan 1983: 26). However, she recognises that while 'melodrama' does help to surface ideological elements there is a lack of resolution of events within the films in a way which benefits women. Using the Lacanian model, Kaplan shows how psychoanalysis can be drawn on to analyse the nature of viewing 'pleasures', noting that

> simply to celebrate whatever gives us sexual pleasure seems to me both too easy and too problematic. We need to analyse how it is that certain things turn us on, how sexuality has been constructed in patriarchy to produce pleasure in the dominance – submission forms, before we advocate these modes.
>
> (Kaplan 1983: 27)

She goes on to discuss the unequal ownership of viewing pleasure and 'desire'. She shows that the 'dominance–submission' dimensions of psychoanalysis can be drawn on to understand the constructed nature of sexuality, as well as the range and differentiated positioning available for women and men. She shows how 'the passivity revealed in women's sexual fantasies is reinforced by the way women are positioned in film' (Kaplan 1983: 28). In the process, she draws on the work of Mary Ann Doane (1981) and outlines Doane's contribution to the debate. Doane shows how, in the classical genres, the female body is sexuality, providing the erotic object for the male spectator. In the woman's film, the gaze must be de-eroticised (since the spectator is now assumed to be female), but in doing this the films effectively disembody the spectator (Kaplan 1983: 28). Doane shows how classic Hollywood genres – westerns and gangster movies, for example – reflect a 'perfect mirror self' for the male spectator with the accompanying control. For the female spectator, the reflection is a 'powerless victimised figure' with a complete lack of control and self worth. As Mulvey (1975: 12–13) notes, 'The male figure is free to command the stage ... of spatial illusion in which he articulates the look and creates the action.'

Kaplan goes on to point out that the early 1980s saw a shift in terms of the male subject in traditional Hollywood film. Men, she argues, became the object of woman's gaze in films such as *Urban Cowboy* and *Saturday Night Fever*, and she identifies actors such as Robert Redford in *The Electric Horseman* as the object of 'female desire'. However, as she notes, the shift in emphasis, with the man being set up as sex object, simply results in the woman taking on the 'masculine' role and acting as bearer of the gaze. In this role, Kaplan observes, the woman always loses her traditionally 'feminine' characteristics, e.g. motherliness, kindness, etc. She adopts 'masculinist' characteristics which deny her femininity. Kaplan argues that even in a supposedly 'feminist' film such as *My Brilliant Career* the crude patterning of oppositions is apparent, in the contextualisation of issues, within the framework of patriarchal power relations, i.e. men's desire carrying power. Kaplan (1983: 29) notes that 'This positioning of the two sex genders in representation clearly privileges the male (through the mechanisms of voyeurism and fetishism, which are male operations, and because his desire carries power/ action where woman's usually does not)'. She goes on to make the point that such substitution does nothing to change established positions and structures.

Kaplan uses the concept of patriarchy unproblematically and her analysis is pre-postfeminist in its lack of deconstruction of feminist and filmic categories, e.g. patriarchy, 'the gaze', signifier and signified. This enables Kaplan to proceed to discuss two Freudian concepts – voyeurism and fetishism – in a problematic but undeconstructed way. Further, Kaplan (1983: 31) notes, 'the sexualization and objectification of women is not simply for the purposes of eroticism; from a psychoanalytic point of view, it is designed to annihilate the threat that woman...poses'.

Kaplan claims that fractures in the feminist film community emerged around the intersection of psychoanalysis and feminism. Some feminists objected to drawing on theories originally devised by men. Julia LeSage argues that the Lacanian model has been problematic in reifying women, 'in a childlike position that patriarchy had wanted to see them in'; for LeSage, the Lacanian framework establishes 'a discourse which is totally male' (cited in Kaplan 1983: 32).[6] Other feminists have advocated an opening up of the debate to focus on women spectators. In this context Kaplan reviews a range of debates and 'positions' from within feminist writing and critique.[7] Despite the fact that Kaplan's writing cannot be identified as postfeminist, she recognises the range of debates within feminism which have produced feminist pluralism. Judith Barry and Sandy Flitterman 'have argued that feminist artists must avoid claiming a specific female power residing in the body of women and representing "an inherent feminine artistic essence which could find expression if allowed to be explored freely"' (Barry and Flitterman 1980: 37, cited in Kaplan 1983: 33).

The feminist community of the 1980s identified a range of feminist challenges and alternatives to conventional film and filmic practices. Arbuthnot and Seneca (1982) articulate a need for feminist films 'that at once construct woman as spectator without offering the repressive identifications of Hollywood films and that satisfy our craving for pleasure' (Kaplan 1983: 33). Kaplan notes that in order to problematise Hollywood images and in order to understand 'how it is that women take pleasure in objectification, one has to have recourse to psychoanalysis' (Kaplan 1983: 34). Kaplan claims that psychoanalytic methodology is an essential first step in the feminist project of challenging the patriarchal discourses of Hollywood film.

Another feminist theorist who, like Mulvey, has drawn on Freudian and Lacanian psychoanalytic accounts is Mary Ann Doane. She has employed a more sophisticated version of psychoanalytic theory in analysing the male gaze. Doane claims that female subjectivity and voyeurism is impossible within patriarchal society and thus 'the reversal of the gaze' is not feasible. As Doane (1982: 42) comments, 'the male striptease, the gigolo – both inevitably signify the mechanism of reversal itself, constituting themselves as aberrations whose acknowledgment simply reinforces the dominant system of aligning sexual difference with a subject/object dichotomy'. Doane's point of emphasis is different from Mulvey's: while Mulvey's is on the female/passive, male/active binary, Doane considers the concepts of 'proximity' and 'distance'. She maintains 'that in cinematic theory there is a certain distance which needs to be maintained between film and spectator' (Mahoney 1994: 69). This distance also needs to be established to assume a voyeuristic or fetishistic position. However, the impact of psychoanalytic theory on theories of the feminine, from Freud to Irigaray, constructs women as lacking the 'necessary distance for voyeurism or fetishism' (*ibid.*). Van Zoonen shows how, 'Drawing on the Lacanian model, Doane maintains that the capacity to establish this distance is located in the appreciation of sexual difference that takes place in childhood' (van Zoonen 1994: 91). As female specificity is characterised by proximity, women lack the capacity to establish a voyeuristic position.

Given this position, Doane argues that the only possibilities for female spectatorial pleasure are firstly masochistic, resulting from an over-identification with the image or narcissistic resulting from becoming the object of one's own desire. Mulvey (1981) in a later article (produced as a result of criticism of her earlier position) 'also claims that the female gaze can only be a masochistic adaptation of the male spectator position enforced by the voyeuristic/fetishistic economy of narrative cinema in a patriarchal order' (van Zoonen 1994: 91–92). Doane goes further than Mulvey, in maintaining that the female gaze can gain control of the image by two means. She contends that a distance can be established by the female spectator by adopting the male spectatorial position, which Doane calls 'transvestism', or by using femininity as a mask. In the latter example, Doane draws on the psychoanalytic concept of the 'masquerade', which she argues facilitates the creation of a distance between the self and image.

Stephen Heath (1986) maintains that it is only in the 1980s that the idea of 'the masquerade' gained significant attention and currency. He argues that the concept gained wider currency within the development of the debates around female sexuality and feminist critiques of psychoanalysis. The concept has been particularly valuable in the area of representation, particularly in relation to film and cinema. Heath draws on Joan Riviere's article 'Womanliness as a Masquerade' (1926) to understand the concept of masquerade.

In summarising Riviere's analysis of masquerade, Heath (1986: 48) states that its concern is with 'women who wish for masculinity' and who may then put on 'a mask of womanliness' as a defence, 'to avert anxiety and the retribution feared from men'. The case developed by Riviere is of a successful intellectual woman who adopts the mask, i.e. the stereotypical patterning of femininity (womanliness) as a defensive strategy, because she has successfully adopted masculinist discourse and behaviour. As Heath (1986: 48) maintains, 'The problem can be solved by reference to Oedipal rivalry.' In adopting a public and successful intellectual position the woman rivals and can be seen 'symbolically' to take the place of her father (to have castrated him). However, the woman attempts to placate him by adopting the trappings of womanliness, e.g. flirting, anticipating reprisals, etc. Riviere states 'it was an unconscious attempt to ward off the anxiety which would ensue on account of the reprisals she anticipated from the father figure after her intellectual performance' (cited in Heath 1986: 37). As Riviere goes on to note, the woman's life consisted alternatively of both masculine and feminine behaviours.

Riviere further develops the explanation around the Oedipal situation and, as Heath maintains, in summarising the position Riviere's 'masquerade' involves 'the mask of womanliness, as a defence, to avert anxiety and the retribution feared from men', 'disguising herself' as merely a castrated woman; 'masquerading as guiltless and innocent'; masquerading in a feminine guise (Heath 1986: 38, 41). In Heath's summary, 'A woman identifies as a man – takes on masculine identity – and then identifies herself after all as a woman – takes up the feminine identity' (1986: 49). Riviere's own position as regards the masquerade is, as Heath acknowledges, an ambiguous one. She at times appears critical; at other times as answering 'the essential nature of fully developed femininity' (Heath 1986: 43).

As Heath maintains, the position is a complex one; 'masquerade' is within a woman's domain, but it has been usurped by the man. As Heath (1986: 50) notes, 'Collapsing genuine womanliness and masquerade together, Riviere undermines the integrity of the former with the artifice of the latter.' He goes on to analyse the central issue around 'masquerade': the status of the feminine – the identity of the woman. Heath argues that masquerade is a representation of femininity; but, as he goes on to say, 'femininity is representation, the representation of the woman' (Heath 1986: 53). The main contribution of psychoanalysis is its representation of identity as precarious.

Heath considers 'the masquerade' in relation to cinema, citing the work of Josef von Sternberg, particularly his direction of Marlene Dietrich in *Morocco*, Max Ophuls' *Madam de*, and Hitchcock's *Suspicion* and *Rebecca* as all representative of masquerade. Heath (1986: 58) argues, 'the fetishization of the masquerade that the cinema captures is the male distance: having positioned the woman as phallus, as the term for the fantasy of the man, her identity for him'. Heath cites the work of Mary Ann Doane (1982) in relation to the positioning of the female spectator. Doane (1982: 87) maintains that 'The effectivity of masquerade lies precisely in its potential to manufacture a distance for the image to generate a problematic within which the image is manipulable, producible and readable by the woman.' She notes that theories of female spectatorship are rare, and that 'spectatorial desire in contemporary film theory is generally delineated as either voyeurism or fetishism, as precisely a pleasure in seeing what is prohibited in relation to the female body' (Doane 1982: 76). Doane (1982: 77) points out that filmic theory and the cinematic institution have in common with Freudian theory 'the eviction of the female spectator from a discourse purportedly about her (the cinema, psychoanalysis)'.

Doane, in reference to the work of Joan Riviere, whom she acknowledges was the first to theorise the concept of masquerade, shows that 'the masquerade of femininity is a kind of reaction-formation against the woman's trans-sex identification [her transvestism]' (Doane 1982: 81). Doane argues that the concept of the 'masquerade' as discussed in Riviere's work, in the process of exaggerating or 'flaunting' femininity, establishes a distance between women and femininity: 'womanliness is a mask which can be worn or removed' (*ibid.*). The masquerade's resistance to patriarchal positioning would therefore lie 'in its denial of the production of femininity as closeness' (*ibid.*). Doane argues that the growing demand for a theorisation and elaboration of female spectatorship is a result of the necessity to understand fully the position in order to dislocate it. She sees 'masquerade' as playing an important role in this process.

Mulvey (1993) further extends Doane's argument in a more recent development of the concepts of fetishism and masquerade. She claims that the alignment between femininity and masquerade receives its strongest statement in the Hollywood cinema, 'investing as it does in the power wielded by eroticism in the marketplace' (Mulvey 1993: 17). Mulvey maintains that this can be seen in the shift that has taken place from the fetishisation to the commodification of the female body, through links between Hollywood cinema and the conscious marketing of the female spectator. In this context, the cinema acts as a link between 'the movie star as object of desire and the commodities associated with her as objects of desire, for the women watching the screen and looking in shop windows' (*ibid.*).

FEMINIST AND FILMIC CRITIQUES OF PSYCHOANALYTIC THEORY

Both Mulvey's and Doane's perspective of pleasurable female spectatorship is essentially negative, and the concept of unmediated pleasure for the female spectator is inconceivable within the psychoanalytic framework. The types of critiques which have emerged on the use of psychoanalytic theory by Mulvey and Doane have come from a number of directions – from feminist and non-feminist film theorists, and from theorists working in the area of post-colonialism and anti-racism.

One of the criticisms of psychoanalytic film theory emerging from mainstream film theorists, as well as feminist film theorists, is the implicit assumption within psychoanalytic film theory that media texts contain univocal meanings. Van Zoonen (1994: 92) contends that the pleasures of the male spectatorial position is a 'direct result of the way they are positioned by the cinematographic mode of address'. She notes that in this situation the text–spectator relation is determined by the visual and narrative discourses of the text which produced fixed gendered subjectivities, allowing for a limited range of responses (e.g. voyeurism and identification) and in the process ignoring the ambiguities and tensions which frame the text. Thus both textual discourses and the discourses of spectatorship are confined by a closed and predetermined frame of reference. The primary determinant of spectatorship is gender, which assumes primacy over factors such as 'race, sexuality, class, cultural capital and individual life histories beyond the Oedipal stage' (ibid.).

This raises some important issues, because even using the concept of gender alone, a universal response to mainstream Hollywood cinema in terms of spectatorial pleasure cannot be considered. Feminists working in the area of anti-racism and post-colonialism have questioned the relevance of the debate to their concerns (Roach and Felix 1988; Gaines 1994). Some leading theorists in the field have moved, more recently, to incorporate issues of race and ethnicity in their work (Modleski 1993). Van Zoonen (1994: 94) maintains that Doane's (1991) analysis maintains that both 'women and blacks constitute an enigma and a threat to the patriarchal unconscious that can only be contained by violent repression'. She claims that Doane's psychoanalytic account of the collective unconscious, while explaining the nature of sexism and racism, can be seen at the same time as ethnocentrically 'preoccupied with the pathological character of white patriarchal society' (1994: 94). Within this framework women and blacks are seen as 'different', 'other' and 'deviant'.

POST-COLONIAL AND ANTI-RACIST CRITIQUES IN FEMINIST FILM THEORY

One of the most thoroughgoing critiques of psychoanalytic theory in terms of its white middle-class binary (female/male) frame of reference is provided by Jane Gaines in an essay titled 'White Privilege and Looking Relations: Race and Gender in Feminist Film Theory' (1994).[8] Gaines considers the problems inherent in psychoanalytic theory for explaining race and ethnicity and its implications for feminist film theory more generally. She claims that the psychoanalytic model functions to ignore or marginalise 'considerations that assume a different configuration' (Gaines 1994: 177). In this context Gaines maintains that the Freudian–Lacanian scenario serves to 'eclipse the scenario of race–gender relations in African-American history, since the two accounts of sexuality are fundamentally incongruous' (ibid.). Further, the model universalises and reaffirms patterns of familial relations based on 'white middle class norms'.

174

The psychoanalytic model establishes gender as central in its analysis of oppression by positing the central binary opposition as between male/female. As Gaines notes: 'to the extent that it works to keep woman from seeing other structures of oppression it functions ideologically' (*ibid.*). In this context Gaines explains how psychoanalytic theory was incorporated into the theoretical work of writers such as Claire Johnston (1973) and Laura Mulvey. As Gaines (1994: 178) comments, 'In retrospect, we understand that the apparent intransigence of the theory of cinema as patriarchal discourse as it developed out of these essays is the legacy of the Althusserian theory of the subject.' Psychoanalytic theory served to provide a version of the construction of the subject which supplemented that of classical Marxism.

In an unqualified attack on Gaines' position, Modleski (1993) claims that Gaines has a strong ideological axe to grind in her attack on psychoanalytic film theory, maintaining that psychoanalysis cannot be used to discuss the issue of race in film theory adequately. In her essay 'Cinema and the Dark Continent: Race and Gender in Popular Film' (1993), Modleski aimed to show that Gaines' claim lacks foundation.

Drawing on the work of the post-colonialist writer Homi Bhabha (1984, 1986, 1988, 1994), Modleski shows that his post-colonialist critiques of colonialist discourses draw on a number of psychoanalytic concepts and frames of reference. Modleski (1993: 74) claims that 'Homi Bhabha has shown how colonialist discourse... involves a process of mimicry that is related psycho-analytically to the mechanism of fetishization.' She maintains that by 'mimicry' Bhabha seems to imply the imposition of one nation's values, structures and language on another – a colonised nation. The process of imposition does not imply the complete obliteration of difference but speaks of 'a desire for a subject of a difference that is almost the same, but not quite' (Bhabha 1984: 131). The position emphasised by Bhabha is one of ambivalence. Elsewhere Bhabha states that

> it is the force of ambivalence that gives the colonial stereotype its currency: ensures its repeatability in changing historical and discursive conjunctures; informs its strategies of individuation and marginalization; produces that effect of probabilistic truth and predictability which, for the stereotype, must always be in *excess* of what can be empirically proved or logically construed. Yet the function of ambivalence as one of the most significant discursive and psychical strategies of discriminatory power – whether racist or sexist, peripheral or metropolitan – remains to be charted.
>
> (Bhabha 1994: 66)

The development of the 'problematics of difference and sameness' as developed by Bhabha parallel the debates that have emerged in feminist theory. Modleski notes that Bhabha work is important in highlighting 'the psycho-social dynamics of colonialism and racism', establishing the relevance of psychoanalysis to areas which have previously been understood as outside its sphere. However, she

175

observes that, while Bhabha draws on concepts which have emerged from feminist theorisation of sexual difference, he himself neglects and dismisses gender and feminist issues.

This issue has been acknowledged, if not more fully addressed, in Bhabha's text *The Location of Culture* (1994), which reflects his engagement with elements of poststructuralism as well as psychoanalytic theory. As Bhabha (1994: 74) comments, 'The force of colonial and post-colonial discourse as a theoretical and cultural intervention in our contemporary moment represents the urgent need to contest singularities of difference and to articulate diverse "subjects" of differentiation.' However, the theoretical emphasis of Bhabha's work remains undifferentiated in his use of the category 'race' and he references only male post-colonialist, poststructuralist and anti-racist writers in this context – notably Edward Said, Franz Fanon and Michel Foucault.

Michele Wallace (1993) is critical of the current debates around the issue of the representation of race from both within and outside the black community. She contends that

> it may even be that the economic and political victimization of the urban and rural black poor in the US and worldwide is somehow exacerbated by the deeply flawed and inadequate representations of 'race' currently sponsored by both blacks and non-blacks in both 'high' and 'low culture'.
>
> (Wallace 1993: 654)

Wallace (1993: 655) maintains that the debates around race and sexuality need to be 'reunited in discussions of post-colonial "minority" discourse', and she argues that this is where debates in the area of black feminist cultural production should be situated. Gaines (1994: 176) also sees a shift in the location of debates concerning psychoanalytic theory and its intersection with discourses in the area of race and ethnicity. She claims that the debate has shifted from film studies to African and African-American studies,[9] and maintains that there is already a strong black feminist literary theory and cultural studies emerging, but also a parallel development in both critical and creative work on film and video art.[10]

Wallace contends that it is imperative that debates around a number of discourses within 'Marxist cultural criticism, structuralism, psychoanalysis, deconstruction and postmodernism' (Wallace 1993: 659) are incorporated into the development of a critical practice designed to deal with 'the complexities of racial/sexual politics as a constellation of increasingly global issues' (*ibid.*). However, Gaines is more critical about the implications of psychoanalytic theory and Marxist models for an analysis of race and sexuality. She claims that, while race has been incorporated into Marxist models more smoothly than has sexuality, the interpretation of racial conflict as an aspect of class struggle is unsatisfactory, particularly to Marxist feminists who want to understand the exact nature of the intersection of gender and race. As Gaines (1994: 180) notes, the 'oppression of women of colour remains incompletely grasped by the classical Marxist paradigm'.

FEMALE SPECTATORSHIP, PLEASURES AND RESISTING PLEASURES: POSTFEMINIST RESISTANCES TO PSYCHOANALYTIC DISCOURSES

The limitations of psychoanalytic theory for addressing issues raised by women of colour and lesbian feminists within debates in the area of feminist film theory became increasingly articulated around the issue of female spectatorship, particularly the pleasures gained from contesting dominant readings of text. Gaines (1994: 179) shows how the fragmentation of a unified feminist response to psychoanalytic theory was made apparent in the objections raised by lesbian feminists in the US to 'the operation of the classic realist text in terms of the tensions between masculinity and femininity'. The assumptions inherent in psychoanalytic theory regarding male spectatorial pleasures were contested by lesbian feminists, who argued that lesbian spectatorial pleasures were negated through this process. Gaines observes that such pleasures could never be 'construed as anything like male voyeurism'; in addition lesbian spectatorship 'would significantly change the trajectory of the gaze' (*ibid.*).

Gaines observes that lesbian feminists have consistently claimed that because psychoanalytic theory can only understand 'pleasure' in terms of the male/female binary, it is unable to conceive of lesbian and gay spectatorial pleasures. She contends that it is a product of what Monique Wittig calls 'the heterosexual assumption, or the straight mind', which Gaines (1994: 79) describes as 'that unacknowledged structure not only built into Lacanian psychoanalysis, but also underlying the basic divisions of Western culture, organizing all knowledge...'[11] Gaines points out that women of colour, already a marginalised group in terms of mainstream feminist analysis, remain unacknowledged and unassimilated by the central elements of psychoanalytic theory. She notes that attempts by feminism to articulate 'difference' consistently include work by lesbian and black feminists as evidence of feminism's more inclusive discourses. However, as Gaines (1994: 179–180) comments, 'the very concept of "different perspectives", while validating distinctness and maintaining woman as common denominator, still places the categories of race and sexuality in theoretical limbo'.

'PLEASURES' AND POPULAR CULTURAL TEXTS

Female spectatorial pleasure has been theorised outside the framework of psychoanalytic film theory. Some feminist film theorists and cultural theorists have claimed that female spectatorial pleasures can be found in particular genres and filmic texts. Modleski (1984: 104) maintains that feminists 'can look for clues to women's pleasure which are already present in existing forms even if this pleasure is currently placed at the service of patriarchy'. This particular approach highlights the attempt by some feminists working in the area of popular culture to attempt to identify strategies which resist dominant constructions of women's pleasure through pre-existing popular forms of mass entertainment.

One such popular cultural genre is melodrama. Van Zoonen (1994), drawing on Byars' (1991) analysis of 1950s melodrama, shows that many technical and narrative aspects of the Hollywood melodrama, for example *mise en scène*, characters and the narrative itself, establish a very different 'text–spectator' relation to the model of male voyeuristic spectatorship. In addition, van Zoonen notes that films with strong female leads, or characters with strong friendship bonds between women, offer different possibilities for female spectatorial pleasure. In these instances the emphasis is on the way different aspects of the text, for example narrative or visual devices, offer different 'readings'. As van Zoonen (1994: 96) comments, 'how these readings will be actualized by real audiences depends on their particular characteristics and viewing contexts and is not determined by the psychoanalytic drama inscribed by the text'.

Two analyses of films which adopt this approach are Arbuthnot and Seneca's (1982) analysis of the film *Gentlemen Prefer Blondes*[12] and Stacey's (1987) analysis of the film *Desperately Seeking Susan*.[13] Arbuthnot and Seneca, in their analysis of *Gentlemen Prefer Blondes*, aim to shift the emphasis from an analysis of male viewing pleasures to female pleasures of the classic narrative filmic text. They identify a range of feminist pleasures, including female friendship and the tension between 'male objectification and women's resistance'. Similarly, in Stacey's analysis of *Desperately Seeking Susan* she claims there is no way that traditional psychoanalytic film theory can account for the fascination both female protagonists express for each other. As van Zoonen (1994: 96) points out, the film is not about sexual difference but about difference between women, and it is this type of difference for which Lacanian psychoanalysis can provide no explanations. In a later work, Stacey (1991) outlines two feminist positions on identification within a broader conception of pleasures.

The first position is exemplified in Mulvey's work which, as Stacey notes, criticises 'identification of any kind for reproducing sameness, fixity and the confirmation of existing identities' (Stacey 1991: 148). Stacey rejects the psychoanalytic framework and claims that it is possible to reclaim identification as a site of resistance 'by seeing it as involved in the production of desired identities' (Mahoney 1994: 70), and thus as potentially empowering. She claims that female spectators can experience the pleasures of identification from films with leading female film stars such as Doris Day and Bette Davis. Mahoney notes that these 'pleasures can arise from acknowledged differences between spectator and star; worshipping the star as goddess or desiring to overcome the gap between them; or they can come from a denial of the distance between self and ideal, namely the widely recognised pleasure of losing oneself in the film' (*ibid.*).

REPRESENTATIONS OF 'RACE' AND BLACK WOMEN IN POPULAR CULTURE

Popular cultural forms such as film have frequently served as vehicles to represent issues around race and ethnicity and to confirm representations of racial stereotypes. Modleski (1993: 78) maintains that popular film is also used to explore 'the highly charged taboo relationship between black men and white women'. In this context Modleski uses the film *Gorillas in the Mist* as an example. In a summary which draws constant parallels with the film *King Kong*, Modleski outlines what she describes as the film's bizarre psychosocial dynamics. She claims that psychoanalytic theory cannot be dismissed as an analytic framework for dealing with issues of race, even though those who have used psychoanalysis may be racially biased.

Many feminist writers may find problematic Modleski's rather crude application of some of the conceptual repertoire of psychoanalytic film theory to the analysis of race within popular film. Certainly Modleski's earlier work, *Loving with a Vengeance: Mass Produced Fantasies for Women* (1984), where she considered forms of entertainment produced specifically for women, such as *Harlequin* romance or soap operas, has been the subject of considerable criticism from within feminist film and media theory.

Modleski (1993: 78) does raise the issue of the 'representation of black women in popular film looking especially at the ways in which the black woman functions as the site of the displacement of white culture's (including white women's) fears and anxieties'. In addition, in developing a point raised by Claire Johnston regarding the absence of women as women in 'patriarchal cinema', Modleski notes that this has been much more literally the case for black women than for white, and that black women in film are in the most marginalised position. As she observes, 'when present at all [the black woman] has served as a signifier of (white) female sexuality or of the maternal ("Mammy")' (Modleski 1993: 85). Michele Wallace, while not dealing directly with the implications of psychoanalytic film theory, considers attempts by popular cultural forms to mainstream, depoliticise and 'colonise' black feminist literary texts (see Chapter 7).

What these diverse analyses share is an attempt to rescue female pleasures in popular cultural forms. Bryars (1991: 20) recommends 'an approach that enables us to hear strong feminine, resisting voices even within mainstream cultural artifacts'. It is clear that psychoanalytic theory has annihilated the potential for female pleasure and even 'the resistance which women have constructed out of inbuilt contradictions in patriarchal popular culture' (van Zoonen 1994: 97). As more feminist film theorists and cultural theorists have recognised these limitations, what van Zoonen has called 'Mulvey's dark and suffocating analysis of patriarchal cinema' has been increasingly challenged by more subversive and more empowering forms of female spectatorship.

179

POSTFEMINIST PLEASURES IN FEMALE SPECTATORSHIP

The ambiguity in the term 'female spectatorship' can be seen in many of the debates outlined, and is addressed by Christine Gledhill in her article 'Pleasurable Negotiations' (1988). Gledhill (1988: 67) contends that 'Female spectatorship elides conceptually distinct notions: the "feminine spectator", constructed by the text, and the female audience, constructed by the socio-historical categories of gender, class, race and so on'. This distinction is an important one for understanding the nature of the female spectator and the concept of a diverse or differentiated audience response more generally. It also has implications for pleasures and resisting pleasures experienced by differently positioned 'readers'.

The subject positionings constructed by different texts clearly relate to whether the text (and its inscribed pleasures) is produced for male or female spectators. One area where the male body becomes the object of spectatorial pleasure is television sport and sports photography. Van Zoonen (1994: 99) observes that 'textual devices can modify a full-blown subordination of the male body'. She also draws on the work of Ien Ang (1983), who shows how sports photography establishes the boundaries for visualising the male body within patriarchy. Ang (1983: 421, cited in van Zoonen 1994) maintains that 'These pictures are a compromise between activity and passivity; the male body tolerates the transformation into an object of visual desire only when it is in motion.' Van Zoonen (1994: 104) contends that the way in which the male body presents itself to the female spectator within a patriarchal framework shows that a 'reversal of masculine structures of looking which is based on identification and voyeurism does not produce an equivalent female voyeurism'. She maintains this confirms the inadequacy of the psychoanalytic model for the female spectator, and shows that despite 'contradictions within patriarchal culture', the dominant visual economy is still organised along traditional gender lines.

In a study that highlights the positioning of female spectators within an area designed for masculine viewing pleasure – telerugby – Star (1988) considers the 'symbolic annihilation' of women as viewers of Television New Zealand (TVNZ)'s Rugby World Cup. In this article Star draws on gender theory for an analysis of 'the positioning' of the audience. In doing so, she draws parallels between 'soap-opera' which she argues within the context of media theory is aimed at a female audience and 'sportsopera' which she maintains is aimed at a male audience because of its masculinist discourses, e.g. violence, action, death, masculinity, authority and nationalism

> Because of our strongly gender marked conditioning, male and female subjects have different positions in relation to all these discourses. The convergence of discourses in a text and the subject positions offered viewers mark soap opera and sports opera as gender directed.
>
> (Star 1988: 187)

Women and men, she says, will experience the same action in different ways.

Star contends that the masculinist discourses of television and rugby could usefully be called 'master discourses to stress their hegemonic and phallocratic functions' (*ibid.*). Master discourses are linked with both formal 'compulsory' institutions as well as more informal patternings, e.g. 'gendered body language, "compulsory heterosexuality" and everyday "chatter" ' (*ibid.*).[14] Using master discourses in a hegemonic sense, Star is able to show how 'outsider' or 'resisting' readings can attempt to resist or challenge dominant discourses and 'to make conscious and explicit what has remained unconscious in the dominant discourse, e.g. the racist unconscious, the sexist unconscious' (Star 1988: 188).

Margaret Morse (1983, 1985), in writing about the discursive nature of television, maintains television only pretends to hold a real discourse with viewers. Morse further argues that 'the stories told by televised sports discourse are a new form of fiction which masquerades as interpersonal discursive contact' (Star 1988: 190). Star, while agreeing with Morse, wants to go further and maintains that they may be seen as simulations (after the model of Baudrillard) which are an invention of dominant groups. She claims that 'Television is a cultural artifact. Far from presenting the world as it naturally is, television with its capacity to eavesdrop, survey, record, censor, silence, order, transmit etc... is fruitfully approached as what Michel Foucault would term the apparatus of power' (Star 1988: 189).

In discussing 'sportsopera' within the framework of gendered TV discourse, Star clearly identifies the masculinist discourses around TVNZ's Rugby World Cup, which include: racism, heterosexism, the celebration of masculine mythic values, nationalistic and warring discourse and violence. Extending her debate to televised sport more generally, she argues that it is an area of programming which is a male preserve: 'Dominated by male sports and male commentators, celebrating macho values, male bodies and prowess, televised sport clearly targets male viewers' (Star 1988: 191).

The discursive location of women in televised sport is a problematic one. Morse (1983: 44) defines the position as follows: 'Sport remains a male preserve, a place of "autonomous masculinity", freed even from dependence, on woman as other to another identity.' Star (1988: 192) disagrees with Morse and maintains that women are integral to the masculinist discourse of televised sport (sportsopera). As she comments, 'Women are...thoroughly built into sports-opera, as an all-but-invisible otherness, a backdrop, the essential gestalt without which the discourse of masculinity would not function' (*ibid.*). Televised sport, and in particular sportsopera, involves the 'symbolic annihilation of women'. The discourses of televised sport address a male viewer, as Star (1988: 193) notes: 'The viewer situated in the voice over discourse is male. Women are excluded by mode of address.' Star also discusses the wider 'power-knowledge' base of 'rugby hegemony', the real corridors of rugby power, e.g. clubs, bars, locker rooms, hotel bedrooms, where the 'dirty discourse' occurs. Star maintains that it is the ability of males to control knowledge of and speech about 'the dirty discourse of rugby' which establishes the 'power-knowledge' base of the masculinist discourse of rugby. Star carefully grounds her analysis within Umberto Eco's model of 'phatic speech' or 'chatter'.[15]

There are parallels between sportsopera (televised rugby texts) and soap opera. Star (1988: 194) notes both are cheap to produce and deliver large audiences. 'Classic serial narrative structure moves relentlessly towards closure: equilibrium, disequilibrium, resolution. In soap opera the "closure" is always temporary. Often more enigmas are thrown up than are resolved, giving continuing uncertainty.' Similarly she argues the televised rugby text has a limited possibility of 'closure'. As she notes, 'Soaps and sportsopera both have lots of little climaxes' (*ibid.*). Within media theory soaps have frequently been portrayed as female, and it is argued that the reason for this is 'the perspective and experience of female characters are central to the narrative' (*ibid.*).[16] Sportsopera, Star contends, similarly operates to create the characteristic male melodrama.

It is claimed that there are other parallels between soap opera and sportsopera in their discursive location of the female and male viewer. Star claims that in both genres committed and sustained viewing is required in order to identify with key characters (players) and to become embroiled in the narrative (game). She notes that 'Tania Modleski has commented that the classical Hollywood male narrative maximised actions and minimised dialogue. Televised rugby fitted this model perfectly...' (Star 1988: 195).

As mentioned above, one of the most interesting dimensions of Star's work is her use of Umberto Eco's concept of sports 'chatter'. She argues that Eco's use of sports discourse is useful as it operates on a number of different levels: at the level of the sport itself, i.e. the discourses of the players; at the level of the discourses of the spectator, i.e. the discourses around watching sport; the discourse of 'meditated sport' or media discussions of sport; and discourse on discourse, i.e. when the players or media discuss mediated sport. Eco (1969) argues that present-day sport is dominated by the last three discursive levels, which are removed from the sport itself. As Eco maintains, at these latter levels we enter the realm of hyper-reality in which sport itself might well not exist:

> So sport as practice, as activity, no longer exists, or exists for economic reasons (for it is easier to make an athlete run than to invent a film with actors who pretend to run); and there exists only chatter about chatter about sport.
>
> (Eco 1969: 162)

It is at this level that Eco's work is interesting for the general debate, i.e. 'in the realm of hyper-reality it is the images of sport which become more important than the sport itself' (Star 1988: 196). Star goes on to show that it is at this level that the ideas of Eco (and Baudrillard) can be seen to parallel the (now contested) debates of feminist theorists such as Ang and Modleski who maintain that soaps create an opportunity for women to share 'legitimate' time and interests together, established around television (soap) discourses. As Star contends, ' . . . soap opera maintains this binary, positive-male/negative-female structuring because, even though the supposed concerns of women are foregrounded, they remain firmly tied to phallocratic, capitalist, heterosexual definitions' (*ibid.*).

Star draws further analogies between sportsopera and soap opera through the introduction of (characters) – *player-types*. The distance between image and reality is collapsed; details of lives beyond (rugby) are filtered through the master discourse of rugby or the nature of soap. As Star (1988: 198) notes, 'the impression of intimacy such technology can provide is distinctly hyper-real in that viewers come to know electronic images and value them as highly if not more highly than the actual game'. She also notes that there is a greater degree of flexibility and space for characters to change. However, Star maintains that in 'classical male narrative, such changes must be linked to cause and effect'. In the case of rugby, argues Star, changes have been gradual: 'In the popular consciousness of postcolonial New Zealand, rugby is synonymous with tradition and stability, possibly associated for many with a golden age free from various modern traumas'. Star also notes that, despite the fact that rugby sportsopera is a 'male form', the viewing figures for females are high. She notes that non-feminist women are not only interested but 'flattered' to be part of the masculinist discourses of rugby. Star states that the whole area of female viewing pleasures in relation to sportsopera needs researching.[17]

Star states that the masculinist discourses of telerugby are intersected by other factors such as race, ethnicity and nationality. All the male presenters were white and Pakeha (and generally former players). As Star notes, 'Maori women, and persons whose sexual identity is not heterosexual, were completely invisible' (*ibid.*). The media have dealt with the 'threat' of feminism in two ways: by processes of accommodation and ridiculing. Star maintains that Roland Barthes's concept of 'inoculation' is useful here: the 'process by which an apparent show of tolerance . . . protects against the risk of "a more general subversion" ' (Star 1988: 199). Star maintains that feminists have developed a similar concept: 'recuperation'. She shows that this process of incorporation or 'recuperation',[18] as used by feminist theorists, is highlighted in the stereotype of the 'new woman' as used by advertisers, in television fiction, entertainment and in public service programmes. The stereotype is 'white, dresses for heterosexually identified men, is competitive, aggressive, materialistic, individualistic and reverses roles with males' (*ibid.*). The threat of the 'new woman' stereotype has resulted in her 'neutralisation' in a variety of different ways: falling for some inferior-status male (e.g. the Mildred Pierce model); being exposed as a lesbian (e.g. the Sister George model); 'finding herself' pregnant or in a traditional family setting (e.g. the Cagney and Lacey model).[19]

Star cites the work of Julie d'Acci, who has criticised two assumptions of liberal feminists: first, that media should reflect and positively portray 'real-life' improvements in women's position; and second, that representing 'successful' women as role models, particularly women from different ethnic backgrounds, will necessarily have an impact on the 'real situation' of women. There is rarely any discussion of the relationship between 'representation' and 'real life' within these theoretical debates. As d'Acci (1987: 205) maintains, 'Appeals for equal rights, equal pay and individualism become appeals for equality of representation [in the media].' Star notes that the representation of 'real life' in this way does not mean that the media escapes the discourses of 'bourgeois phallocracy'. As she comments, 'Rather it is positive to argue that they become collapsed into an unreal world of media simulation and hyper-reality in the manner explored by McLuhan, Debord, Baudrillard, Eco *et al.*' (Star 1988: 199).

Star observes that, in terms of age, physical appearance, body types, etc., there is a much broader range of television 'professional male types' available for men than there is for women. In addition, she notes (1988: 200), 'the new woman stereotype is most frequently represented in a commodity context and almost unfailingly with a man. Her "liberation" and well being are strongly equated with consumption.' In considering feminist work on male and female newsreaders, Holland (1987) maintains that 'the treatment of women in the media is still dominated by the central problem of situating women as sexual' (Star 1988). Star concludes in maintaining that neither news, nor current affairs, nor TV sport are overtly about sex, but that gender and sexuality are a subtext in all three. She claims that the discourses of rugby make this apparent.

In a later article, Star (1992) further develops the concept of the differentiated audience for telerugby and the concept of 'resisting pleasures' or 'reading against grain'. She shows how it is possible to gain pleasure from textual discourses such as the technical or physical aspects of the game (of rugby) without being implicated and positioned as a viewer by the machismo and sexism of the sports text. Gledhill (1988: 67) notes that 'recent work suggests that the textual possibilities of resistant or deconstructive reading exist in the processes of the mainstream text'. This process occurs when the viewer or reader refuses to be constructed by the text. Star (1992) theorises the concepts of 'pleasures' and 'resisting pleasures' available to feminist audiences within the context of viewing telerugby.

In analysing TVNZ's Rugby World Cup 1987 viewing figures, Star notes that it attracted a strong female following. In every age category (except among teenagers) the figures for female viewers matched those for males. In the teenage group male viewing figures were six points less than female viewing figures. Star notes that

> in so far as telerugby can be said to address women at all it speaks to 'good' women playing out 'natural' patriarchal roles (girl friend, follower, wife, mother, etc.). The kinds of pleasures available to this group include: sex; familiarity; nostalgia; security; patriotism; recognition and approval; vicarious success through 'their' males, the catharsis available to those

who love and understand the game; and the satisfaction of believing themselves 'normal'.

(Star 1992: 125)

Star notes, by contrast, that a different set of pleasures can emerge from different groups of women viewers. Oppositional or 'resisting pleasures' emerge from feminist viewers who, in the process, 'surface' issues of racism, sexism, violence, homophobia and machismo in rugby and telerugby.

Star contextualises the symbolic cultural significance of World Cup Rugby in New Zealand, and maintains World Cup Rugby can be placed within the popular culture 'traditions' of male spectacle, where the superhero has been 'writ large', e.g. *Superman, Last of the Mohicans, The Unforgiven*. Star notes that telerugby draws on a tradition in which contempt for women was a prominent feature: 'The old Pakeha hypermasculine narratives of war, violence, sacrifice and death remain central despite loud cries by the NZ Rugby Football Union... and TVNZ in the form of "New Image" rugby' (Star 1992: 126). Drawing on Umberto Eco's terms, Star comments that World Cup 1987 telerugby 'chatter' was overwhelmingly by, for and about men.

In terms of theorising women viewers in relation to telerugby, Star in her earlier article (1988) argues that women are not just silenced but 'symbolically annihilated' in telerugby. She reviews three theoretical models which feminists have developed in order to understand the questions of female audiences. The first is a 'socio-historical' model which emerged from the social sciences and which portrayed women in a filmic or televisual text as a 'reflection' of socioeconomic and political circumstances.[20] The second model is the psycho-analytic or 'semiotic model', and is associated with the work of Laura Mulvey (1975). The third model identified by Star is typified in the work of Linda Williams (1988) and Christine Gledhill (1988), who attempt to transcend both approaches. Star outlines how Williams and Gledhill employ 'hegemonic' explanations to patriarchal capitalism. As Star (1992: 128) shows, 'since hegemony is never total and always open ended the meanings preferred by dominant groups are constantly needing to be reimposed in the face of resistance from disadvantaged groups'.

Williams and Gledhill show that the concept of 'the media audience' does not simply result from the imposition of the ideas of ruling groups, e.g. white, male, middle-class, media magnates via their global 'organisation and control of the culture industry'. Star claims that they maintain that instead of addressing issues of 'dominant ideology' which could be assumed to be unified and consistent, 'feminists need to unmask the series of varied strategies which are necessary to keep ideologies dominant in response to changing historical circumstances, especially the challenges of resisting groups' (*ibid.*).

Star maintains that the media are 'sites of constant negotiation' around money and pleasure which she sees as operating at three interacting levels: institutional, textual and receptional. While understanding the interaction between these levels as significant, Star focuses on the issue of reception/negotiation in terms of understanding the concept of a differentiated audience. She maintains that

> one of the problems of feminist discussions of female spectatorship up until recently has been the tendency to confuse the viewer constructed by the text (which is the outcome of negotiations at the first two levels) with the female audience as socio-historically situated, according to race, class, sexual preference and so on, which occurs at negotiations at this level (Gledhill, 1988; Kuhn, 1982).
>
> (Star 1992: 130)

Star argues that televised rugby texts can be interpreted or 'read' in a variety of different ways by different groups, and she goes on to show how these different groups experience different 'pleasures' from viewing. She identifies the following groups: Maori and Pacific Island women, Pakeha, lesbian, heterosexual, working-class, able-bodied, disabled, married, young/old, non-sportswomen, rugby buffs, feminists, non-feminists.

PLEASURES AND 'RESISTING PLEASURES'

Star argues that for the heterosexual audience the issue is sex (and masculinity): the principal object of the television 'gaze' in telerugby is male bodies. She notes one of the few explicit women's accounts of pleasures in watching 'Aussie Rules football' on television:

> What attracted my interest were the images of male bodies. Here were barely clad, eyeable male bodies in top anatomical nick. The cameras follow their rough and tumble disport with relentless precision, in wide angle, close-up and slow motion replay. With the commentary turned down and some music the imagery may be released from its imposed fixated meaning and the performance enjoyed, as choreographed spectacle: lyrical, flagrantly masculine, and erotic.
>
> (Poynton and Hartley 1990: 150)

However, as Beverley Poynton points out in her analysis of the 'pleasures in watching Aussie football, the text is not in fact constructed for women's voyeuristic enjoyment'. Poynton argues, as does Star, that male sports texts like 'telerugby' are primarily constructed for men to gaze at men.[21]

THE 'FEMALE GAZE' AS MOCKERY OF MACHISMO

Lorraine Gamman and Margaret Marshment, in *The Female Gaze: Women as Viewers of Popular Culture* (1988), maintain that feminist theorists argue that the concept of 'the female gaze' as mockery of machismo offers spectators the possibility of identifying with the 'pleasures' of activity without the sort of voyeurism associated with the 'male gaze' position of the classic Hollywood cinema. However, Star makes a clear distinction, not fully established in earlier feminist theories (e.g. Kaplan, Mulvey), between feminist and non-feminist spectators.

Star argues there is a major difference between the pleasures available to feminists and non-feminists. Feminists can experience the multiple pleasures of 'resisting pleasures', she says, and ' "Resisting viewings" are the pleasures of viewing against the grain, that is in contradiction to the messages you are expected to receive from the text' (1992: 134). She maintains that feminists get pleasure from being critical, from 'naming' behaviour using the feminist theoretical repertoire, e.g. homophobic, macho, phallocentrism. Star argues that lesbian feminists, who are not open to feeling sexually attracted to men, have a different approach to viewing telerugby and distinctive pleasures are available:

> Rugby viewing or spectating can be a lesbian occasion . . . I have listened to the positive words that many different lesbians use to describe male bodies in action. We will use words like 'super', 'powerful', 'gutsy', 'outstanding', or 'absolutely brilliant' to describe a move or a skill (seldom a physique). We never use the more explicitly sexual adjectives I have heard some heterosexual women use like 'hunk', 'spunk', 'physical', 'gorgeous', 'well-hung', or 'turn-on' for male athletes. Instead, we tend to use the first set of words equally to describe females and males, but reserve sexual words solely for women athletes.

> (Star 1992: 136)

Star argues that Maori women, both feminist and non-feminist, watch telerugby from a different perspective. She cites the work of Jacqueline Bobo (1988) who 'in her discussion of black women's positive reception of *The Color Purple* . . . shows how those in an oppressed position grow used to constructing something positive from the few media scraps they may have' (Star 1992: 134). For Maori, rugby is one of the too few spaces on television where Maori people are seen to be successful. Maori women as audience celebrate and support Maori men's success: 'Another pleasure comes from some Maori women's understanding and love of rugby and in some cases participation in the game' (Star 1992: 135).

Thus different audiences bring 'different frameworks of understandings' to their readings of telerugby. The concept of 'pleasures' and 'resisting pleasures' is an important one in media theory, highlighting the significance of the differentiated audience. In addition, media forms are recognised as 'sites of struggles' around which constant 'negotiation' takes place, these negotiations occurring at institutional and textual levels and at the level of reception.

CONCLUSION

This chapter has considered feminist and postfeminist debates in the area of media and film theory. Second wave feminist interventions into mainstream cinema were centred on debates around psychoanalytic theory. Both feminist theorists and practitioners drew on the repertoire of dominant discourses in an attempt to challenge their mode of address and their assumptions. For postfeminist theorists these interventions were problematic in their uncritical use of a language and body of concepts which reinforced a model of binary opposition. Postfeminist discourses around film and media, through their intersection with post-colonialism and anti-racism, articulate difference and challenge dominant discourses in the area of spectatorship, pleasures, and media and filmic texts. Postfeminist debates in the area of media and film theory aim to establish a multivocalism for both feminist theorists and practitioners.

9

POSTFEMINISMS AND CULTURAL SPACE: SEXUALITY, SUBJECTIVITY AND IDENTITY

INTRODUCTION

At an earlier point in this book, it was established that cultural studies, and in particular debates around representation, provided a focal point for the coalescing of a number of debates including feminism, poststructuralism, postmodernism and post-colonialism. Popular cultural forms especially were identified as useful for framing debates around identity, sexuality, ethnicity and image. In this sense popular cultural forms can be seen as 'sites of opposition' and 'sites of resistance' for a range of groups who wish to open up the possibilities for the creation of new sites of meaning and knowledge. Thus representational issues emerging from popular cultural forms can be seen as actively involved in different subaltern or subcultural groups' attempts to establish new identities. In this context both postmodernist and postfeminist theoretical debates encourage an approach to identity where both meanings and identities are fluid, not fixed. Two bodies of theory intersect around these debates: one emerging from feminist debates concerned with gender and sexuality which coalesce around gay and lesbian politics, and the other from cultural studies, concerned with debates linking representations and identities within newly defined cultural spaces. This final chapter is concerned to investigate the possibilities and potential for the emergence of new identities and coalitions, and examines debates in the area of sexuality, pornography and representational politics.

SEXUALITY, SUBALTERN IDENTITY AND 'PERFORMATIVITY'

The influence of poststructuralism on feminist debates has made earlier debates around identity, sexuality and representation problematic. However, as Patton (1993: 82) notes, the poststructuralist debate itself came under attack from gender theorists such as Judith Butler (1990a), Donna Haraway (1991) and Sandra Harding (1986), who 'sought to take the anti-essentialist arguments all the way down' (Patton 1993: 82). As Patton comments, these theorists have 'demonstrated that even the supposed biological referents of gender ("sex" in genotype) are themselves socially constructed' (*ibid.*). These two areas of debate – the feminist poststructuralist critique of identity and the subsequent debates emerging from the 'gender theorists' within feminism – need to be examined.

Second wave feminist theorising focused on the social construction of gender categories and drew a distinction between 'sex', which was taken to be universal and biological, and 'gender' which was understood as culturally variable but, as Bailey (1993: 100) notes, still at some level, fundamental: 'Because these gender differences between male and female roles are then seen as social rather than biological, they are changeable by human agency.' This distinction between a conception of a biological 'eternal nature' and a socially constructed model of gender was increasingly challenged by 'feminists, poststructuralists and philosophers and historians of science' (*ibid.*). As Bailey comments, the sociocultural and historical characteristics of both sex as a biological category as well as gender became a central issue in the debate.

The work of Michel Foucault, particularly his 'genealogy of sexuality and sex' as outlined in *The History of Sexuality* (1981a), has contributed to feminist debates in the area. There are a number of dimensions of Foucault's work more generally which have been valuable in advancing feminist debates. These include: his disruption of fixed and stable categories of sexuality and sex; his conceptualisation of new forms of power; his relationship between power and pleasure; and his articulation of the link between resistance and identity.

Bailey (1993: 102) claims that, while Foucault does not examine the relationship of gender to bodies and identity directly, his analysis lends itself to these debates. Foucault understands bodies as related 'to the production, transmission, reception and legitimation of knowledge about sexuality and sex'. His rejection of 'transhistorical' categories undermines traditional conceptions of 'the cultural relationship between women, bodies and sexuality' (*ibid.*). This position challenges feminist essentialist positions around a conception of a 'transhistorical female essence', and his genealogical account of bodies renders incoherent a conception of 'bodily vulnerability of women to men across time and culture' (Bailey 1993: 106).

Foucault's genealogical critique has implications for conceptions of identity. Bailey (1993: 105) contends that 'by documenting the discontinuities of history, he dispels the shadow of a monolithic, transcendent culture from which marginalised groups and individuals must wrest the rights to their "identities" '. We will return to this point shortly.

Bardo (1993a) shows how Foucault's *History of Sexuality* articulates Foucault's theory of new forms of power, including 'discipline', 'normalisation' and 'biopower', which explain how power and identity are related. His conception of power in his later work (see Chapter 3) understood power as productive and plural. Bordo (1993a: 192) maintains that this productive conception of power can be seen in 'new forms of culture and subjectivity, new openings for potential resistance to emerge'. As Foucault (1983) claims, where there is power there is also resistance: 'Jana Sawicki (1988: 186) points out that Foucault's notions of power are eminently compatible with feminist understandings of the personal as political' (Bailey 1993: 115).

Before going on to assess Foucault's analysis of power, resistance and the proliferation of identities, his relationship between power and pleasure can also be seen as having also important implications for feminist politics. Bordo (1993a: 192) claims that a Foucauldian framework of power and pleasure do not cancel one another and that such a model facilitates an understanding of compliance as well as contestation and resistance. She argues that women may themselves contribute to 'the perpetuation of female subordination... by participating in industries and cultural practices' (*ibid.*) which contribute to their own lack of power. In this context Bordo draws on the Foucauldian concept of 'docile bodies'; that is, women may experience an illusion of power, while being rendered 'docile'. However, she shows that this 'very "docility" can have consequences that are personally liberating and/or culturally transforming' (*ibid.*). She provides two examples of such instances:

the woman who goes on a rigorous weight-training programme in order to achieve a currently stylish look may discover that her new muscles also enable her to assert herself more forcefully at work. Or... 'feminine' decorativeness may function 'subversively' in professional contexts which are dominated by highly masculinist norms (such as academia).

(*ibid.*)

Bordo thus confirms Foucault's contention that power relations are 'unstable' and that 'resistance is perpetual and hegemony precarious'.

Foucault's theorisation of the relationship between bodies and power highlights the problematic nature of feminism's earlier analysis of 'pleasure'. As Bordo (1993a: 193) observes, second wave feminist discourses which put a premium on the oppressiveness of femininity 'could not be expected to give much due to the *pleasures* of shaping and decorating the body or their subversive potential'. Linked to this, she says, has been the implications of Foucault's work for conceptualisations of representation: 'Foucault has been attractive to feminists for his later insistence that cultural representation is ubiquitous and perpetual' (*ibid.*). Bordo claims that Foucault has been of interest to two 'waves' of Foucauldian-inspired feminism: the first wave emphasised concepts such as ' "discipline", "docility", "normalisation" and "bio-power" ', while a second emphasised elements of deconstruction including ' "intervention", "contestation", "subversion" ' (*ibid.*).

The relationship between power and resistance in Foucault's work has implications for conceptualisations of identity. Bailey (1993: 116), drawing on Foucault, claims that his contention that 'all discourses give rise to resistance offers a more fluid, more partial "identity"...'[1] Bailey drawing on Sawicki (1988: 186-190) notes that Foucault's conception of 'identity as historically constructed' is compatible with an analysis of identity by lesbian feminists.

191

However, the reconstruction of identities which has emerged from lesbian feminism has been formulated as an 'identity politics', based on a 'hierarchical distinction from other identities', such as gay men. Sawicki claims that this model limits the potential for alliances between lesbians and gay men, which could reinforce and 'strengthen local struggles'. Bailey (1993: 116) highlights the way that Foucault's conceptualisation of ' "homosexuality" as an identity constructed through the hegemonic discourses on sexuality and sex has exploded the confines of this limited identity, constituted by, and enabling, a gay community which encompasses many other political identities and differences'.

IDENTITY AND 'PERFORMATIVITY': THE WORK OF JUDITH BUTLER

My recommendation is not to solve this crisis of identity, but to proliferate and intensify this crisis.

(Butler 1990a: 121)

Perhaps the most significant challenge to the concept of gendered identities is contained in the work of the postmodern feminist theorist Judith Butler, particularly her conception of gender as 'performativity'.

Martin (1992: 101) draws on Judith Butler's work on the 'deconstruction of feminist identity politics and its foundationalist premises' and her call for 'the disaggregation of sex, gender, sexual identity and desire' (*ibid.*). Butler argues that division along gender lines is simply the articulation of repeated performances of culturally sanctioned acts of gender. She states that

The deconstruction of identity is not the deconstruction of politics; rather it establishes as political the very terms through which identity is articulated. This kind of critique brings into question the foundationalist frame in which feminism as an identity politics has been articulated. The internal paradox of this foundationalism is that it presumes, fixes, and constrains the very 'subjects' that it hopes to represent and liberate.

(Butler 1990a: 148)

Drawing on aspects of poststructuralist analysis, Butler shows that the plurality of discursive domains within which women are located establishes diversity around issues of 'subjectivity', 'identity' and 'difference'. As Martin (1992: 103) maintains, ' "the subject of feminism" cannot be thought of as a stable, unified, or internally coherent woman, or lesbian', without in the process ignoring the range of discourses within which 'subjects are constituted'. Butler maintains, however, that resistance to and subversion of dominant hegemonies can only emerge ' "within the practices of repetitive signifying"', not from claims to independent and discrete identities' (Martin 1992: 103). Martin, in a comprehensive summary of Butler's work, shows how Butler's argument stresses the importance of 'surfacing' and making 'visible the complexities that already exist', but which are rendered invisible by dominant discourses 'with deep investments in defining viable subjects' (1992: 105).

Butler's (1990a: 137) radical conception of identity advances a model which creates spaces for a range of sexual identities – including gay, queer, lesbian identities – which act to destabilise the unity of identity categories, exposing 'the regulatory fiction of heterosexual coherence'. As such, Butler claims that she is not interested in 'difference *qua* difference', nor in 'celebrating each and every new possibility *qua* possibility', but in 'redescribing those possibilities that already exist, but which exist within cultural domains designated as culturally unintelligible and impossible' (Butler 1990a: 148–149, cited in Martin 1992: 103).

It is in this context that aspects of performativity within homosexual practices 'such as drag and butch-femme roles, become privileged sites for the re-description of "possibilities that already exist" ' (*ibid.*). It is the identification of gay men and lesbians with butch/femme roles that act to subvert essentialist notions of identity. As Martin (1992: 104) claims, Butler's conceptions of drag[2] and butch-femme roles show that 'a model of signification might displace the debates over whether gay and lesbian sexual practices constitute imitations or the real thing...'. Both drag and butch-femme are seen as performative in that neither can be seen as imitative since, as Martin shows, all performances are 'imitations of fantasized ideals, hence masquerades' (*ibid.*).

For Butler, heterosexuality is itself a masquerade. She claims that 'drag is subversive to the extent that it reflects on the imitative structure by which hegemonic gender is itself produced, and disputes heterosexuality's claim on naturalness and originality' (1993a: 125). However, both 'drag' and 'butch-femme' are problematic conceptually and in their application, which reflects difficulties with the concept of performativity. Modleski (1991: 158) claims that Butler 'speaks of a situation in which "the anatomy of the performer is... distinct from the gender of the performer, and both of these are distinct from the gender of the performance", which suggests a "dissonance ... between sex and gender, and gender and performance" ' (Butler 1990a: 137, cited in Modleski 1991: 158).

In her application of the concept of drag in her now famous analysis of the film *Paris is Burning*, a film on the subcultural practices of black and Hispanic gays, Butler (1993a) recognises that these representations are ambivalent and she acknowledges that they could be 'read' as being of homophobic, misogynistic and racist origins.[3] The butch-femme as an example of 'the performative' is also problematic. Teresa de Lauretis claims that 'The butch-femme role playing is exciting not because it represents heterosexual desire but because it doesn't; that is to say in mimicking it, it shows the uncanny distance like the effect of ghosting, between desire (heterosexually represented as it is) and the representation' (cited in Modleski 1991: 158).[4]

Modleski notes that the contrast between the approach of Butler and de Lauretis, both lesbian feminists, both theorising the issue of gender identity, is an interesting one. In contrast to Butler's emphasis on gender as 'performativity', de Lauretis, far from deconstructing the concept of gender, is concerned to understand the means by which women become 'gendered' and in the process serve as 'sources of empowerment' for other women.

Martin is an advocate of Butler's performative account of gender, and of the separation of the analytically and politically distinct categories of sexuality and gender. As Martin contends the normalisation of sex and gender works to obliterate pluralities and, while not wanting to dismiss lesbian feminist positions such as Adrienne Rich's, she recognises the limitations of this position in terms of sexual desire and sexual essentialism. However, Martin does not subscribe fully to Butler's deconstruction of gender as 'a significant social marker' (1992: 117). There are also other criticisms of Butler's position from those like Benhabib (1992), who argue from a somewhat 'modernist' perspective that it involves a concept of identity without a subject. However, for Butler, the identification of a subject in any real sense limits the possibilities of diversity. For Butler (1990a: 121) the answer to the issue of both identity and representation is to 'proliferate and intensify the crisis and she calls for a chaotic multiplicity of representations'.

THE PROLIFERATION OF IDENTITIES AND REPRESENTATIONS

Biddy Martin, in her article 'Sexual Practice and Changing Lesbian Identities' (1992), considers the politics of 'authentic' and feminist lesbian identities, emphasising the complexity of same-gender eroticism. She argues that we need to denaturalise heterosexuality as part of destabilising the powerful homo–heterosexuality opposition. Martin seeks to contextualise lesbian and gay identity and politics within the right-wing backlash in the early 1990s in the US. As she notes,

> The effort to open up the public realm to a discussion and appreciation of sexual diversity and variation challenges the epistemological and political terms in which homosexuality and other 'perversions' have been closeted for the benefit of 'the ambient heterosexual population', or what Cindy Patton, in *Inventing Aids*, calls 'a repressive administrative state'.
>
> (Martin 1992: 95)

Drawing on a lecture by Susie Bright, editor of the lesbian porn magazine *On Our Backs*, Martin ponders how this provided an interesting opportunity 'to further consider changing lesbian identities'. Martin expresses the problematics of sexual identity framed by the rigid sexual categorisation of 'the right', but also from within the lesbian community itself, through its demand for stability and internal coherence and the 'uniqueness of lesbian identity'. She argues that not only has this obscured sexual differences, but it has also 'generated an active resistance to knowing what we fantasise, desire, do and think' (1992: 97).

A range of different positions including lesbian feminist, sex radicals and 'queer identities' represented debates around identity and sexuality in the 1970s and 1980s. The lesbian feminist position represents a model of identity where the categories of sex, gender and sexual identity are inextricably linked, with clearly defined 'sexualities'. Women's 'essential feminine identity' is cast in terms which clearly distinguish it from the masculine identity. The collective and unitary identity of the lesbian feminists led them to identify not with their sexuality but with their gender. This led them to reject any sense of identification with gay men or 'sex radicals'. Thus women's sexual, and specifically lesbian, identity is framed in opposition to masculine sexuality. The authenticity of women's and lesbian identity was seen as distorted and denigrated by pornography. The work of Adrienne Rich and Catherine MacKinnon convey slightly different views within this anti-pornography position.

Adrienne Rich (1980: 650) held that lesbianism is a 'profoundly female experience' which has a parallel in motherhood and is linked to clearly identified characteristics of 'womanhood';. This emphasis on the 'essential' characteristics of femininity – for example, 'emotional', 'gentle', 'nurturing' – can be seen as repressive of both sexuality and 'desire'. Biddy Martin (1992: 10) maintains that the 'collapse of sexuality and gender' appears to remove the importance of desire and replaces it with the desexualised concept of 'identification'. The collapsing of sexuality and gender in Rich (1980: 648) is significant for her objective, which is to erode any potential differences between lesbian women and feminist women by establishing a 'lesbian continuum' which includes 'women identified women' and heterosexual women. Modleski (1991: 151), drawing on what Bersani calls 'the pastoralizing' and 'domesticating' of sexuality, claims that Rich's analysis presents a desexualised model of lesbian identity. (Kemp 1994: 3)

MacKinnon (1989), while dealing with the issue of power and pleasure, defines these categories as the prerogative of men and used by men to sexualise hierarchy. MacKinnon (like Rich) collapses the categories of sex and gender, making little distinction between the 'sexuality of men' and 'male sexuality'. As Kemp (*ibid.*) notes for Mackinnon, sexuality is about the dominance of men over women as she indicates, 'dominance eroticized defines the imperatives of its masculinity, submission eroticized defines its femininity' (1989: 318). She thus elides sex, gender and sexuality and this is clearly extended to her analysis of pornography.

The essentialist model of identity as theorised by Rich and MacKinnon's position was clearly a problematic one for both lesbian sexuality and identity. However, the work of Rich, MacKinnon and others should not be totally dismissed. Martin (1992: 101) shows how Adrienne Rich's writing in the 1970s challenged traditional conceptions and definitions of lesbianism. Martin argues that the revisiting of a number of discourses around sexuality, and sexual identity, such as the 'renewed emphasis on sex, on alignments with gay men, and on sexual practices such as "butch-femme" roles does not represent a simple return from women identification to minoritizing models of gender inversion'. She indicates that the now much criticised work of lesbian and feminist writers of the 1970s has made it possible for lesbian writers and theorists to engage with a wide range of 'sexual, textual and theoretical explorations' as part of the increasingly contested nature of lesbian identity and politics.

It would be mistaken to convey a model of broad-based agreement within feminism or lesbian feminism in the 1970s. The model of 'sexual essentialism' was challenged by writers such as Gayle Rubin (1984). Rubin is representative of the lesbian sadomasochistic position and stressed the separation of sexuality from gender. She calls for the re-evaluation of radical lesbian identities and the construction of new queer identities, advocating the 'appreciation of erotic diversity and more open discussion of sexuality', and as Kemp (1994: 5) shows, Rubin claims that 'variation is a fundamental property of all life, from the simplest biological organisms to the most complex human formations' and she challenges the concept of 'sexual essentialism' with 'benign sexual variation' (1984: 303).

In stark contrast to lesbian feminists such as Rich and MacKinnon, who stress the repressive nature of 'compulsory heterosexuality' and female submission, Modleski (1991: 152) claims that 'the sex radicals tend to emphasize the individual "free choice" in matters of sexual behaviour, including such activities as lesbian sadomasochism, which many women denounce as acting out oppressive patriarchal relations of dominance and subordination'.

The position of sex radicals such as Rubin leads to a defence of most sexual practices (including paedophilia). As Modleski comments, this leads them to identify more with 'stigmatized erotic populations' than with radical feminists. Rubin (1984: 305) advocates s/m (sadomasochism) as legitimate practice and argues that s/m practice is based on consensual agreement. Modleski (1991: 157) claims that 'lesbian sadomasochism enacts a complex dynamic in which existing gender arrangements are simultaneously contested and preserved – preserved partly in order to *be* contested'. She claims that there is thus a one-sidedness in the debates around sadomasochism, whether these are from the position that understands 'lesbian sadomasochism as replicating existing gender inequalities' or from the position held by those, such as Parveen Adams who, Modleski maintains, hold that 'the lesbian sadomasochist has entirely succeeded in separating sexuality from gender' (*ibid.*). One of the difficulties for lesbian sadomasochists is that, while they criticise the strict binary conception of male power and oppression typical of the lesbian feminist position, they appear to ignore the issues of power and control intrinsic to their own position. The implications of s/m debates for postfeminism will be considered more fully below.

The deconstruction of the reified and prescriptive nature of lesbian sexuality as developed in these debates opened up feminism to a recognition and articulation of difference represented in a range of critiques emanating from within and outside feminism. For writers and theorists such as Susie Bright and Judith Butler, and for others working in the same area, lesbianism cannot be understood as an 'absolutely separate identity with separate foundations and internal homogeneity' (Martin 1992: 105). The implications of such a position would mean, as Martin notes, complicity 'with the repressive, even deathly operations of normalization and exclusion, even of lesbians' own fantasies, pleasures and practices' (*ibid.*).

What becomes clear is that Martin is challenging the same totalising tendencies, based on a seemingly fragile coherence, that she implies characterise lesbian identities, as women of colour and lesbian feminists did of second wave feminism. The crude binary opposition, a characteristic feature of the uncritical use of terms such as 'patriarchy' and 'oppression', is replaced in Martin's work by the critique of homo–heterosexual opposition. Drawing on Bright's lecture, Martin highlights how 'investments in sexual identity categories become stumbling blocks in current discussions of sexual practices and pleasures' (Martin 1992: 97). In this context, Martin argues, the construction of homosexuality and lesbianism as marginal, leaves the naturalising tendencies of heterosexuality unchallenged and contains 'difference in a third static category'.

Martin (1992: 98) goes on to note that the need for uniformity of identity and claims to authenticity based on 'separate foundations in a world outside of heterosexuality, operates as a defence against the continued marginalisation, denial and prohibition of women's love and desire for other women'. Martin asks whether this strategy is the best one 'to challenge heterosexism and misogyny, or an effective strategy to defend against annihilation' (*ibid.*). She claims that the constant effort needed to maintain the category intact clearly highlights both its instability as a 'unitary category, and its lack of fixed foundations' (*ibid.*: 98–99), and this emphasis on unity makes for difficulties in terms of understanding 'the complexity of social realities, fantasies, desires, pleasures and practices' (*ibid.*). Debates within lesbian feminism around pornography, sadomasochism, etc. have been late in 'surfacing', due to the attempt to maintain internal coherence. Martin cites Greta Christina's work on bisexuality, *Drawing the Line*, which

> [points] to important ways in which the politicization of bisexuality and appropriation of the term 'queer' opens up new alignments, or realignments across categories of gender and sexual identity. These new alignments co-exist and contend with other constructions of lesbian identity, including those that emphasise the gender specificity of lesbians' experiences and oppression and the differences between lesbians and gay men.

> (Martin 1992: 110)

As Martin shows, questions of the contested nature of lesbian identity have become more visible, as part of the more contested nature of identity within feminist theory and politics. Martin notes that heterosexist and anti-homophobic readings of homosexuality have, on one level, been characterised by contradictions, but 'contradictions that remain available for manipulation in the service of power/knowledge' (*ibid.*).

Debates around the proliferation and diversification of identities and representations can be seen to have coalesced around the area of gay/lesbian politics. In this context there has been an opening up of a series of new debates around the area of political theory and practice. Moynihan (1994: 17) contends that the 'gay movement and the more recently declared "queer nation" share political objectives around resistance to the marginalisation of homosexuality as excluded and demonic Other'. She claims that after that their political projects diverge, and the gay movement is primarily associated with 'the assertion of difference on the basis of rights assumptions: that people have the right to be accepted regardless of sexual preference' (*ibid.*). Moynihan distinguishes between this position and that of the 'queer nation', who she maintains 'reads that implicit desire to become part of the mainstream as a form of cooptation. In contrast, they identify as "queer" ie., with the transgressive, and as "nation" as separate and autonomous' (*ibid.*).

The issue of identity is a crucial part of the politics of both gays and the queer nation. Moynihan, drawing on the work of Cindy Patton (1993), shows how the emphasis on a 'rights based politics' implies a concept of identity and acts to constrain difference. The queer nation rejects these constraints and understands itself in terms of performativity. As Moynihan (1994: 17) notes, this 'location of identity in performance is an important move, both politically and theoretically for it entails a refusal to be individuals or subjects of liberal, Western homosexuality'. For the queer nation, as Moynihan shows, 'identity belongs to "nation" as a collective, formulated through collective alliance. It also moves the political away from acting subjects to the performative... to what people do rather than who they are' (*ibid.*).

This becomes important in the issue of gay and lesbian sexual practices such as 'drag' 'butch-femme roles' and sadomasochistic practices. Joan Nestle's work *A Restricted Country* (1987) highlights some of these issues. She considers butch-femme roles in the 1950s and sees them not as ' "phony heterosexual replicas", but "complex erotic statements" that signalled erotic choices' (Nestle 1987: 100, cited in Martin 1992: 107). Martin notes that in her account of butch-femme roles Nestle does not understand them 'as expressions of some underlying gender core or identification, or as imitations of heterosexual gender complementarities, but as the thoroughly performative construction of a public erotic culture in defiance of the injunction to be normal heterosexual women' (Martin 1992: 111). Nestle contextualises this view within a model which aims to 'restore queerness to lesbianism'. As Martin states,

> Nestle writes about choices and modes of survival, about erotic and social competencies, about concrete struggles and pleasures, and about political alignments among lesbians, gay men, sex workers (including prostitutes and porn writers) and other sexual minorities that have been effaced by the emphasis on lesbianism as gender identification.
>
> (Martin 1992: 109)

The rearticulation of the erotic into sexual politics around lesbianism can also be seen in the increasing focus on s/m practices among lesbians. Martin (1992: 99) notes that in her lecture at Cornell, Susie Bright claimed that 'lesbians' anxieties about penetration and its potentially heterosexual or male implications are now old news'. Lewis and Adler maintain that the shift in acceptance of s/m practices within lesbian relations has partly led to, and partly been the result of, changes in lesbian culture and identity (1994: 433–4). Kemp (1994: 7) shows that they maintain that s/m practices have reinscribed power into lesbian relationships and they provide a feminist critique of these relations and practices. Modleski (1991: 149) claims 'that powerlessness and masochism have different ideological valences for women than for gay men'. Drawing on the work of Kaja Silverman, Modleski, while recognising that Silverman 'overstates the case for the subversive potential of even male masochism, observes that since masochism is so close to the norm for women, it is unlikely to have the radical force it has for men' (*ibid*.).[5] She goes on to comment that there is a qualitative difference in lesbian s/m relations and heterosexual relationships, commenting that the former do not carry the 'weight of male physical and economic power behind them' (1991: 154).

While recognising the importance of the new 'militant' politics of sexuality, Martin maintains that some of the patterns of exclusion, which were apparent in feminism's 'exclusive focus on gender', are emerging in the new politics of sexuality. One of the casualties is 'gender' itself. Martin maintains that the new radical politics of sexuality is often 'formulated against feminism', rather than in relation to it. She argues that 'to define a politics of sexuality as if gender were no longer a social marker or as if feminist analysis and politics had not been critical to current developments seems willfully blind' (Martin 1992: 117). As Martin comments in referencing the work of Nestle, Lorde, Goldsby and Bright, to 'put desire back into history', as Nestle advocates, 'means refusing to abstract it out of the complex relations through which sexuality is constructed and enacted' (*ibid*.).[6]

Martin considers a range of erotic literature and maintains that both literature and pornography are potentially positive in their implications: first, in terms of proliferating the range of representations and practices available; second, in terms of understanding these representations and practices as challenging binary models of sex and sexuality; third, as a means of subverting dominant cultural forms and establishing new discourses, representations and identities.

POPULARISING REPRESENTATIONAL POLITICS: MADONNA AND THE TEXTUAL POLITICS OF DIFFERENCE

It is against this theoretical background and the demand for a proliferation of representations of sexualities that the emergence of Madonna as a 'gay icon' can be read. As Hann (1995: 5) comments, 'Madonna embodies one accessible point in popular culture where representations of homoerotica, bisexuality, s/m, sexual freedom etc reach the wider public'. The central element in Madonna's 'positioning' is her 'ambivalence'. On one level Madonna can be 'read' as the 'traditional erotic spectacle for male fantasies'; at another level 'her ambivalence is thought to create spaces for a lesbian/gay oppositional reading' (*ibid.*). In this context Madonna's representations can be seen as a 'site of contestation' for a range of identities and practices. As Hann contends, this is seen 'as positive by many gays and lesbians fighting for their identity and rights in the midst of a conservative backlash in the West', and reifies essentialist 'ideals of identity' (*ibid.*). It is the sense of ambiguity that belongs to the politics of the 'queer nation'.

Lisa Henderson's article 'Justify Our Love: Madonna and the Politics of Queer Sex' (1993) raises many of the issues around Madonna's status as a 'queer icon', including: the idea of cultural representations as 'sites of contestation'; Madonna as a signifier of sexual resistance; Madonna as the embodiment of 'strategies of proliferation and diversity'; and Madonna as encouraging the expression of lesbian lust and fantasies.

Schwichtenberg (1993: 6) claims that much of Madonna's later work (*Express Yourself, Vogue, Justify My Love*, the *Blond Ambition Tour* and *Truth or Dare*) deals explicitly with representations of sexuality that have particular resonance for gay and lesbian audiences. She argues that they 'recontextualise those elements, within gay history, fantasy and political struggle' (*ibid.*). Schwichtenberg claims that the Madonna paradigm provides the impetus to shift 'the margins to the centre' and thus 'it highlights the complexities of gay and lesbian politics and pleasures as they are lived, constructed and contested' (*ibid.*).

Henderson draws on the censorship controversy around *Justify My Love* as a centrepiece within which to examine a number of discourses that situate Madonna within the context of the sex and pornography debates. Henderson, arguing from an anti-antipornography position, 'affirms the pleasures of Madonna's gay-directed rearticulations and visibility; however she concedes that, unlike Madonna, gay and lesbian people represent an oppressed minority of whom sex-identification entails tremendous risk' (Schwichtenberg 1993: 6).

Henderson contextualises Madonna in relation to the gay community. She notes that Madonna, unlike Robert Mapplethorpe, has never identified herself as a gay artist. Madonna, also unlike Mapplethorpe, has 'circulated bits and pieces of lesbian and gay subculture in popular genres to popular audiences. Especially for many young gay people in the United States Madonna came closer than any other contemporary celebrity to being an above ground queer icon' (Henderson 1993: 108). Henderson considers Madonna's 'positioning' in relation to gay politics and the gay community and in relation to the essential ambiguity in much of Madonna's work. She notes that for many lesbians and gays the lyrics of *Justify My Love* (among others) articulate the gay community's 'refusal to await sanction, from [Jessie] Helms, or the church, to have sex and to forge their identities through the medium of sexual politics' (Henderson 1993: 122). However, as Henderson goes on to point out, the messages in Madonna's lyrics are double-edged, both liberating and conforming, and Madonna remains 'the essential female spectacle' appealing to heterosexual male fantasy. Henderson claims that 'Many of *Justify My Love*'s sexual gestures depend on dominance and subordination for their effect, overturning the standard of mutuality in much feminist and humanist rethinking of sexual relationships' (*ibid.*).

The issue of pornography is raised by Henderson (1993: 115) in the context of a broader discussion of sexual freedom, questions of legitimacy, and the political significance of pornography and sexual practices '(penetration, sadomasochism, lesbian butch/femme roles)'. She outlines the anti-pornography and the anti-antipornography[7] positions as follows: 'In characterising the antipornography stance, I have noted elsewhere that female subordination in patriarchy is assumed to be both the cause and effect of the female degradation in pornography (Henderson, 1991: 3)' (*ibid.*). Henderson indicates that for the anti-antipornography lobby the suppression of pornography is part of a broader definition of sexual expression, including lesbian sex. She claims that as with 'earlier songs and videos (e.g. *Open Your Heart, Express Yourself* and *Hanky Panky*), *Justify My Love* can thus be read from the anti-antipornography position, which separates power and coercion rather than power and sex' (Henderson 1993: 115–116).

Henderson also shows how *Justify My Love* is available for lesbian reading, now codified as 'oppositional reading'.[8] As she states, 'however gratifying even a glimpse of eroticism may be, lesbian viewers hardly need to await pop culture's nervous forays into homosexuality in order to produce their own erotic identifications' (*ibid.*). Henderson, in drawing on this range of cultural contexts, shows the lesbian and gay appeals of *Justify My Love*; however, as she indicates, 'the context is created through, not despite its contradictions and volatilities' (*ibid.*).

Henderson considers how Madonna, and in particular *Justify My Love*, is articulated by the gay press in terms of lesbian and gay politics and identity. Many writers in the gay press, she notes, go to the heart of Madonna's appeal to lesbian and gay audiences:

> These include her willingness to act as a political figure as well as a popular one and to recognise that such fraught domains as sex, religion, and family, are indeed political constructions, especially for lesbian and gay audiences. Like politics, the sex in Madonna's repertoire is conspicuously *there*.
>
> (Henderson 1993: 117)

Within the gay press Henderson (1993: 119) shows that Madonna becomes 'a queer icon whose very sensibilities are "gay" and whose ironies resonate with particular power in lesbian and gay imaginations'. Don Shewey (1991: 44), who interviewed Madonna for *The Advocate*, a national lesbian and gay magazine, claims that 'Hollywood doesn't really get Madonna. She doesn't fit any past models of Hollywood stardom' (cited in Henderson 1993: 119).

Another group of writers in mainstream publications, feminist writers, have also focused on where Madonna and *Justify My Love* fit into contemporary feminist politics. Their critiques reflect the more ambivalent relationships between Madonna and feminism around 'sexual pleasure and representation'. Henderson, however notes that gay writers give Madonna a more generous appraisal. Michael Musto[9] acclaims Madonna's 'artifice and multiplicity as a bridge between lesbian and gay fans':

> Her pride, flamboyance and glamour reach out to gay guys as much as her butch/femme dichotomy and her refusal to be victimised strike a cord in lesbians. As a result, Madonna – the great leveller, a breath mint and candymint – is the first superstar to appeal equally to both camps.
>
> (cited in Henderson 1994: 121)

Henderson notes in conclusion that, despite Madonna's appeal to the gay community, gay and lesbian writers remain sceptical about the double edge of Madonna's appeal. Henderson (1993: 123) argues that 'Madonna's penchant for metamorphosis beckons to us to recognise and toy with our own self-construction', but, as she points out, the 'universe' available to most people is a much more limited one. In addition Madonna's 'plasticity' carries with it many of 'the oppressive meanings of consumer society', as well as retaining the greater audience and greatest profit. As Henderson notes, 'It is difficult finally to acknowledge the divided self and engage the pleasure of masquerade while at the same time fighting a strikingly antagonistic, legal and social system' (ibid.). She maintains that

> Madonna cannot be seen to be the answer to significant social and political problems but in terms of articulating and problematising the issue of representation for the lesbian and gay community, she has captured the politically powerful ground of the popular.
>
> (Henderson 1993: 124)

Patton, like Henderson, contextualises the debate around lesbian and gay identity and politics and its representations within a political and theoretical context. Patton identifies the same critiques of the internal operations and theoretical framework developed within lesbian and gay politics as developed within feminism. She claims that by 'the end of the 1980s, much of the theoretical work in lesbian and gay studies de-essentialized the once apparently stable "homosexuality" ' (Patton 1993: 82). The process of self-reflection was further developed by poststructuralist and postmodernist debates. As Patton notes

> poststructuralist work appeared to undercut the claims of the most visible gay and lesbian rights organisations that had, for more than two decades, hitched their wagons to the rhetoric and practices of postwar US Minority politics ... lesbian and gay critics were caught between the desire for theoretical clarity and the hope for political and cultural freedom.
>
> (Patton 1993: 82)

Schwichtenberg (1993: 6) claims that, for Patton, Madonna's *Vogue* serves as a touchstone from which she develops a poststructuralist theory that explains the formation of subaltern memory in relation to gay politics, identity and representation. Schwichtenberg shows how 'Patton explores the tensions between Madonna's liberation body politic in *Vogue* and the live experience of voguing as a kind of "folk" dance that originated among black and Hispanic queens (a particular gay, subaltern formation)' (*ibid.*).

Patton's theory explores the possibilities of cultural representations around Madonna's video *Vogue*. As such it offers a number of openings for debates in the area of popular culture and gay cultural identity and representation. Patton's analysis positions debates around Madonna's appropriation and commodification of elements of gay, popular and cultural identity against debates which understand her position as establishing 'sites of resistance' in popular culture. In addition, Patton's (1993: 86) analysis of voguing establishes new ways of conceptualising gay identity because of its link to non-white gay culture. Finally Patton draws on the work of Michel Foucault[10] to develop the concept of 'lieux de memoire'.[11] As Schwichtenberg (1993: 6) comments, Patton gives a 'provocative and nuanced account of the political stakes invested in popular embodiments of subaltern memory'.

Patton outlines the theoretical debates that frame the analysis of black and gay culture in the 1980s and 1990s, and positions Madonna and Madonna's work in relation to these wider debates. She observes that

> where some critics have viewed *Vogue* and Madonna's work in general as parasitic on, variously, black and gay culture and even on feminism, I will suggest that she re-routes through mass culture quotidian critiques of dominant culture (in this case voguing's critique of whiteness and of gender) making them more available as places of resistance...
>
> (Patton 1993: 83)

Patton at one and the same time undertakes an ideological critique of 'voguing' as an art form, and a textual analysis of Madonna's music video *Vogue*. She goes on to say that

> what seemed vital about the diffusion of voguing through release of the video was the battle it sparked over control of the popular memory of homosexuality, for a new generation of queens. Young gay men and women were coming out through their imitation of voguing and Madonna. They were learning to remember their bodies in a critique of gender that is autonomous of gay liberation and feminism.
>
> (Patton 1993: 86)

Patton charts the 'popular history of homosexuality' in terms of homosexual subcultures which she maintains 'developed elaborate signifiers of membership' (1993: 87).[12] *Vogue* and voguing, she notes, is positioned at a site of intersection of race and gender in terms of its representation and history:

In both its intertextual components and in the hype about the video's subject – voguing – *Vogue* constitutes a site of memory reconstituting Afro-Latin and gay history due to: (1) its prominence and popularity, (2) its self-referential claims to being a kind of history and (3) its intertextual linkages.

(Patton 1993: 92)

Patton develops the theme of history in terms of the text itself, maintaining that *Vogue* can be 'read' in historical terms because of its use of black-and-white photography and 'retro' costuming. In addition, Patton claims that the listing of the names of iconic figures from gay male culture are both a traditional form of history and a traditional mode of establishing one's lineage and thus one's authority to speak. However,

textual analysis provides us with only a glimpse of the ways in which popular cultural artifacts connect with a wide range of memories and folk knowledges; textual analysis is mute at the moment that we try to understand how dancers operate in the lieux de memoire.

(Patton 1993: 97)

In conclusion, Patton (1993: 98) notes that, while the 'moves of voguing deconstruct gender and race', *Vogue* itself makes it problematic to understand why such a process of deconstruction is necessary. As she indicates, 'in constructing its historicity, *Vogue* alludes to a popular memory of repression that it then anxiously undercuts by atomizing and dequeening the performance of the dance' (*ibid.*).

The weight of both Henderson and Patton is on the capabilities of cultural readers. Kemp (1994: 11) comments that, while putting emphasis on the importance of diverse cultural readers, this in itself cannot provide a complete analysis of how meaning is created. A fuller explanation would also take account of the processes that create these readers, as they cannot be understood as completely free agents. As he claims, 'To suggest this would be to ignore the possibility that cultural products can exert any normalising influence, and that the intended meanings of culture might have effects upon audiences' (*ibid.*).

THE POLITICAL IMPORTANCE OF AMBIVALENCE IN THE SEXUAL POLITICS OF RACE AND ETHNICITY

The emphasis on cultural readings and the implication for the 'polyvocal quality' of texts is central for debates around both sexual and cultural representations and identities. Mercer (1992: 23) claims that the struggle for identity and agency always 'entails the negotiation of ambivalence'. Debates around the political importance of ambivalence have been particularly important in theories of sexual and cultural representation around race and ethnicity (Bhabha 1984, 1994; Mercer 1994) and post-colonialism. This last section of the chapter

204

considers some of these debates, particularly as they have coalesced around the work of Robert Mapplethorpe. It also considers the framing of debates within feminism around the issue of pornography and the implications of debates around sexuality and identity for feminist theorising.

PORNOGRAPHY AND CULTURAL SPACE: FRAMING THE DEBATES

If there ever was a quintessential postfeminist issue, pornography is it.
(Modleski 1991: 135)

Modleski's comment is an interesting one in reflecting on the debates around pornography that preoccupied feminism in the 1970s and early 1980s. It is insightful, if by it she means that the issue of pornography encapsulated debates around sexuality, identity and representation, which have (at least, in part) defined the postfeminist agenda.

Second wave feminist debates on pornography can broadly be divided into two 'camps': the 'anti-pornography' camp, a position held by writers such as Catherine MacKinnon, Andrea Dworkin and Adrienne Rich; and the 'anti-antipornography' camp which tended, at least in the 1970s and 1980s, to be associated with 'sex radical' Gayle Rubin. Perhaps more interesting than the assumptions behind these positions were the implications of these debates for issues of sexuality and identity.

The anti-pornography position which occupied a prominent space in second wave feminist debates around the issue of representation, became part of a feminist orthodoxy in the 1970s and early 1980s and is still represented in feminist debates in the 1990s.[13] The anti-pornography position is based on a model which sees pornography as an expression of male power and oppression within patriarchy. It is a model which understands pornography as a representation of oppressive fantasies, that objectifies women and leads to violence. Catherine MacKinnon (1987: 172) claims that pornography 'institutionalizes the sexuality of male supremacy, fusing the eroticization of dominance and submission with the social construction of male and female'. In fact both Andrea Dworkin (1981–1987) and Catherine MacKinnon (1987, 1989) understand pornography as itself a form of violence against women.

Elsewhere MacKinnon, in an article entitled 'Sexuality, Pornography and Method: Pleasure under Patriarchy' (1989), outlines a model of pornography which implies a direct link between pornography as a representational form and violence against women, particularly rape. Thus for MacKinnon pornography is directly linked to male sexuality and is 'inextricably linked to victimizing, hurting, exploiting' (MacKinnon 1989: 328, citing Dworkin). Other advocates of the anti-pornography position, such as Suzanne Kappeler (1986), claim that all representations of women within a framework of patriarchal commodity capitalism are degrading and violent and by definition pornographic.

The anti-pornography model can be characterised as follows: it assumes a unitary, undifferentiated concept of pornography, making no distinction between different forms; it is based on a simple binary model which understands all pornography as a reflection of male sexuality; it assumes a single transparent, undifferentiated meaning regardless of gender, race/ethnicity, sexuality or class; it assumes a simple cause/effect model which implies that pornography as representation will lead to violence; finally it makes assumptions about women's sexuality, seeing women as passive victims, while at the same time denying opportunities for resistance.

The anti-pornography movement is a pro-censorship movement, with groups like Women Against Pornography (WAP) demanding censorship legislation. One of the unintended consequences of such demands is the casting of women as 'victims' and the 'authorizing' of the State to intervene further in issues of sexuality and identity. In both the UK and the US such debates have been appropriated by 'the Moral Majority' to restrict and control a range of services and art forms seen as 'morally corrupting'. Examples include the work of Robert Mapplethorpe, lesbian feminist art, abortion information, etc.

The anti-antipornography position or the anti-censorship position is represented in the work of Vance (1984) and Burstyn, among others.[14] This position can be characterised in the following way: it makes a distinction between pornography and erotica; it attempts to counter the representations of women in pornography by working 'within'; it challenges the uniformity of sexual representations of women by advocating a proliferation of sexual representations; it establishes cultural spaces within the context of representational forms and identity. The proliferation of sexual representations of women has produced what Gayle Rubin (1984: 303) calls an 'appreciation of erotic diversity and more open discussion of sexuality'.

CULTURAL REPRESENTATIONS AND MARGINALISED IDENTITIES

Debates in the 1970s and 1980s surrounding the issue of pornography highlighted conflicts of interest between lesbian feminists and gay men. What was sometimes overlooked in the radical feminist (psychoanalytically driven) relationship between pornography and the 'male gaze' was the privileging of a particular racial group in these debates, namely white men. This model of the dominant gaze of the white gay man has been drawn on by a number of writers and theorists in their analysis of the representation of black sexual identity. Hooks, in her analysis of Isaac Julien's film *Looking for Langston*, contends that the 'gaze of the white [gay] male as it appears in the film is colonizing, it does not liberate' (1993: 69). She goes on to question whose or what 'desire is expressed when the only frontal nudity seen in the film appears as secondhand image – the pictures of naked black men taken by wealthy white photographer Robert

Mapplethorpe?' (*ibid.*). Hooks' position retains a strong commitment to a modernist representational model which privileges reality over fantasy and assumes a univocal reading of the text. As she argues, 'Though acknowledged, Mapplethorpe's vision is simply not compelling when it is displayed within a framework where the prevailing image is that of the black male body defining itself as subject, not as object' (*ibid.*).

The anti-pornography movement, typical of feminist initiatives of the 1970s, while problematic in its links with the 'New Right's' demands for censorship, was important in its politicisation of the issue of sexual representation. While the movement remained an essentially white middle-class movement, the issues of race and racism emerged in critiques from women of colour and Third World women. Mercer (1994: 131) notes that these same critiques did not emerge in the gay movement, and he comments that 'white gay men retain a deafening silence on race'. Mercer maintains, 'this is not surprising, given the relatively depoliticized culture of the mainstream gay "scene" ' (*ibid.*).

Mercer considers many of the issues that have characterised debates within feminism, particularly in the work of writers such as bell hooks. He notes that the issue of 'freedom of choice' within sexual libertarianism reflects racial privilege and is embodied in the white-dominated 'consumer-oriented character of the metropolitan gay subculture' (Mercer 1994: 133). He contends that this subculture in many ways is no different to mainstream culture in terms of the way it 'positions' and represents black men. Mercer claims that 'As black men we are implicated in the same landscape of stereotypes which is dominated and organized around the needs, demands and desires of white males' (*ibid.*). He shows that the same 'narrow repertoire of "types", is available to the black man including the supersexual stud and the sexual "savage" on the one hand, or the delicate, fragile and exotic "oriental" on the other' (*ibid.*).

The confinement of gay black men to these stereotypes is reflected in different representational forms, particularly gay pornography. Mercer raises the dilemma faced by gay black men in this context: 'what interests us are the contradictory experiences that the porno-photo-text implicates us in, as pornography is one of the few spaces in which erotic images of other black men are made available' (*ibid.*). He maintains that the repetition of the stereotypes of black men in gay pornographic forms 'betrays the circulation of "colonial fantasy" (Bhabha, 1984)' (*ibid.*).

MAPPLETHORPE AND THE IMPLICATIONS OF AMBIVALENCE

It is within this context that Mercer develops a critique of the work Robert Mapplethorpe. His images of *Black Males* (1983) 'as the stereotypical conventions of racial representation in pornography are appropriated and abstracted into the discourse of art photography' (Mercer 1994: 134). Mercer claims that Mapplethorpe's work can be seen as reinforcing and reiterating the terms of 'colonial fantasy' and thus constructing the black man as serving the racist fantasies of the 'white male gaze'. (Hann 1995: 8).

While recognising the importance of the concept of 'the colonial fantasy' as articulated by Bhabha and developed by Mercer in its implications for black identity, Mercer does move beyond a position which 'fixes' a conception of black identity within this model. He maintains that 'black readers may appropriate pleasures by reading against the grain, overturning signs of otherness into signifiers of identity. In seeing images of other black men coded as gay, there is an affirmation of our sexual identity' (Mercer 1994: 135–136).

Mercer's reconceptualisation of Mapplethorpe's work is in part a reassessment of Mapplethorpe's own position, as a member of the gay community and his subsequent death from AIDS, and partly Mercer's redefinition of the nature of the text. As Hann (1995: 9) comments, drawing on Mercer's (1992) earlier work, 'it does make a difference who is speaking because if Mapplethorpe can be recognised as a queer advocate then his representations can be empowering'. Hann goes on to note that one of the main reasons behind Mercer's rereading of Mapplethorpe's work is that his previous critique could be appropriated by the 'New Right'.

In addition, Mercer recognises the importance of 'ambivalence' in reading texts. As Hann (1995: 9) claims, Mercer 'privileges this as an important political position reminding us that the struggle for identity and agency always "entails the negotiation of ambivalence" (Mercer, 1992: 23)'. She notes that 'Mercer argues for the importance of any representations that expose what Spivak calls the "epistemic violence" of the denial of difference, the false stability of the centre' (*ibid.*). In this context Mercer suggests a textual model that advocates 'aesthetics of ambivalence' (Gaines 1992: 29).

FANTASY, PORNOGRAPHY AND REPRESENTATION

In an article entitled 'The Force of Fantasy: Feminism, Mapplethorpe, and Discursive Excess', Judith Butler (1990b) considers the issue of pornography, and in particular the work of Robert Mapplethorpe, against the backdrop of feminist debates around pornography, representation and fantasy. She contends that within the anti-pornography position there is an 'implicit theory' which 'relies upon a representational realism that conflates the signified of fantasy with its (impossible) referent' (Butler 1990b: 105). She claims that it is this theory of fantasy which informs those branches of feminism which call for censorship against pornography and which 'appears to inform New Right efforts to prohibit federal funding of artists like Robert Mapplethorpe' (*ibid.*).

Butler contends that the effort to limit 'representations of homoeroticism' in the federally funded art world, 'in an effort to censor the phantasmatic', inevitably leads to its production. Drawing on the work of Jacqueline Rose, Butler (1990b: 108) shows how 'the phantasmatic is also precisely that which haunts and contests the borders which circumscribe the construction of stable identities'. Fantasy offers the possibility of the fragmentation or proliferation of identifications which challenges the very 'locatability of identity'.

It is within this context that Butler challenges the implications for both representations and identity of the anti-pornography position. As she contends,

> the effort to impute a causal or temporal relation between the phantasmatic and the real raises a set of problems... [The] view that fantasy motivates action rules out the possibility that fantasy is the very scene which *suspends* action and which, in its suspension, provides for a critical investigation of what it is that constitutes action.
>
> (Butler 1990b: 113)

The anti-pornography position, in its assumptions about cause and effect, offers no possibilities for alternative interpretations because it is based on the claim that the text permits a single interpretation and understands the 'construction of the pornographic text as a site of univocal meaning' (*ibid.*). Butler notes that it is this 'postulation of a single identificatory access' to representation that carries with it a stabilisation of gender identity. She claims that 'the political task is to promote a proliferation of representations, sites of discursive production, which might then contest the authoritative production produced by the prohibitive law' (1990b: 119).

CONCLUSION

Postfeminist and postmodernist debates, while not necessarily advocating 'the death of the subject', recognise that the epistemological framing of the subject as an object of knowledge increases as differentiation proliferates division. These unitary categories which characterised 'identity politics' have been increasingly challenged as identity becomes more fluid and fragmented, undermined by contrasts such as that between gay and straight, female and male, and black and white. This increasing fluidity has impacted on both the range and meaning given to representations. The proliferation of representations emerging from cultural forms are partly the result of popular cultural forms emerging as 'sites of resistance'. As Dyer (1993: 2) notes, cultural forms can no longer be seen to have a single determinate meaning and are understood in different ways by different cultural and subcultural groups. However, he recognises that 'the complexity of viewing/reading practices in relation to representation' does not imply that there is 'equality and freedom in the regime of representation'. As Butler (1990b: 121) contends, it is the very proliferation and deregulation of representations as part of a process towards the production of a chaotic multiplicity of representations which will undermine the restriction of the terms of political identity.

CONCLUSION

Postfeminism as a frame of reference may become accepted in time as an obvious successor to second wave feminism, representing conceptual and theoretical diversity and encapsulating a range of diverse political and philosophical movement for change. Postfeminism, along with postmodernism and post-colonialism, has been important in establishing a dynamic and vigorous area of intellectual debate, shaping the issues and intellectual climate that has characterised the move from modernity to postmodernity in the contemporary world. These anti-foundationalist movements for change have challenged academic culture's modernist discourses and led to a paradigm shift away from the liberal humanist models of the Western Enlightenment which have framed academic culture's discourses.

Despite feminism's modernist foundations, second wave feminism's interventions certainly posed challenges to dominant academic discourses, identifying a number of 'sites of struggle' and opening up a number of 'sites of resistance' for feminist discourses. However, second wave feminism was limited by its own political agenda and modernist inclinations.

Postfeminism has emerged as a result of critiques from within and outside feminism. It has encouraged an intellectually dynamic forum for the articulation of contested theoretical debates emerging from within feminist theorising, as well as from feminism's intersection with a number of critical philosophical and political movements including postmodernism and post-colonialism.

What can be seen as the unsettling of the intellectual discipline of feminism by theoretical challenges from its 'margins' or, from subaltern discourses, has forced feminism to be more responsive to a range of political and ethical challenges. As Yeatman contends, 'feminist theory has matured to the point where it is able to subject its own premises to an ironical skeptical and critical mode of analysis' (1994: 49).

The 'paradigm shift' from feminism to postfeminism can be seen in a number of different directions: first, in the challenges posed by postfeminism to feminism's epistemological foundationalism; second, in postfeminism's shift away from specific disciplinary boundaries; and third, in postfeminism's refusal to be limited by representational constraints. All these dimensions of

210

postfeminism have been investigated in the chapters of this text. It is Teresa de Lauretis who best captures the shift from feminism to postfeminism:

> A feminist theory begins when the feminist critique of ideologies becomes conscious of itself and turns to question its own body of writing and critical interpretations, its basic assumptions of terms and the practices which they enable and from which they emerge. This is not merely an expansion or a reconfiguration of boundaries, but a qualitative shift in political and historical consciousness. This shift implies, in my opinion, a dis-placement and a self-displacement: leaving or giving up a place that is safe, that is 'home' (physically, emotionally, linguistically and epistemologically) for another place that is unknown and risky, that is not only emotionally but conceptually other, a place of discourse from which speaking and thinking are at best tentative, uncertain and unguaranteed. But the leaving is not a choice: one could not live there in the first place.
>
> (de Lauretis 1988: 138–139)

NOTES

INTRODUCTION

1 *Second wave feminism*: a term coined by Marsha Weinman Lear to refer to the formation of women's liberation groups in America, Britain and Germany in the late 1960s. The term 'second wave' implies that 'first wave' feminism ended in the 1920s.

   Disillusionment with the politics of Civil Rights, the anti-war movement and Students for a Democratic Society led American women to form their own consciousness-raising groups. This activity is encapsulated in the slogan 'the personal is political'. Sara Evans claims that, in its trajectory from Civil Rights to Women's Liberation, the second wave recapitulated the history of first wave feminism in the sense that a struggle for racial equality was midwife to both feminisms.

   The main change in second wave feminist theory since 1970 has been the move from minimising differences between men and women to celebrating a woman-centred perspective. Second wave feminism currently is committed to radically extending egalitarianism based on a sophisticated understanding of the oppressiveness of imposed gender division. Second wave feminism is a radical transformation project and aims to create a feminised world.

   (Adapted from Humm 1989: 198)

1 CONSENSUS AND CONFLICT IN SECOND WAVE FEMINISM: ISSUES OF DIVERSITY AND DIFFERENCE IN FEMINIST THEORISING

1 Fraser and Nicholson (1990: 22) draw on Lyotard's identification of modernism with 'grand narratives' and they maintain:

   The postmodern condition is one in which 'grand narratives' of legitimisation are no longer credible. By 'grand narratives' he [Lyotard] means in the first instance, overarching philosophies of history like the Enlightenment story of the gradual but steady process of reason and freedom . . . The story guarantees that some sciences and some politics have the right pragmatics and, so are the *right* practices.

2 Fraser and Nicholson (1990) maintain that all the general theories of the sexual division of labour are modernist, and that, as grand narratives, they represent specific historical and cultural constructions.

3 Underlying the text is an exploration of the relationship between theorising and feminism. It is a critique of the theoretical grounding and paradigmatic conventions of modernist feminism, and is essentially a critique of feminism's emphasis on causality and the idea that cause can be found only at the level of social structure.
4 The specificity of the female body, particularly its connection to reproduction, is central in these arguments.
5 Socialist feminists locate subjectivity and consciousness (following Marx) not in a biological or philosophical essence but in human activity, primarily as it is organised under capitalism.

4 PSYCHOANALYTIC THEORY, SEMIOLOGY AND POSTFEMINISM

1 Grosz (1990a) references Irigaray (1984, 1985a, 1985b).
2 Kaplan (1983) explains the operation of the 'dominating power of the male gaze' in *Camille* (1936), *Blonde Venues* (1932), *Lady from Shanghai* (1946) and *Looking for Mr Goodbar* (1977).
3 For a more detailed analysis, see Jane Feuer (1980) '*Daughter Rite*: Living with Our Pain and Our Love', *Jump Cut* 23; R.B. Rich and Linda Williams (1981); and Annette Kuhn (1982).
4 See Sandy Flitterman and Jacquelyn Suter (1989) 'Textual Riddles: Woman as Enigma or Site of Social Meanings? An Interview with Laura Mulvey', *Discourse* 1, pp. 86–127.
5 See Jane Weinstock (1980) 'She Who Laughs First, Laughs Last', *Camera Obscura* 5 (Spring), pp. 100–110.
6 See Constance Penley (1977) 'The Avant-Garde and Its Imaginary', *Camera Obscura* 2 (Fall), pp. 3–33; see also Kaja Silverman (1983) *The Subject of Semiotics* New York: Oxford University Press.

5 THE 'LANDSCAPE OF POSTFEMINISM': THE INTERSECTION OF FEMINISM, POSTMODERNISM AND POST-COLONIALISM

1 I am grateful to Angela McRobbie (1994) for this concept.
2 Michèle Montrelay (1970) 'Recherches sur la fémininité', *Critique* 278 (July), trans. Parveen Adams as 'Inquiry into Femininity', *M/F* 1 (1978), reprinted in *Semiotext(e)* 10 (1981), p. 232.
3 Nicholson (1992) highlights parallels between Frederic Jameson's (1984) position and her own in establishing a continuity between modernism and postmodernism.
4 Benhabib cites Judith Butler's (1990a) *Gender Trouble: Feminism and the Subversion of Identity* for a provocative application of a Foucauldian framework for gender analysis.
5 See Stuart Hall (1992b) for an analysis of 'new ethnicities'.
6 See Gayatri Chakravorty Spivak (1992).

7 POSTFEMINISM AND POPULAR CULTURE: REPRESENTATIONS AND RESISTANCE

1 For Kristeva's position on the postmodern see 'Postmodernism?' *Bucknell Review*, 25:11 (1980) pp. 136–41.

2　*Huyssen references a paper given by Stuart Hall at the conference on mass culture at the Centre for Twentieth Century Studies, Spring 1984.*

3　Huyssen notes that the Frankfurt School, characterised by the work of Theodor Adorno and Max Horkheimer, emphasised features of mass culture such as streamlining technological reproduction and administration, which he claims popular psychology would ascribe to the realm of masculinity rather than femininity. For a more detailed exposition on the work of the Frankfurt School, see Theodor W. Adorno (1975) 'Culture Industry Reconsidered', *New German Critique* 6 (Fall) 12; Max Horkheimer and Theodor W. Adorno (1982) *Dialectic of Enlightenment*, New York: Continuum.

4　See Teresa de Lauretis (1985), 'The Violence of Rhetoric: Considerations on Representation and Gender', *Semiotica* (Spring), special issue on the rhetoric of violence.

5　See Pierre Bourdieu (1984) *Distinction*, London/New York: Routledge & Kegan Paul.

6　See J. McGuigan (1992) *Cultural Populism*, London: Routledge.

7　See Mikhail Bakhtin (1968). Kaplan (1993:149) draws on Bakhtin's theory of the mask and the distinctions he makes in this regard:

> He noted that the mask in romanticism was terrifying because it deceived, it hid the 'real' subject, it distorted and concealed identity; but the mask in ancient folklore represented play, the recognition of the changeability and nonfixity of the subject. Although Bakhtin carefully locates these differing conceptions of the mask in history, I reintroduce them for a Foucauldian genealogy of the mask – the mask as representing what history, in fact, shows – namely, that there is no stable identity (Foucault 1979)'.

8　See Michel Foucault (1981a) *The History of Sexuality*, Harmondsworth: Penguin. Kaplan cites the 1979 edition of the same book.

9　Mandzuik (1993: 173–174) notes that

> This text was part of an advertising campaign featured on MTV during the 1990 election season. The various ads featured rock stars in fifteen-second messages that protested censorship and advocated freedom of speech. The series ostensibly was intended to convince the music television audience, presumably young adults, to vote in the current election. All of the advertisements ended with a still shot displaying 'Rock the Vote' slogan, which itself was shadowed by a large check mark signifying the act of checking a choice on a ballot. Madonna's particular text, however, contained a curious mixture of messages, crossing such interventionist politics with a diverse set of articulations of 'Americanness'.

10　See Kevin Sessums (1990) 'White Heat', *Vanity Fair* (April), p. 208.

11　The broader debate around postfeminism, gay and lesbian and representational politics and 'cultural space' is dealt with more fully at a later point in this text (see Chapter 9). However, the issue of gay cultural representations as they have been articulated around Madonna as a 'gay cultural icon' are significant here for the debates around postfeminism and subcultural identities.

8　POSTFEMINIST VARIATIONS WITHIN MEDIA AND FILM THEORY

1　E. Ann Kaplan, in her book *Women and Film* (1983), charts the realist debate in feminist film. She observes that the documentary film has been the traditional exemplar of the realist film. Kaplan notes that, of the few women who made films in Hollywood, by far the largest number of films by American women have taken the cinéma vérité documentary form. She also notes that the documentary form of realist film has provoked much theoretical debate. However, Kaplan fails to make a clear conceptual distinction between feminist film and films by and about women. The attack upon realism arose out of the perception that realist women's documentaries in the conventional forms did not work strategically. Kaplan argues that those who had provided a critique of convential realism such as Johnston, and others such as Mulvey and Wollen in Britain, developed a new feminist avant-garde, which, while drawing on earlier avant-garde traditions (e.g. Russian formalism, surrealism, Brecht) and 'counter-cinema' directors (e.g. Godard), 'was new in its combination of semiology, structuralism, Marxism and psychoanalysis' (Kaplan 1983: 138).

2 In psychoanalytic theory, 'narcissism' means 'extreme love of self'. *Primary narcissism*, in which sexual energy is directed toward the self, is characteristic of the pre-genital stages of psychosexual development, whereas *secondary narcissism* refers to feelings of pride experienced when the ego identifies with the ideas of the supergo. Mulvey draws on the Lacanian conception of narcissism where the process of identification parallels the 'mirror stage' in Lacanian theory. In 'On Narcissism', *Telos* 44 (Summer 1980), sociologist Stanley Aronowitz argues that the sense of autonomy gained from a self-affirmative narcissism is necessary for sexual and political liberation. This radical departure from the negative attitude towards narcissism evidenced by Freud is also found in French psychoanalyst Sarah Kofman's article (1980) 'The Narcissistic Woman: Freud and Firard', *Diacritics* 10 (Byars 1994: 107, n.13).

3 See the summary of Mulvey's analysis of voyeurism in 'Is the Gaze Male?', in Kaplan (1983).

4 In 'Instincts and Their Vicissitudes', one of Freud's later works, he further developed his theory of scopophilia where the pleasure of the look is transferred to others.

5 See Mulvey (1993) for a recent analysis of fetishism.

6 See Julia LeSage (1978) 'Women and Film: A Discussion of Feminist Aesthetics', in *New German Critique* 13.

7 Kaplan draws on the work of Judith Mayne (1981) 'The Woman at the Keyhole: Women's Cinema and Feminist Criticism', *New German Critique* 23, pp. 27–43; Arbuthnot and Seneca (1982); Julia Kristeva (1980) 'Woman Can Never Be Defined', in Elaine Marks and Isabelle de Courtivron (eds) *New French Feminisms*, Sussex: Harvester Press; and Barry and Flitterman (1980: 37).

8 Gaines' essay originally appeared in *Screen* 29(4) (Autumn 1988), pp. 12–27. It is this version of the essay which was critiqued by Modleski.

9 These debates can be traced through the work of Henry Louis Gates (ed.) (1984) *Black Literature and Literary Theory*, New York: Methuen, and (1991) 'Critical Fanonism', *Critical Inquiry* 17 (Spring); Homi Bhabha (1987), 'What Does the Black Man Want?' *New Formations* 1 (Spring).

10 See, for instance, Patricia Hill Collins (1991) *Black Feminist Thought: Knowledge, Consciousness and the Politics of Empowerment*, New York: Unwin Hyman; Cheryl A. Wall (ed.) (1989) *Changing Our Own Words: Essays on Criticism, Theory and Writing by Black Women*, New Brunswick, NJ: Rutgers University Press; Michele Wallace (1990) *Invisibility Blues: From Pop to Theory*, New York: Verso; Able Sharon Lark (1988) 'Black Women Filmmakers Defining Ourselves: Feminism in Our Own Voice'; and Jacqueline Bobo (1988) '*The Color Purple*: Black Women as Cultural Readers', both in Pribram (1988); Karen Alexander (1991), 'Fatal Beauties: Black Women in Hollywood', in Christine Gledhill (ed.) *Stardom: Industry of Desire*, New York: Routledge.

11 See Monique Wittig (1980) 'The Straight Mind', *Feminist Issues* (Summer), pp. 107–111.

12 See Arbuthnot and Seneca (1982). *Gentlemen Prefer Blondes* is a Hollywood film, made in 1953 and starring Marilyn Monroe and Jane Russell as showgirls.

13 *Desperately Seeking Susan* (1984) stars Madonna in the lead role and Rosanna Arquette as the 'suburban housewife'.

14 See Eco (1969).

15 Star uses Eco's concept of 'chatter' as a mechanism, code or communication which acts as a 'fill-in', maintaining a bond or link until another topic or issue arises which can act to reinforce the process of 'male-bonding'. Star makes the point that under some circumstances sport chatter 'is as much capable of engaging the mechanisms of identification and acting out as is the game' (Star 1988: 203, n.18). She argues that Eco's 'chatter' resembles Heidegger's 'idle talk' and the semiologists use of 'phatic speech':

> Sport chatter is an example of how we are spoken by pre-existing language. Principally it involves the discussion of sport as something seen... Chatter about sport may take place 'outside' the media, in the media or about the media, in different combinations.
>
> (Star 1988: 196)

16 Some feminist theorists (Modleski 1984; Ang 1985; Root 1986) have suggested that 'the succession of deferred resolutions and climaxes in soaps is connected with the endless broken and often frustrating nature of women's work in the home, raising children and caring for other dependents' (Star 1988: 194). This is now a highly contested area of feminist theorising, with many feminist 'media' theorists challenging the idea of 'soaps as female'.

17 Star (1992) went on to undertake this research herself. The work appears as 'Undying Love, Resisting Pleasures: Women Watch Telerugby' in R. du Plessis (ed.) (1992) *Feminist Voices*, Auckland: Oxford University Press.

18 See Baehr and Dyer (1987) and Holland (1987).

19 For 'the Mildred Pierce model', see E. Ann Kaplan (1983); for 'the Sister George model', Vitto Russo (1981) *The Celluloid Closet: Homosexuality in the Movies*, New York: Harper & Row; for 'the Cagney and Lacey model', see Julie d'Acci (1987).

20 For example, see G. Tuchman, A.K. Daniels and J. Benet (eds) (1978) *Hearth and Home*, New York: Oxford University Press.

21 Star's work has been centrally concerned with this area, and she maintained that, 'despite protestations to the contrary, men in rugby e.g. players, journalists and followers have been appreciating each other's body in a thoroughgoing aesthetic and erotic manner for many years' (Star 1992: 133). This point is more fully developed in Star (1991) 'Man-on-Man: Denying Homoeroticism in Telerugby', a paper delivered at the Australian Teachers of Media Conference, Melbourne.

9 SEXUALITY, PORNOGRAPHY AND CULTURAL SPACE

1 Foucault maintains: 'there is a plurality of resistances, each of them a special case: resistances that are possible, necessary, improbable; others that are spontaneous, savage, solitary, concerted, rampant, or violent; still others that are quick to compromise, interested or sacrificial; by definition, they can only exist in the strategies field of power relations' (Bailey cites the 1978 version of Foucault's *The History of Sexuality*, vol. 1 *An Introduction*, New York: Vintage Books, page 96).

2 Butler (1990a:137) contends that 'As much as drag creates a unified picture of "woman", it also reveals the distinctness of those aspects of gender experience which are falsely naturalized as a unity through the regulatory fiction of heterosexual coherence.'

3 Cindy Patton describes Jenny Livingston's *Paris is Burning* (1991) as follows:

> ...a Wisemanesque documentary about ball culture,...one of the first mass-distributed, sympathetic sets of images of black gay men. However, it avoids the crucial battle over interpretation of voguing by constituting itself as a dictionary of terms and insisting that voguing is about imitating rather than deconstructing gender.
>
> (Patton 1993: 101)

4 See Teresa de Lauretis (1989) 'The Essence of the Triangle or, Taking the Risk of Essentialism Seriously: Feminist Theory in Italy, the US, and Britain', *differences* 1(2) (Summer), pp. 22–27.

5 See Kaja Silverman (1988), 'Masochism and Male Subjectivity', *Camera Obscura* 17, p. 36.

6 See Nestle (1987); Jackie Goldsby (1990) 'What it Means to be Coloured Me', *Outlook* 9; Audre Lorde (1982) *Zami: A New Spelling of My Name*, Trumansberg, NY: The Crossing Press; and Katie King (1988) 'Audre Lorde's Lacquered Layerings: The Lesbian Bar as a Site of Literacy Production', *Cultural Studies*, 2, pp. 321–342.

7 The anti-pornography and anti-antipornography literature is vast but the following references are provided by Henderson. For an introduction to the first position see Dworkin (1981), Lederer (1980), Cole (1989), and Leidholdt and Raymond (1990). On the second position, see Vance (1984), V. Burstyn (ed.) (1987) *Women Against Censorship*, Vancouver: Douglas McIntyre, and *Feminist Review* (1990).

8 Oppositional reading is similar to Star's (1992) concept of 'resisting pleasures' or 'reading against the grain'. Oppositional readings, as Henderson notes (1993: 125, n. 7), can acquire political force but she notes they may also constitute a valuable form of personal resistance even in the absence of a movement.

9 See Michael Musto (1991) 'Immaculate Connection', *Outweek*, 20 March, pp. 35–42, 62. Henderson's quote comes from page 36.

10 See M. Foucault (1989) 'Film and Popular Memory', in Sylvère Lotringer (ed.) *Foucault Live*, Foreign Agent Series, New York: Semiotext(e).

11 Patton (1993: 90) claims that Foucault (1989; see previous note) 'is also interested in the relation between popular memory, the administration of history, and local resistance. For Foucault, mass media and fragmentation of traditional social units also constitute a new formation; the critical issue is the ways in which popular culture functions as a site of struggle for the control of popular memory'.

12 Patton cites the work of Michel Foucault on *The History of Sexuality* as establishing a major current of gay and lesbian history which considers homosexuality to be of recent genesis: 'Its emergence is situated variously by different scholars between the seventeenth and nineteenth centuries. Against this current is a...group of scholars who view homosexuality as pancultural and transhistorical and only marginally different in its forms' (Patton 1993: 100, n. 7).

13 See D. Russell (ed.) (1993) *Making Violence Sexy: Feminist Views on Pornography*, Buckingham: Open University Press, and Smith (1993).

14 See note 7 of this chapter.

BIBLIOGRAPHY

Abbott, P. and Wallace, C. (1990) *An Introduction to Sociology: Feminist Perspectives*, London/ New York: Routledge.

Acker, J. (1989) 'Making Gender Visible', in R. Wallace (ed.) *Feminism and Sociology*, London: Sage.

Adam, I. and Tiffin, H. (1990) *Past the Last Post: Theorising Post-Colonialisms and Post-Modernism*, Calgary: University of Calgary Press.

Alcoff, L. (1988) 'Cultural Feminism Versus Post-Structuralism: The Identity Crisis in Feminist Theory', *Signs* 13(3), pp. 405–436.

Alice, L. (1995) 'What is Postfeminism? or, Having it Both Ways', in L. Alice (ed.) *Feminism, Postmodernism, Postfeminism: Conference Proceedings*, Massey University, New Zealand, pp. 7–35.

Ang, I. (1983) 'Mannen ob zicht: Marges van het vrouwelijk voyeurisme' *Tijdschrift voor Vrouwenstudies (Journal of Women's Studies)* 4(3), pp. 418–435.

——(1985) *Watching 'Dallas': Soap Opera and the Melodramatic Imagination*, London: Methuen.

Arbuthnot, L. and Seneca, G. (1982) '"Pre-text and Text" in *Gentlemen Prefer Blondes'*, *Film Reader* 5, reprinted in P. Erens (ed.) (1990) *Issues in Feminist Film Criticism*, Bloomington: Indiana University Press.

Ashcroft, B., Griffiths, G. and Tiffin, H. (eds) (1995) *The Post-Colonial Studies Reader*, London: Routledge.

Baehr, H. and Dyer, G. (eds) (1987) *Boxed in: Women and Television*, London: Pandora.

Bakhtin, M. (1968) *Rabelais and His World*, Cambridge, MA: MIT Press.

Bailey, M.E. (1993) 'Foucauldian Feminism: Contesting Bodies, Sexuality and Identity', in C. Ramazanoglu (ed.) *Up Against Foucault: Explorations of Some Tensions Between Foucault and Feminism*, London/New York: Routledge.

Barrett, M. (1987) 'The Concept of Difference', *Feminist Review* 26 (Summer), pp. 29–42.

——(1988) Comment on a Paper by Christine Delphy, in C. Nelson and L. Grossberg (eds) *Marxism and the Interpretation of Culture*, Chicago: University of Illinois Press.

——(1990) 'Feminism's Turn to Culture', *Woman: A Cultural Review* 1, pp. 22–24.

——(1991) *The Politics of Truth: From Marx to Foucault*, Stanford: Stanford University Press.

——(1992) 'Words and Things: Materialism and Method in Contemporary Feminist Analysis', in M. Barrett and A. Phillips (eds) *Destabilizing Theory: Contemporary Feminist Debates*, Cambridge: Polity Press.

Barrett, M. and Coward, R. (1982) Letter and Discussion, *M/F* 7.

Barrett, M. and McIntosh, M. (1985) 'Ethnocentrism and Socialist Feminist Theory', *Feminist Review* 20, pp. 23–47.

Barrett, M. and Phillips, A. (eds) (1992) *Destabilizing Theory: Contemporary Feminist Debates*, Cambridge: Polity Press.

Barry, J. and Flitterman, S. (1980) 'Textual Strategies: The Politics of Art Making', *Screen* 21(2).

Bartky, S.L. (1988) 'Foucault, Femininity and the Modernisation of Patriarchal Power', in I. Diamond and L. Quinby (eds) *Feminism and Foucault: Reflections on Resistance*, Boston: Northeastern University Press.

—— (1990) *Femininity and Domination: Studies in the Phenomenology of Oppression*, London: Routledge.

Baudrillard, J. (1983) *In the Shadow of the Silent Majorities or The End of the Social and Other Essays*, trans. Paul Foss, Paul Patton and John Johnston, New York: Semiotext(e).

—— (1988) *Jean Baudrillard: Selected Writings*, ed. M. Poster, Stanford: Stanford University Press.

—— (1990) *Seduction*, London: Macmillan (first published in France by Editions Galilée [1979]).

Bell, A. and McLennan, G. (eds) (1995) 'National Identities: From the General to the Pacific', *Sites* 30, pp. 1–8.

Belsey, C. and Moore, J. (eds) (1989) *The Feminist Reader – Essays in Gender and the Politics of Literary Criticism*, London: Macmillan.

Benhabib, S. (1986) *Critique, Norm and Utopia*, New York: Columbia University Press.

—— (1992) *Situating the Self: Gender, Community and Postmodernism in Contemporary Ethics*, Cambridge: Polity Press.

—— (1994) 'Feminism and The Question of Postmodernism', in *The Polity Reader in Gender Studies*, Cambridge: Polity Press.

Benhabib, S. and Cornell, D. (eds) (1987) *Feminism as Critique*, Oxford: Blackwell/ Minneapolis: University of Minnesota Press.

Bennett, T. (1980) 'Popular Culture: A "Teaching Object" ', *Screen Education* 34, pp. 17–29.

—— (1981a) 'Popular Culture', *Themes and Issues (1)*, Milton Keynes: Open University Press.

—— (1981b) 'Popular Culture', *Themes and Issues (2)*, Milton Keynes: Open University Press.

—— (1986) 'Introduction: Popular Culture and "The Turn to Gramsci" ', in T. Bennett, C. Mercer and J. Woollacott (eds) *Popular Culture and Social Relations*, Milton Keynes: Open University Press.

Best, S. and Kellner, D. (1991) *Postmodern Theory: Critical Interrogations*, London: Macmillan.

Bhabha, H. (1984) 'Of Mimicry and Man: Ambivalence of Colonial Discourse', *October* 28 (Spring), pp. 125–133.

—— (1985) 'Signs Taken for Wonders: Questions of Ambivalence and Authority Under a Tree Outside Delhi, May 1817', in F. Barker (ed.) *Europe and Its Others*, vol. 1, *Proceedings of the Essex Conference on the Sociology of Literature*, July 1984, Colchester: University of Essex; also *Critical Inquiry* 12, pp. 144–165.

—— (1986) 'The Other Question: Difference, Discrimination and the Discourse of Colonialism', in F. Barker, P. Hulme, M. Inversen and D. Loxley (eds) *Literature, Politics and Theory: Papers from the Essex Conference, 1976–84*, London: Methuen.

—— (1988) 'The Commitment to Theory', *New Formations* 5, pp. 5–23.

—— (ed.) (1990a) *Nation and Narration*, London: Routledge.

—— (1990b) 'DissemiNation: Time, Narrative and the Margins of the Modern Nation', in H. Bhabha (ed.) *Nation and Narration*, London: Routledge.

—— (1994) *The Location of Culture*, London: Routledge.

Bobo, J. (1988) '*The Color Purple*: Black Women as Cultural Readers', in E.D. Pribram (ed.) *Female Spectators: Looking at Film and Television*, London: Verso.

Bordo, S. (1990) 'Postmodernism and Gender Scepticism', in L. Nicholson (ed.) *Feminism/ Postmodernism*, New York/London: Routledge.

—— (1993a) 'Feminism, Foucault and the Politics of the Body', in C. Ramazanoglu (ed.)

219

Up Against Foucault: Explorations of Some Tensions Between Foucault and Feminism, London/ New York: Routledge.

——(1993b) '"Material Girl": The Effacements of Postmodern Culture', in C. Schwichtenberg (ed.) *The Madonna Connection*, NSW: Allen & Unwin.

Braidotti, R. (1991) *Patterns of Dissonance: A Study of Women in Contemporary Philosophy*, Cambridge: Polity Press.

——(1992) 'On the Feminist Female Subject of From She-Self to She-Other', in G. Bock and S. James (eds) *Beyond Equality and Difference: Citizenship, Feminist Politics and Female Subjectivity*, London: Routledge.

——(1994) 'Radical Philosophies of Sexual Difference: Luce Irigaray', in *The Polity Reader in Gender Studies*, Cambridge: Polity Press.

Brennan, T. (ed.) (1990) *Between Feminism and Psychoanalysis*, London: Routledge.

——(1993) *History After Lacan*, New York/London: Routledge.

Burchell, G., Gordon, C. and Miller, P. (eds) (1991) *The Foucault Effect: Studies in Governmentality*, London: Harvester Wheatsheaf.

Burgin, V., Donald, J. and Kaplan, C. (eds) (1986) *Formations of Fantasy*, London: Methuen.

Butler, J. (1990a) *Gender Trouble: Feminism and the Subversion of Identity*, New York/London: Routledge.

——(1990b) 'The Force of Fantasy: Feminism, Mapplethorpe, and Discursive Excess', *Differences* 2(2) (Summer), pp. 105–125.

——(1990c) 'Gender Trouble, Feminist Theory and Psychoanalytic Discourse', in L. Nicholson (ed.) *Feminism/Postmodernism*, New York/London: Routledge.

——(1992) 'Contingent Foundations: Feminism and the Question of "Postmodernism"', in J. Butler and J.W. Scott (eds) *Feminists Theorise the Political*, New York/London: Routledge.

——(1993a) *Bodies That Matter: On the Discursive Limits of Sex*, New York: Routledge.

——(1993b) 'Imitation and Gender Insubordination', in D. Fuss (ed.) *Inside Out: Lesbian Theories/Gay Theories*, New York: Routledge.

Butler, J. and Scott, J.W. (eds) (1992) *Feminists Theorise the Political*, New York/London: Routledge.

Byars, J. (1994) 'Feminism, Psychoanalysis, and Female-Oriented Melodramas of the 1950s', in D. Carson, L. Dittmar and J.R. Welsch (eds) *Multiple Voices in Feminist Film Criticism*, Minneapolis/London: University of Minnesota Press.

—— Byars (1991) *All That Hollywood Allows: Reading Gender in 1950s Melodrama*, Chapel Hill: University of North Carolina Press.

Brunsdon, C. (1991/2) 'Pedagogies of the Feminine: Feminist Teaching and Women's Genres', *Screen* 32(4), pp. 364–382.

Cain, M. (1993) 'Foucault, Feminism and Feeling: What Foucault Can and Cannot Contribute to Feminist Epistemology', in C. Ramazanoglu (ed.) *Up Against Foucault: Explorations of Some Tensions Between Foucault and Feminism*, London/New York: Routledge.

Caine, B., Grosz, E. and de Lepervance, M. (eds) (1988) *Crossing Boundaries: Feminism and the Critique of Knowledge*, Sydney: Allen & Unwin.

Caine, B. and Pringle, R. (eds) (1995) *Transitions – New Australian Feminisms*, NSW: Allen & Unwin.

Campbell, K. (ed.) (1992) *Critical Feminism: Arguments in the Disciplines*, Milton Keynes: Open University Press.

Carby, H. (1982) 'White Woman Listen! Black Feminism and the Boundaries of Sisterhood', in Centre for Contemporary Cultural Studies *The Empire Strikes Back: Race and Racism in '70s Britain*, London: Hutchinson.

Carson, D., Dittmar, L. and Welsch, J.R. (eds) (1994) *Multiple Voices in Feminist Film Criticism*, Minneapolis/London: University of Minnesota Press.

Chodorow, N. (1979) *The Reproduction of Mothering: Psychoanalysis and the Sociology of Gender*, Berkeley: University of California Press.

——(1985) 'Beyond Drive Theory', *Theory and Society* 14(3), pp. 271–321.

Cixous, H. (1981a) 'The Laugh of the Medusa', in E. Marks and I. de Courtivron (eds) *New French Feminisms*, Sussex: Harvester Press.

——(1981b) 'Sorties', in E. Marks and I. de Courtivron (eds) *New French Feminisms*, Sussex: Harvester Press.

Cole, S.G. (1989) *Pornography and the Sex Crisis*, Toronto: Amanita.

Curry, R. (1990) 'Madonna from Marilyn to Marlene – Pastiche and/or Parody?', *Journal of Film and Video* 42(2) (Summer), pp. 15–30.

d'Acci, J. (1987) 'The Case of Cagney and Lacey', in H. Baehr and G. Dyer (eds) *Boxed in: Women and Television*, London: Pandora.

de Beauvoir, S. (1972) *The Second Sex*, Penguin: Harmondsworth.

de Lauretis, T. (1984) *Alice Doesn't: Feminism, Semiotics, Cinema*, Bloomington: Indiana University Press.

——(1986) 'Feminist Studies/Critical Studies: Issues, Terms and Contexts', in T. de Lauretis (ed.) *Feminist Studies/Critical Studies*, London: Macmillan.

——(1987) 'The Technology of Gender', in T. de Lauretis *Technologies of Gender: Essays on Theory, Film and Fiction*, Bloomington: Indiana University Press.

——(1988) 'Displacing Hegemonic Discourses: Reflections on Feminist Theory in the 1980s', *Inscriptions* 3(4), pp. 127–145.

——(1990) 'Eccentric Subjects: Feminist Theory and Historical Consciousness', *Feminist Studies* 16(1), pp. 115–151.

——(1993) 'Upping the Anti [*sic*] in Feminist Theory', in S. During (ed.) *The Cultural Studies Reader*, New York/London: Routledge.

——(1994) 'Rethinking Women's Cinema: Aesthetics and Feminist Theory' (1985), in D. Carson, L. Dittmar and J.R. Welsch (eds) *Multiple Voices in Feminist Film Criticism*, Minneapolis/London: University of Minnesota Press.

Dempster, E. (1988) 'Women Writing the Body: Let's Watch a Little How She Dances', in S. Sheridan (ed.) *Grafts: Feminist Cultural Criticism*, London: Verso.

Derrida, J. (1978a) *Writing and Difference*, London: Routledge and Kegan Paul.

——(1978b) 'Speculations – On Freud', *Oxford Literary Review* 3(2), pp. 78–97.

Dews, P. (1979) 'The Nouvelle Philosophie and Foucault', *Economy and Society* 8(2), pp. 127–71.

——(1984) 'Power and Subjectivity in Foucault', *New Left Review* 144, pp. 72–95.

di Stefano, C. (1990) 'Dilemmas of Difference: Feminism, Modernity and Postmodernism', in L. Nicholson (ed.) *Feminism/Postmodernism*, New York/London: Routledge.

Diamond, I. and Quinby, L. (eds) (1988) *Feminism and Foucault: Reflections on Resistance*, Boston: Northeastern University Press.

Doane, M.A. (1981) 'The Woman's Film: Possession and Address', in P. Mellencamp, L. Williams and M.A. Doane (eds) *Re-Visions: Feminist Essays in Film Analysis*, Los Angeles: American Film Institute.

——(1982) 'Film and Masquerade: Theorizing the Film Spectator', *Screen* 23(3/4) (September/October), pp. 74–88.

——(1987) *The Desire to Desire: The Women's Film of the 1940s*, London: Macmillan Press.

——(1991) *Femmes Fatales: Feminism, Film Theory, Psychoanalysis*, London: Routledge.

Donaldson, L.E. (1988) 'The Miranda Complex: Colonialism and the Question of Feminist Reading', *Diacritics* 18(3) pp. 65–77.

During, S. (1985) 'Postmodernism or Postcolonialism?', *Landfall*, pp. 366–380.

——(ed.) (1993a) *The Cultural Studies Reader*, New York/London: Routledge.

——(1993b) 'Postmodernism or Post-Colonialism Today', in T. Docherty (ed.) *Postmodernism, A Reader*, New York: Harvester Wheatsheaf.

—— (1995) 'Postmodernism or Post-Colonialism Today', in B. Ashcroft, G. Griffiths and H. Tiffin (eds) *The Post-Colonial Studies Reader*, London: Routledge; also *Textual Practice* 1(1) (1987), pp. 32–47.

Dworkin, A. (1981) *Pornography: Men Possessing Women*, New York: Pedigree.

—— (1987) *Intercourse*, New York: The Free Press.

Dyer, R. (1986) *Heavenly Bodies: Film Stars and Society*, New York: St Martin's Press.

—— (1993) *The Matter of Images: Essays on Representations*, London/New York: Routledge.

Easthope, A. and McGowan, K. (eds) (1992) *A Critical and Cultural Theory Reader*, NSW: Allen & Unwin.

Eco, U. (1969) *Travels in Hyperreality*, London: Picador.

—— (1984) 'A Guide to the Neo-Television of the 1980s', *Framework* 25, pp. 18–27.

Eichler, M. (1986) 'The Relationship Between Sexist, Non-Sexist, Woman Centred and Feminist Research', in T. McCormack (ed.) *Studies in Communication* 3, Toronto: JAI Press.

—— (1988) *Non-Sexist Research*, London: Allen & Unwin.

Faludi, S. (1992) *Backlash*, London: Vintage.

Felski, R. (1989) 'Feminism, Postmodernism, and the Critique of Modernity', *Cultural Critique* 13, pp. 33–56.

Feminist Review (1990) special issue,'Perverse Politics: Lesbian Issues' 34 (Spring).

Fiske, J. (1987a) *Television Culture*, New York: Routledge.

—— (1987b) 'British Cultural Studies and Television', in R. Allen (ed.) *Channels of Discourse: Television and Contemporary Criticism*, Chapel Hill: University of North Carolina Press.

—— (1989a) *Reading the Popular*, London: Unwin Hyman.

—— (1989b) *Understanding Popular Culture*, London: Unwin Hyman.

—— (1992) 'Cultural Studies and the Culture of Everyday Life', in L. Grossberg, C. Nelson and P. Treichler (eds) *Cultural Studies*, New York: Routledge.

Flax, J. (1987) 'Postmodernism and Gender Relations in Feminist Theory', *Signs* 12(4), pp. 621–643.

—— (1990a) *Psychoanalysis, Feminism and Postmodernism in the Contemporary West*, Berkeley: University of California Press.

—— (1990b) 'Postmodernism and Gender Relations in Feminist Theory', in L. Nicholson (ed.) *Feminism/Postmodernism*, New York/London: Routledge.

—— (1992a) 'Beyond Equality: Gender, Justice and Difference', in G. Bock and S. James (eds) *Beyond Equality and Difference: Citizenship, Feminist Politics and Female Subjectivity*, London: Routledge.

—— (1992b) 'The End of Innocence', in J. Butler and J.W. Scott (eds) *Feminists Theorise the Political*, New York/London: Routledge.

Foster, H. (ed.) (1983) *The Anti-Aesthetic: Essays on Postmodern Culture*, Port Townsend: Washington Bay Press.

Foucault, M. (1972) *The Archaeology of Knowledge*, London: Tavistock.

—— (1973a) *The Birth of the Clinic*, London: Tavistock.

—— (1973b) *The Order of Things: An Archaeology of the Human Sciences*, New York: Vintage Books.

—— (1977) *Discipline and Punish*, Harmondsworth: Penguin.

—— (1980) *Power/Knowledge: Selected Interviews and Other Writings 1972–1977 by Michel Foucault*, ed. C. Gordon, trans. C. Gordon, L. Marshall, J. Mepham and K. Soper, Sussex: Harvester Press.

—— (1981a) *The History of Sexuality*, vol. 1, *An Introduction*, Harmondsworth: Penguin.

—— (1981b) 'The Order of Discourse', in R. Young (ed.) *Untying the Text: A Post-Structuralist Reader*, London: Routledge.

—— (1982) 'The Subject and Power', trans. L. Sawyer, in H.L. Dreyfus and P. Rainbow (eds) *Michel Foucault: Beyond Structuralism and Hemeneutics*, Chicago: University of Chicago Press.

—— (1988) 'On Power', in L. Kritzman (ed.) *Michel Foucault: Politics, Philosophy, Culture: Interviews and Other Writings 1977–84*, London: Routledge.

—— (1991) 'Politics and the Study of Discourse', in G. Burchell, C. Gordon and P. Miller (eds) *The Foucault Effect*, Sussex: Harvester Press.

Fraser, N. (1989) *Unruly Practices: Power, Discourse and Gender in Contemporary Social Theory*, Cambridge: Polity Press.

—— (1992) 'The Uses and Abuses of French Discourse Theories for Feminist Politics', *Theory, Culture and Society*, 9, pp. 51–71.

Fraser, N. and Nicholson, L. (1988) 'Philosophy: An Encounter Between Feminism and Postmodernism', *Communication* 10/3(4), pp. 345–394.

—— (1990) 'Social Criticism Without Philosophy: An Encounter Between Feminism and Postmodernism', in L. Nicholson (ed.) *Feminism/Postmodernism*, New York/London: Routledge.

Friedan, B. (1963) *The Feminine Mystique*, New York: W.W. Norton.

Gaines, J. (1992) 'Competing Glances: Who is Reading Robert Mapplethorpe's Black Book?' *New Formations 16*.

—— Gaines (1994) 'White Privilege and Looking Relations: Race and Gender in Feminist Film Theory', in D. Carson, L. Dittmar and J.R. Welsch (eds) *Multiple Voices in Feminist Film Criticism*, Minneapolis/London: University of Minnesota Press.

Gallop, J. (1982) *Feminism and Psychoanalysis: The Daughter's Seduction*, London: Macmillan.

Gallop, J. and Burke, C. (1980) 'Psychoanalysis and Feminism in France', in H. Eisenstein and A. Jardine (eds) *The Future of Difference*, Boston: G.K. Hall.

Game, A. (1991) *Undoing the Social: Towards a Deconstructive Sociology*, Milton Keynes: Open University Press.

Gamman, L. and Marshment, M (eds) (1988) *The Female Gaze: Women as Viewers of Popular Culture*, London: The Women's Press.

Gatens, M. (1986) 'Feminism, Philosophy and Riddles Without Answers', in C. Pateman and E. Grosz (eds) *Feminist Challenges: Social and Political Theory*, NSW: Allen & Unwin.

Gatens, M. (1991) *Feminism and Philosophy*, Cambridge: Polity Press.

—— (1994) 'The Dangers of a Woman-Centred Philosophy', in *The Polity Reader in Gender Studies*, Cambridge: Polity Press.

Gates, Jr., H. (1987) 'Authority, (White) Power and the (Black) Critic: It's All Greek to Me', *Critical Critique* 7, pp. 19–46.

Gavey, N. (1989) 'Feminist-Poststructuralism and Discourse Analysis: Contributions to Feminist Psychology', *Psychology of Women Quarterly* 13, pp. 459–475.

Giddens, A. (1987) *Social Theory and Modern Sociology*, Cambridge: Polity Press.

Giroux, H.A. (1993) 'Living Dangerously: Identity, Politics and the New Cultural Racism: Towards a Critical Pedagogy of Representation, *Cultural Studies* 7(1), pp. 1–27.

Gledhill, C. (1988) 'Pleasurable Negotiations', in E.D. Pribram (ed.) *Female Spectators: Looking at Film and Television*, London: Verso.

—— (1991) *Stardom: Industry of Desire*, London: Routledge.

Gordon, C. (ed.) (1980) Power/Knowledge: Selected Interviews and Other Writings 1972–1977 by Michel Foucault, trans. C. Gordon, L. Marshall, J. Mepham, K. Soper, Sussex: Harvester Press.

Grant, J. (1987) 'I Feel Therefore I Am: A Critique of Female Experience as the Basis for a Feminist Epistemology', *Women and Politics* 17 (Fall), pp. 99–114.

Grimshaw, J. (1986) *Feminist Philosophers: Women's Perspectives on Philosophical Traditions*, Sussex: Wheatsheaf.

—— 1993) 'Practices of Freedom', in C. Ramazanoglu (ed.) *Up Against Foucault: Explorations of Some Tensions Between Foucault and Feminism*, London/New York: Routledge.

223

Grossberg, L. (1993) 'The Formations of Cultural Studies', in V. Blundell, J. Shepherd and I. Taylor (eds) *Relocating Cultural Studies*, London/New York: Routledge.

Grossberg, L., Nelson, C. and Treichler, P. (eds) (1992) *Cultural Studies*, New York: Routledge.

Grosz, E. (1986) 'What is Feminist Theory?', in C. Pateman and E. Grosz (eds) *Feminist Challenges: Social and Political Theory*, NSW: Allen & Unwin.

——(1988) 'The In(ter)vention of Feminist Knowledges', in B. Caine, E. Grosz and M. de Lepervance (eds) *Crossing Boundaries: Feminism and the Critique of Knowledge*, Sydney: Allen & Unwin.

——(1989) *Sexual Subversions: Three French Feminists*, Sydney: Allen & Unwin.

——(1990a) 'Contemporary Theories of Power and Subjectivity', in S. Gunew (ed.) *Feminist Knowledge: Critique and Construct*, London: Routledge.

——(1990b) 'A Note on Essentialism and Difference', in S. Gunew (ed.) *Feminist Knowledge: Critique and Construct*, London: Routledge.

Gunew, S. (ed.) (1990) *Feminist Knowledge: Critique and Construct*, London: Routledge.

Gunew, S. and Yeatman, A. (eds) (1993) *Feminism and the Politics of Difference*, NSW: Allen & Unwin.

Halberg, M. (1992) 'Feminist Epistemology: An Impossible Project', extracted in S. Hall, D. Held and D. McGrew (eds) *Modernity and Its Futures*, Cambridge: Polity Press.

Hall, S. (1980) 'Cultural Studies: Two Paradigms', *Media, Culture and Society* 2, pp. 57–72.

——(1987) 'Minimal Selves', in L. Appignanesi (ed.) *Identity*, ICA Documents 6, London: Institute of Contemporary Arts.

——(1992a) 'Cultural Studies and Its Theoretical Legacies', in L. Grossberg, C. Nelson and P. Treichler (eds) *Cultural Studies*, New York: Routledge.

—— (1992b) 'The Question of Cultural Identity', in S. Hall, D. Held and D. McGrew (eds) *Modernity and Its Futures*, Cambridge: Polity Press.

Hall, S., Held, D. and McGrew, D. (eds) (1992) *Modernity and Its Futures*, Cambridge: Polity Press.

Hann, S. (1995) 'Pornography, Identity and Cultural Space', unpublished seminar paper, Massey University, New Zealand.

Haraway, D. (1985) 'A Manifesto for Cyborgs: Science, Technology and Socialist Feminism in the 1980s', *Socialist Review* 80 (March/April), pp. 65–108.

——(1988) 'Situated Knowledges: The Science Question in Feminism and the Privilege of Partial Perspective', *Feminist Studies* 14(3), pp. 575–599.

—— (1991) *Simians, Cyborgs and Women: The Reinvention of Nature*, New York: Routledge.

Harding, J. (ed.) (1986) *Perspectives on Gender and Science*, Lewes: Falmer Press.

Harding, S. (1986) *The Science Question in Feminism*, Ithaca: Cornell University Press.

——(1987) *Feminism and Methodology*, Milton Keynes: Open University Press.

——(1990) 'Feminism, Science and the Anti-Enlightenment Critique', in L. Nicholson (ed.) *Feminism/Postmodernism*, New York/London: Routledge.

——(1991) *Whose Science? Whose Knowledge?* Milton Keynes: Open University Press

——(1993) 'Reinventing Ourselves as Other: More New Agents of History and Knowledge', in L. Kauffman (ed.) *American Feminist Thought at Century's End – A Reader*, Oxford: Blackwell.

Hartsock, N. (1990) 'Foucault on Power: A Theory for Women?', in L. Nicholson (ed.) *Feminism/Postmodernism*, New York/London: Routledge.

Harvey, S. (1978) *May '68 and Film Culture*, London: British Film Institute.

——(1981) 'An Introduction to *Song of the Skirt*', *Undercut* 1.

Haskell, M. (1973) *From Reverence to Rape: The Treatment of Women in the Movies*, New York: Holt, Rinehart & Winston.

Hatzimanolis, E. (1993) 'Timing Differences and Investing in Futures in Multicultural

(Women's) Writing', in S. Gunew and A. Yeatman (eds) *Feminism and the Politics of Difference*, NSW: Allen & Unwin.

Heath, S. (1986) 'Joan Riviere and the Masquerade', in V. Burgin, J. Donald and C. Kaplan (eds) *Formations of Fantasy*, London: Methuen.

Hekman, S. (1990) *Gender and Knowledge: Elements of a Postmodern Feminism*, Cambridge: Polity Press.

Henderson, L. (1991) 'Lesbian Pornography: Cultural Transgression and Sexual Demystification', *Women and Language* 14(1) (Spring), pp. 3–12.

——(1993) 'Justify Our Love: Madonna and the Politics of Queer Sex', in C. Schwichtenberg (ed.) *The Madonna Connection*, NSW: Allen & Unwin.

Holland, P. (1987) 'When a Woman Reads the News', in H. Baehr and G. Dyer (eds) *Boxed in: Women and Television*, London: Pandora.

hooks, b. (1984) *Feminist Theory: From Margin to Center*, Boston: South End Press.

——(1990) *Yearning: Race, Gender and Cultural Politics*, Boston: South End Press.

——(1992) *Black Looks: Race and Representation*, Boston: South End Press.

——(1993) 'Seductive Sexualities: Representing Blackness in Poetry and on Screen', in L. Kauffman (ed.) *American Feminist Thought at Century's End – A Reader*, Oxford: Blackwell.

Hoy, D.C. (1986) *Foucault: A Critical Reader*, Oxford: Blackwell.

Humm, M. (1989) *The Dictionary of Feminist Theory*, Hemel Hempstead: Simon & Schuster.

Hutcheon, L. (1988) *A Poetics of Postmodernism: History, Theory, Fiction*, London/New York: Routledge.

—— (1994) 'The Post Always Rings Twice: The Postmodern and the Postcolonial', *Textual Practice* 18(2) (Summer), pp. 205–238.

——(1995) 'Circling the Downspout of Empire: Post-Colonialism and Postmodernism', in B. Ashcroft, G. Griffiths and H. Tiffin (eds) *The Post-Colonial Studies Reader*, London: Routledge; also *Ariel* 20(40), (1989), pp. 149–175.

Huyssen, A. (1984) 'Mapping the Postmodern', *New German Critique* 33, pp. 5–52.

——(1986) *After the Great Divide: Modernism, Mass Culture and Postmodernism*, Bloomington: Indiana University Press.

Irigaray, L. (1977) 'Women's Exile', *Ideology and Consciousness* 1, pp. 24–39.

——(1984) *L'Ethique de la différence sexuelle*, Paris: Editions de Minuit.

——(1985a) *Speculum of the Other Woman*, trans. G. Gill, Ithaca: Cornell University Press.

——(1985b) *This Sex Which is Not One*, Ithaca: Cornell University Press.

Jameson, F. (1984) 'Postmodernism, or the Cultural Logic of Late Capitalism', *New Left Review* 146, pp. 53–92.

Jardine, A. (1981) 'Introduction to Julia Kristeva's 'Women Time''', *Signs* 7(1), pp. 5–12.

Johnston, C. (1973) 'Women's Cinema as Counter-Cinema', in C. Johnston (ed.) *Notes on Women's Cinema*, London: Society for Education in Film and Television.

Jolly, M. (1993) 'Colonising Women and Material Empire', in S. Gunew and A. Yeatman (eds) *Feminism and the Politics of Difference*, NSW: Allen & Unwin.

Jones, A.R. (1984) 'Julia Kristeva on Feminism – The Limits of a Semiotic Politics', in *Feminist Review* 18 (Winter), pp. 56–83.

Kaplan, E.A. (1983) *Women and Film*, New York/London: Routledge.

——(1987) 'Gender Address and the Gaze in MTV', in *Rocking Around the Clock*, London/New York: Routledge.

——(1993) 'Madonna Politics: Perversion, Repression or Subversion? Or Masks and/as Master-y', in C. Schwichtenberg (ed.) *The Madonna Connection*, NSW: Allen & Unwin.

Kappeler, S. (1986) *The Pornography of Representation*, Cambridge: Polity Press.

Kauffman, L. (ed.) (1993) *American Feminist Thought at Century's End – A Reader*, Oxford: Blackwell.

Kelsey, J. (1991) 'Treaty Justice in the 1980s', in P. Spoonley, D. Pearson and

C. Macpherson (eds) *Nga Take: Ethnic Relations and Racism in Aoteoroa/New Zealand*, Palmerston North: Dunmore Press.

——(1993) *Rolling Back the State: Privatisation of Power in Aoteoroa/New Zealand*, Wellington: Bridget Williams Books.

Kemp, S. (1994) 'Pornography, Sexuality and Cultural Space', unpublished seminar paper, Massey University, New Zealand.

——(1995) 'Feminist Standpoint Epistemology, Poststructuralism and Feminist Research: An Introduction', in Department of Sociology, Massey University, New Zealand, *Postgraduate Review 1995* 1, pp. 61–72.

Kristeva, J. (1981) 'Women's Time', trans. A. Jardine and H. Blake, *Signs* 7(1), pp. 13–35.

Kritzman, L. (ed.) (1988) *Michel Foucault: Politics, Philosophy, Culture: Interviews and Other Writings 1977–84*, London: Routledge.

Kuhn, A. (1975) 'Women's Cinema and Feminist Film Criticism', *Screen* 16(3), pp. 107–112.

——(1982) *Women's Pictures: Feminism and Cinema*, London: Routledge & Kegan Paul.

Larner, W. (1993) 'Changing Contexts: Globalization, Migration and Feminism in New Zealand', in S. Gunew and A. Yeatman (eds) *Feminism and the Politics of Difference*, NSW: Allen & Unwin.

——(1995) 'Theorising "Difference" in Aoteoroa/New Zealand', *Gender, Place and Culture* 2(2), pp. 177–190.

Larner, W. and Spoonley, P. (1995) 'Post-colonial Politics in Aoteoroa/New Zealand', in D. Stasiulis and N. Yuval-Davis (eds) *Unsettling Settler Societies*, London: Sage.

Lather, P. (1989) 'Postmodernism and the Discourses of Emancipation: Precedents, Parallels and Interruptions', *Women's Studies Association (New Zealand) Conference Papers 1989*, Lincoln: WSA.

LeSage, J. (1978) 'The Political Aesthetics of the Feminist Documentary Film', *Quarterly Review of Film Studies* 3(4), pp. 507–523.

Lederer, L. (ed.) (1980) *Take Back the Night: Women on Pornography*, New York: Morrow.

Leidholdt, D. and Raymond, J.G. (eds) (1990) *The Sexual Liberals and the Attack on Feminism*, New York: Pergamon.

Lewis, R. and Adler, K. (1994) 'Come to Me Baby or What's Wrong with Lesbian SM', in *Women's Studies International Forum* 17(4) (July–August).

Lovell, T. (1980) 'Realism and Marxist Aesthetics II', in T. Lovell (ed.) *Pictures of Reality: Aesthetics, Politics and Pleasure*, London: British Film Institute.

Lyotard, J.F. (1984) *The Postmodern Condition: A Report on Knowledge*, Minneapolis: University of Minnesota Press.

McCabe, C. (ed.) (1986) *High Theory/Low Culture. Analysing Popular Television and Film*, Manchester: Manchester University Press.

MacDonald, E. (1991) 'The Trouble with Subjects: Feminism, Marxism and the Questions of Poststructuralism', *Studies in Political Economy* 35, pp. 43–71.

MacKinnon, C. (1982) 'Feminism, Marxism, Method and the State: An Agenda for Theory', *Signs* 7(3), pp. 515–544.

——(1987) *Feminism Unmodified: Discourses on Life and Law*, Cambridge: Harvard University Press.

——(1989) 'Sexuality, Pornography and Method: Pleasure Under Patriarchy', *Ethics* 99, pp. 314–346.

McLennan, G. (1992a) 'The Enlightenment Project Revisited', in S. Hall, D. Held and T. McGrew *Modernity and Its Futures*, Cambridge: Polity Press.

——(1992b) 'Sociology After Postmodernism', *Inaugural Address*, Faculty of Social Sciences Occasional Papers, Massey University, New Zealand, pp. 1–22.

——(1994) 'Feminism, Epistemology and Postmodernism: Reflections on Current Ambivalence', in *Sites* 29 (Autumn), pp. 98–124.

——(1995a) *Pluralism*, Milton Keynes: Open University Press.

——(1995b) 'Feminism, Epistemology and Postmodernism: Reflections on Current Ambivalence', *Sociology* 29(2), pp. 391–409.

McNeil, M. (1993) 'Dancing with Foucault: Feminism and Power-Knowledge', in C. Ramazanoglu (ed.) *Up Against Foucault: Explorations of Some Tensions Between Foucault and Feminism*, London/New York: Routledge.

McRobbie, A. (1982a) '*Jackie*: An Ideology of Adolescent Femininity', in B. Waites, T. Bennett and G. Martin (eds) *Popular Culture: Past and Present*, London: Croom Helm/Open University Press.

——(1982b) 'The Politics of Feminist Research: Between Talk, Text and Action', *Feminist Review* 12, pp. 46–57.

——(1986) 'Dance and Social Fantasy', in A. McRobbie and M. Nava (eds) *Gender and Generation*, London: Methuen.

——(1991) *Feminism and Youth Culture: From 'Jackie' to 'Just Seventeen'*, London: Macmillan.

——(1992) 'Post-Marxism and Cultural Studies', in L. Grossberg, C. Nelson and P. Treichler (eds) *Cultural Studies*, New York: Routledge.

——(1994) *Postmodernism and Popular Culture*, London/New York: Routledge.

Mahoney, B (1994) 'Contradiction Without Shame: The Pleasures of Resistance', *New Zealand Journal of Media Studies* 1(2), pp. 68–75.

Mandzuik, R. (1993) 'Feminist Politics and Postmodern Seductions: Madonna and the Struggle for Political Articulation', in C. Schwichtenberg (ed.) *The Madonna Connection*, NSW: Allen & Unwin.

Marks, E. and de Courtivron, I. (eds) (1981) *New French Feminisms*, Sussex: Harvester Press.

Marshall, B.L. (1994) *Engendered Modernity – Feminism, Social Theory and Social Change*, Cambridge: Polity Press.

Martin, B. (1988) 'Feminism, Criticism and Foucault', in I. Diamond and L. Quinby (eds) *Feminism and Foucault: Reflections on Resistance*, Boston: Northeastern University Press.

——(1992) 'Sexual Practice and Changing Lesbian Identities', in M. Barrett and A. Phillips (eds) *Destabilizing Theory: Contemporary Feminist Debates*, Cambridge: Polity Press.

Mayne, J. (1994) 'Feminist Film Theory and Criticism', in D. Carson, L. Dittmar and J.R. Welsch (eds) *Multiple Voices in Feminist Film Criticism*, Minneapolis/London: University of Minnesota Press.

Memmi, A. (1967) *The Colonizer and the Colonized*, Boston: Beacon Press.

Mercer, K. (1992) 'Skinhead Sex Thing: Radical Difference and the Homoerotic Image', *New Formations* 16.

——(1994) *Welcome to the Jungle: New Positions in Cultural Studies*, New York: Routledge.

Millett, K. (1972) *Sexual Politics*, London: Abacus.

Mitchell, J. and Rose, J. (eds) (1982) *Feminine Sexuality: Jacques Lacan and Ecole Freudienne*, London: Macmillan.

Modleski, T. (1983) 'The Rhythms of Reception: Daytime Television and Women's Work', in E.A. Kaplan (ed.) *Regarding Television*, Frederick, MD: University Publications of America.

——(1984) *Loving with a Vengeance – Mass Produced Fantasies for Women*, London/New York: Methuen.

——(1986a) 'Femininity as Mas(s)querade: A Feminist Approach to Mass Culture', in C. McCabe (ed.) *High Theory/Low Culture: Analysing Popular Television and Film*, Manchester: Manchester University Press.

——(1986b) 'The Terror of Pleasure: The Contemporary Horror Film and Postmodern Theory', in T. Modleski (ed.) *Studies in Entertainment: Critical Approaches to Mass Culture*, Bloomington and Indianapolis: Indiana University Press.

—— (1988) *The Women Who Knew Too Much: Hitchcock and Feminist Theory*, New York: Methuen.

—— (1991) *Feminism Without Women: Culture and Criticism in a 'Postfeminist Age'*, New York: Routledge.

—— (1993) 'Cinema and the Dark Continent: Race and Gender in Popular Film', in L. Kauffman (ed.) *American Feminist Thought at Century's End – A Reader*, Oxford: Blackwell.

Mohanty, C.T. (1995) 'Under Western Eyes: Feminist Scholarship and Colonial Discourses', in B. Ashcroft, G. Griffiths and H. Tiffin (eds) *The Post-Colonial Studies Reader*, London: Routledge; also *Boundary* 2, 12(3)/13(1) (Spring/Fall) (1984).

Moi, T. (1985a) *Sexual/Textual Politics*, New York/London: Methuen.

—— (1985b) 'Power, Sex and Subjectivity: Feminist Reflections on Foucault', *Paragraph* 5, pp. 95–102.

—— (ed.) (1987) *French Feminist Thought – A Reader*, Oxford: Blackwell.

—— (1988) 'Feminism, Postmodernism and Style: Recent Feminist Criticism in the United States', *Cultural Critique* 9, pp. 3–22.

—— (1989a) 'Feminist, Female, Feminine', in C. Belsey and J. Moore (eds) *The Feminist Reader*, London: Macmillan.

—— (1989b) 'Men Against Patriarchy', in L. Kauffman (ed.) *Gender and Theory: Dialogues on Feminist Criticism*, Oxford: Blackwell.

Morris, M. (1988) *The Pirate's Fiancée: Feminism Reading Postmodernism*, London/New York: Verso.

—— (1992) 'Cultural Studies', in K.K. Ruthven (ed.), *Beyond the Disciplines: The New Humanities*, Occasional Paper 13, Australian Academy of the Humanities, Canberra, pp. 1–21.

Morse, M. (1983) 'Sport on Television: Replay and Display', in E.A. Kaplan *Regarding Television. Critical Approaches – An Anthology*, Frederick, MD: University Publications of America.

—— (1985) 'Talk, Talk, Talk', *Screen* (March–April), pp. 3–15.

Moynihan, P. (1994) 'Foucault, Politics and the Performative', unpublished paper given at the 'Foucault the Legacy' Conference, Queensland, Australia, July.

Mulvey, L. (1975) 'Visual Pleasure and Narrative Cinema', *Screen* 16(3) (Autumn), pp. 6–18.

—— (1981) 'Afterthoughts on "Visual Pleasure and Narrative Cinema" Inspired by *Duel in the Sun* (King Vidor, 1946)', *Framework* 15–17, pp. 12–15.

—— (1989) *Visual and Other Pleasures*, London: Macmillan.

—— (1991) *'Xala* and Fetishism', unpublished lecture, Humanities Institute, Stony Brook, New York, March.

—— (1992) 'From "Visual Pleasure and Narrative Cinema"' (1975), in A. Easthope and K. McGowan (eds) *A Critical and Cultural Theory Reader*, NSW: Allen & Unwin.

—— (1993) 'Some Thoughts on Theories of Fetishism in the Context of Contemporary Culture', in *October* 65 (Summer), pp. 3–20.

Nash, K. (1994) 'The Feminist Production of Knowledge: Is Deconstruction a Practice for Women?', *Feminist Review* 47 (Summer), pp. 65–77.

Nestle, J. (1987) *A Restricted Country*, New York: Firebrand Press.

Nicholson, L. (ed.) (1990) *Feminism/Postmodernism*, New York/London: Routledge.

—— (1992) 'On The Postmodern Barricades: Feminism, Politics and Social Theory', in S. Seidman and D.G. Wagner (eds) *Postmodernism and Social Theory*, Oxford: Blackwell.

Nochlin, L. (1982) 'The Nature of Realism', in L. Nochlin (ed.) *Realism*, London: Penguin.

Norris, C. (1990) 'Lost in the Funhouse: Baudrillard and the Politics of Postmodernism', in R. Boyne and A. Rattansi (eds) *Postmodernism and Society*, London: Macmillan.

Owens, C. (1983) 'The Discourse of Others: Feminists and Postmodernism', in H. Foster (ed.) *The Anti-Aesthetic: Essays on Postmodern Culture*, Washington: Bay Press.

Parry, B. (1987) 'From Problems in Current Theories of Colonial Discourse', *Oxford Literary Review* 9 (1/2).

——(1995) 'Problems in Current Theories of Colonial Discourse' (1987), in B. Ashcroft, G. Griffiths and H. Tiffin (eds) *The Post-Colonial Studies Reader*, London: Routledge.

Pateman, C. (1988) *The Sexual Contract*, Cambridge: Polity Press.

Pateman, C. and Grosz, E. (eds) (1986) *Feminist Challenges: Social and Political Theory*, NSW: Allen & Unwin.

Patton, C. (1993) 'Embodying Subaltern Memory: Kinaesthesia and the Problematics of Gender and Race', in C. Schwichtenberg (ed.) *The Madonna Connection*, NSW: Allen & Unwin.

Penley, C. (1985) 'Feminism, Film and Theory and the Bachelor Machine', *M/F* 10, pp. 39–61.

Pettman, J. (1988) 'All the Women Are White: All the Blacks Are Men . . . Racism, Sexism and Sociology', paper presented at the Sociological Association Conference, Australia National University, Canberra.

Phillips, A. (1987) *Feminism and Equality*, Oxford: Blackwell.

——(1991) *Engendering Democracy*, Cambridge: Polity Press.

——(1992) 'Universal Pretensions in Political Thought', in M. Barrett and A. Phillips (eds) *Destabilizing Theory: Contemporary Feminist Debates*, Cambridge: Polity Press.

Poster, M. (1984) *Foucault, Marxism and History*, Cambridge: Polity Press.

Poynton, B. and Hartley, J. (1990) 'Male Gazing: Australian Rules Football, Gender and Television', in M.E. Brown (ed.) *Television and Women's Culture: The Politics of the Popular*, Sydney: Currency Press.

Pribram, E.D. (1988) *Female Spectators: Looking at Film and Television*, London: Verso.

——(1993) 'Seduction, Control, and the Search for Authenticity: Madonna's *Truth or Dare*', in C. Schwichtenberg (ed.) *The Madonna Connection*, NSW: Allen & Unwin.

Pringle, R. (1995) 'Destabilising Patriarchy', in B. Caine and R. Pringle (eds) *Transitions – New Australian Feminisms*, NSW: Allen & Unwin.

Pringle, R. and Watson, S. (1990) 'Fathers, Brothers, Mates: The Fraternal State in Australia', in S. Watson (ed.) *Playing the State*, London: Verso.

——(1992) 'Women's Interests and the Post-Structuralist State', in M. Barrett and A. Phillips (eds) *Destabilizing Theory: Contemporary Feminist Debates*, Cambridge: Polity Press.

Probyn, E. (1987) 'Bodies and Anti-Bodies: Feminism and the Postmodern', *Cultural Studies* 1(3), pp. 349–360.

Rabinow, P. (ed.) (1984) *The Foucault Reader*, London: Penguin.

Radway, J. (1984) *Reading the Romance: Women, Patriarchy and Popular Literature*, Chapel Hill/London: University of North Carolina Press.

Ramazanoglu, C. (1986) 'Ethnocentrism and Socialist Feminist Theory: A Response to Barrett and McIntosh', *Feminist Review* 22, pp. 83–86.

——(1989) *Feminism and the Contradictions of Oppression*, London: Routledge.

——(1992) 'Feminist Methodology: Male Reason Versus Female Empowerment', *Sociology* 26(2) (May), pp. 207–212.

——(1993) *Up Against Foucault: Explorations of Some Tensions Between Foucault and Feminism*, London: Routledge.

Ramazanoglu, C. and Holland, J. (1993) 'Women's Sexuality and Men's Appropriation of Desire', in C. Ramazanoglu (ed.) *Up Against Foucault: Explorations of Some Tensions Between Foucault and Feminism*, London/New York: Routledge.

Ransom, J. (1993) 'Feminism, Difference and Discourse: The Limits of Discursive Analysis for Feminism', in C. Ramazanoglu (ed.) *Up Against Foucault: Explorations of Some Tensions Between Foucault and Feminism*, London/New York: Routledge.

Reekie, G. (1994) 'Feminist History After Foucault', unpublished paper presented at the 'Foucault the Legacy' conference, Queensland, Australia, July.

Rich, A. (1980) 'Compulsory Heterosexuality and Lesbian Existence', *Signs* 5(4), pp. 631–660.

Rich, R.B. (1994) 'In the Name of Feminist Film Criticism', in D. Carson, L. Dittmar and J.R. Welsch (eds) *Multiple Voices in Feminist Film Criticism*, Minneapolis/London: University of Minnesota Press.

Riley, D. (1983) *War in the Nursery: Theories of Child and Mother*, London: Virago.

——(1988) *'Am I That Name?' Feminism and the Category of 'Women' in History*, London: Macmillan.

Riviere, J. (1926) 'Womanliness as a Masquerade', in V. Burgin, J. Donald and C. Kaplan (eds) *Formations of Fantasy*, London: Methuen.

Roach, J. and Felix, P. (1988) 'Black Looks', in L. Gamman and M. Marshment (eds) *The Female Gaze: Women as Viewers of Popular Culture*, London: The Women's Press.

Root, J. (1986) *Open the Box*, London: Comedia.

Rosaldo, R. (1974) 'Women, Culture and Society: A Theoretical Overview', in M.Z. Rosaldo and L. Lamphere (eds) *Women, Culture and Society*, Stanford: Stanford University Press.

Ross, A. (1993) 'The Popularity of Pornography', in S. During (ed.) *The Cultural Studies Reader*, New York/London: Routledge.

Rowbotham, S. (1973) *Hidden from History*, London: Pluto Press.

Rowley, H. and Grosz, E. (1990) 'Psychoanalysis and Feminism', in S. Gunew (ed.) *Feminist Knowledge, Critique and Construct*, London: Routledge.

Rubin, G. (1984) 'Thinking Sex: Notes for a Radical Theory of the Politics of Sexuality', in C. Vance (ed.) *Pleasure and Danger – Exploring Female Sexuality*, Boston: Routledge & Kegan Paul.

Russo, M. (1986) 'Female Grotesques: Carnival and Theory', in T. de Lauretis (ed.) *Feminist Studies/Critical Studies*, London: Macmillan.

Said, E. (1989) 'Representing the Colonised: Anthropology's Interlocutors', *Critical Inquiry* 15(2) (Winter), pp. 205–225.

——(1993) *Culture and Imperialism*, London: Vintage.

Sandoval, C. (1991) 'U.S. Third World Feminism: The Theory and Method of Oppositional Consciousness', *Genders* 10, pp. 1–24.

Sawicki, J. (1988) 'Identity Politics and Sexual Freedom: Foucault and Feminism', in I. Diamond and L. Quinby (eds) *Feminism and Foucault: Reflections on Resistance*, Boston: Northeastern University Press.

——(1991) *Disciplining Foucault: Feminism, Power and the Body*, London: Routledge.

Schulze, L., Barton-White, A. and Brown, J.D. (1993) 'A Sacred Monster in Her Prime: Audience Construction of Madonna as "Low-Other" ', in C. Schwichtenberg (ed.) *The Madonna Connection*, NSW: Allen & Unwin.

Schwichtenberg, C. (ed.) (1993) *The Madonna Connection*, NSW: Allen & Unwin.

Sheridan, S. (1995) 'Reading the Women's Weekly: Feminism, Femininity and Popular Culture', in B. Caine and R. Pringle (eds) *Transitions – New Australian Feminisms*, NSW: Allen & Unwin.

Shewey, D. (1991) 'The Saint, the Slut, the Sensation . . . Madonna', *The Advocate*, 7 May, pp. 42–51.

Slemon, S. (1988a) 'Magic Realism as Post-Colonial Discourse', *Canadian Literature* 116, pp. 9–23.

——(1988b) 'Post-Colonial Allegory and the Transformation of History', *Journal of Commonwealth Literature* 23(1), pp. 157–168.

——(1995) 'The Scramble for Post-Colonialism', in B. Ashcroft, G. Griffiths and H. Tiffin (eds) *The Post-Colonial Studies Reader*, London: Routledge; also in C. Tiffin and A. Lawson (eds) *De-Scribing Empire: Post-Colonialism and Textuality* (1994), London: Routledge.

Smart, B. (1983) *Foucault, Marxism and Critique*, London: Routledge.

——(1986) 'The Politics of Truth and the Problem of Hegemony', in D.C. Hoy (ed.) *Foucault: A Critical Reader*, Oxford: Blackwell.

Smith, A-M. (1993) 'What is Pornography? An Analysis of the Campaign Against Pornography and Censorship', *Feminist Review* 43 (Spring), pp. 71–87.

Smith, P. (1987) 'Men in Feminism: Men and Feminist Theory', in A. Jardine and P. Smith (eds) *Men in Feminism*, New York/London: Routledge.

Sontag, S. (1967) *Against Interpretation*, London: Eyre & Spottiswoode.

——(1978) *On Photography*, London: Allen Lane.

——(1983) *Under the Sign of Saturn*, London: Writers and Readers.

——(1985) 'Sontag on Mapplethorpe', *Vanity Fair* 47(5) (July).

Soper, K. (1990) *Troubled Pleasures: Writing on Politics, Gender and Hedonism*, London: Verso.

——(1993) 'Productive Contradictions', in C. Ramazanoglu (ed.) *Up Against Foucault: Explorations of Some Tensions Between Foucault and Feminism*, London/New York: Routledge.

Spivak, G.C. (1983) 'Displacement and the Discourse of Woman', in M. Krupnick (ed.) *Displacement: Derrida and After*, Bloomington: Indiana University Press.

——(1985a) 'Can the Subaltern Speak?: Speculations on Widow Sacrifice', *Wedge* 7(8) (Winter/Spring), pp. 120–130.

——(1985b) 'The Rani of Simur', in F. Barker (ed.) *Europe and Its Others, vol. 1, Proceedings of the Essex Conference on the Sociology of Literature, July 1984*, Colchester, University of Essex.

——(1985c) 'Three Women's Texts and a Critique of Imperialism', *Critical Inquiry* 12(1), pp. 43–61.

——(1986) 'Imperialism and Sexual Difference', *Oxford Literary Review* 8, pp. 1–2.

——(1988) *In Other Worlds: Essays in Cultural Politics*, New York: Methuen.

——(1992) 'French Feminism Revisited: Ethics and Politics', in J. Butler and J.W. Scott (eds) *Feminists Theorise the Political*, New York/London: Routledge.

Spoonley, P. (1995a) 'The Challenges of Post-Colonialism', *Sites* 30 (Autumn), pp. 48–68.

——(1995b) 'Constructing Ourselves: The Post-Colonial Politics of Pakeha', in M. Wilson and A. Yeatman (eds) *Justice and Identity: Antipodean Practices*, NSW: Allen & Unwin.

Stacey, J. (1987) 'Desperately Seeking Difference', in P. Ehrens (ed.) *Issues in Feminist Film Criticism* (1990), Bloomington: Indiana University Press.

——(1990) 'Is the Legacy of Second Wave Feminism Postfeminism?', in *Women; Class and the Feminist Imagination: A Socialist Feminist Reader*, Philadelphia: Temple University Press.

——(1991) 'Feminine Fascinations: Forms of Identification in Star–Audience Relations', in C. Gledhill (ed.) *Stardom: Industry of Desire*, London: Routledge.

Stallybrass, P. and White, A. (1986) *The Politics and Poetics of Transgression*, Ithaca: Cornell University Press.

——(1993) 'Bourgeois Hysteria and the Carnivalesque', in S. During (ed.) *The Cultural Studies Reader*, New York/London: Routledge.

Stanley, L. and Wise, S. (1984) 'Feminist Research, Feminist Consciousness and Experiences of Sexism', *Women's Studies International Quarterly* 2(3), pp. 359–374.

Star (Gifford), L. (1988) 'Sports Opera: Television, New Zealand's Rugby World Cup and the Symbolic Annihilation of Women', in P. Rosier (ed.) *Women's Studies Association Conference Papers*, University of Waikato, New Zealand.

——(1992) 'Undying Love, Resisting Pleasures: Women Watch Telerugby', in R. du Plessis (ed.) *Feminist Voices*, Auckland: Oxford University Press.

——(1994) 'Wild Pleasures: Watching Men on Television', *Women's Studies Journal* 10(1) (March), New Zealand: University of Otago Press.

Stein, A. (ed.) (1993) *Sisters, Sexperts, Queers: Beyond the Lesbian Nation*, New York: Plume.

Stern, L. (1979) 'Points of View: The Blind Spot', *Film Reader* 4, pp. 214–236.

Suleiman, S.R. (1986) '(Re)Writing the Body: The Politics and Poetics of Female Eroticism', in S. Suleiman (ed.) *The Female Body in Western Culture*, Cambridge: Harvard University Press.

Sykes, B. (1984) 'Untitled Article', in R. Rowland (ed.) *Women Who Do and Women Who Don't Join the Women's Movement*, London: Routledge.

Tester, K. (1994) *Media, Culture and Morality*, London/New York: Routledge.

Tetzlaff, D. (1993) 'Metatextual Girl: → Patriarchy → Postmodernism → Power → Money → Madonna', in C. Schwichtenberg (ed.) *The Madonna Connection*, NSW: Allen & Unwin.

Thomas, G. (1993) 'Post-Colonial Interrogations', *Social Alternatives*, 12(3) pp. 8–11.

Tiffin, H. (1995) 'Post-Colonial Literatures and Counter-Discourse', in B. Ashcroft, G. Griffiths and H. Tiffin (eds) *The Post-Colonial Studies Reader*, London: Routledge; also *Kunapipi* 9(3) (1987).

Todd, J. (ed.) (1983) *Women Writers Talking*, New York/London: Holmes and Meier.

Trinh, T. Minh-ha (1988) 'Not You/Like You: Colonial Women and the Interlocking Questions of Identity and Difference', *Inscriptions* 3(4), pp. 71–79.

——(1989) *Woman, Native Other: Writing, Postcoloniality and Feminism*, Bloomington: Indiana University Press.

——(1993) 'All-Owning Spectatorship', in S. Gunew and A. Yeatman (eds) *Feminism and the Politics of Difference*, NSW: Allen & Unwin.

Turner, B.S. (1990) 'Periodization and Politics in the Postmodern', in B.S. Turner (ed.) *Theories of Modernity and Postmodernity*, London: Sage.

van Zoonen, L. (1994) *Feminist Media Studies*, London: Sage.

Vance, C. (1984) *Pleasure and Danger: Exploring Female Sexuality*, New York: Routledge & Kegan Paul.

Vasta, E. (1993) 'The New Cultural Politics of Difference', in C. Lemert (ed.) *Social Theory: The Multi-Cultural and Classic Readings*, Boulder: Westview Press.

Walby, S. (1990) *Theorizing Patriarchy*, Oxford: Blackwell.

——(1992) 'Post-Post-Modernism? Theorizing Social Complexity', in M. Barrett and A. Phillips (eds) *Destabilizing Theory: Contemporary Feminist Debates*, Cambridge: Polity Press.

Walker, J. (1994) 'Psychoanalysis and Feminist Film Theory: The Problem of Sexual Difference and Identity', in D. Carson, L. Dittmar and J.R. Welsch (eds) *Multiple Voices in Feminist Film Criticism*, Minneapolis/London: University of Minnesota Press.

Wallace, M. (1993) 'Negative Images: Towards a Black Feminist Cultural Criticism', in S. During (ed.) *The Cultural Studies Reader*, London/New York: Routledge.

Walters, S.D. (1995) *Material Feminism: Making Sense of Feminist Cultural Studies*, Berkeley: University of California Press.

Waters, S. (1994) ' "A Girton Girl on A Throne": Queen Christina and Versions of Lesbianism, 1906–1933', *Feminist Review* 43 (Spring), pp. 41–60.

Waugh, P. (1989) *Feminine Fictions: Revisiting the Postmodern*, London: Routledge.

——(ed.) (1992) *Postmodernism – A Reader*, New York: Edward Arnold/Hodder & Stoughton.

Weedon, C. (1987) *Feminist Practice and Poststructuralist Theory*, Oxford: Blackwell.

West, C. (1988) 'Marxist Theory and the Specificity of Afro-American Oppression', in C. Nelson and L. Grossberg (eds) *Marxism and the Interpretation of Culture*, Chicago: University of Illinois Press.

——(1989) 'Black Culture and Postmodernism', in B. Kruger and P. Mariani (eds) *Remaking History*, Dia Art Foundations *Discussion Contemporary Culture* 4, Seattle: Bay Press, pp. 87–97.

——(1992) 'The Dilemma of the Black Intellectual', in b. hooks and C. West (eds) *Breaking Bread: Insurgent Black Intellectual Life*, Boston: South End Books.

—— (1993) 'The New Cultural Politics of Difference', in S. During (ed.) *The Cultural Studies Reader,* London/New York: Routledge.

Williams, L. (1988) 'Feminist Film Theory: Mildred Pierce and the Second World War', in E.D. Pribram (ed.) *Female Spectators: Looking at Film and Television,* London: Verso.

Wilson, M. and Yeatman, A. (eds) (1995) *Justice and Identity: Antipodean Practices,* NSW: Allen & Unwin.

Yeatman, A. (1990a) *Bureaucrats, Technocrats, Femocrats: Essays on the Contemporary Australian State,* Sydney: Allen & Unwin.

—— (1990b) 'A Feminist Theory of Social Differentiation', in L. Nicholson (ed.) *Feminism/ Postmodernism,* New York/London: Routledge.

—— (1993) 'Voice and Representation in the Politics of Difference', in S. Gunew and A. Yeatman (eds) *Feminism and the Politics of Difference,* NSW: Allen & Unwin.

—— (1994) *Postmodern Revisionings of the Political,* New York/London: Routledge.

—— (1995a) 'Interlocking Oppressions', in B. Caine and R. Pringle (eds) *Transitions – New Australian Feminisms,* NSW: Allen & Unwin.

—— (1995b) 'Justice and the Sovereign Self', in M. Wilson and A. Yeatman (eds) *Justice and Identity: Antipodean Practices,* NSW: Allen & Unwin.

INDEX

the academy 31, 40–2; cultural politics of 9, 117–21, 128–31, 134
Adams, P. 196
Adler, K. 199
affectivity and reason 118
agency 44, 97, 98, 101–2, 105; and cultural meaning 142; Foucault on 53, 54, 62–4; political 142; and subjectivity 15–16, 105
Alcoff, L. 20, 23, 24, 101
Alice, L. 2, 3, 4, 5
Althusser, L. 47
ambivalence, and sexual politics of race and ethnicity 204–5, 207–8
Ang, I. 4, 180, 182
anti-racism 105, 107–9; and feminist film theory 173–5
Arbuthnot, L. 170, 178
Artaud, A. 135
arts: visual 120, *see also* film theory; pop art
Ashcroft, B. 95–6, 105, 109, 110
autoeroticism 79
autonomy 97
avant-garde 136, 137

Bailey, M.E. 190, 191–2
Bakhtin, M. 149, 158
Barrett, M. 4, 5, 6, 16, 37, 38–9, 43–4, 56, 127; on essentialism v. nominalism debate 23–4; on feminism's 'turn to culture' 7, 8–9; on Foucault 38, 49–51, 52–3; on patriarchy 17
Barry, J. 170
Barthes, R. 85, 119, 120, 135, 148, 183
Bartky, S.L. 35, 56
Baudrillard, J. 36, 98, 120, 140, 153, 160
Bell, A. 106
Belsey, C. 125–6

Benhabib, S. 14, 42–3, 92, 93–4, 99, 101, 102, 103, 113, 118, 194
Benjamin, W. 119, 121
Bennett, T. 142, 143
Benveniste, E. 47
Bhabha, H. 113, 175–6, 204, 207
biculturalism 132–3
biological essentialism 20
bisexuality 81, 197; of the child 70
'black', as a concept 16, 17
black people: and representational practices 145–7, 179, 203–4, 205–7, *see also* ethnicity; race; women of colour
Bobo, J. 187
the body: and postmodernism 155–9; and power 191
Bordo, S. 35, 44–5, 65, 155–8, 189
Bourdieu, P. 143
Braidotti, R. 4, 56, 78, 79, 80, 100, 101
Brecht, B. 164
Bright, S. 194, 196, 199
Brunsdon, C. 144
Bryars, J. 179
butch-femme roles 193, 198
Butler, J. 4, 18, 40, 56, 78, 131, 161, 162, 189, 196; on agency, subject and discourse 101–2; on fantasy and pornography 208–9; on French feminist deconstructivists 83; on gender identity 35, 101; on gender and performativity 22, 192–4; theory of parodic performance 151
Byars, J. 87, 88, 177

Cain, M. 51, 60–1, 62
Campbell, K. 41
Carby, H. 16, 17
Carson, D. 84, 90

234